Handbook for Developing Occupational Curricula

Handbook for Developing Occupational Curricula

Richard F. Bortz
Southern Illinois University

ALLYN AND BACON, INC.
Boston   London   Sydney   Toronto

Library of Congress Cataloging in Publication Data

Bortz, Richard F
  Handbook for developing occupational curricula.
  Includes index.
  1. Career education—United States—Curricula.
2. Vocational education—United States—Curricula.
I. Title.
LC1037.5.B67   375'.0086   80-17148
ISBN 0-205-07118-X

*LC
1037.5
.B67*

Series Editor: *Jeremy Soldevilla*
Managing Editor: *Robert Roen*

Printed in the United States of America

Printing number and year (last digits):
10 9 8 7 6 5 4 3 2 1   85 84 83 82 81 80

To Raisin, whose quiet indifference
and constant companionship was and still
is much appreciated.

Contents

Foreword

This is truly a curriculum development handbook which supports tried and true methods of curriculum development. The occupational curriculum developer is guided step-by-step through the complete development cycle, beginning with occupational analysis and continuing through development of the final curricula products.

Curriculum specialists, occupational teachers, and teacher educators, administrators, and on-the-job training directors will find this handbook very useful in preparing for and carrying out their curriculum development functions. An excellent balance of theory and application techniques is maintained, with the ultimate focus upon the specific step-by-step procedures required to successfully complete the several operations of occupational curriculum development.

Long-range employment spirals and long-range curriculum spirals are effectively utilized to illustrate the parallel nature of the relationship between curriculum and employment. While this is a somewhat new approach to many, it is based upon concepts supported by several writers, including the author who has repeatedly utilized the approach successfully in teaching curriculum development. The curriculum spiral serves as a guide in multiple option curricula development which may range from a single course to comprehensive curricula for a group of functionally related occupations. Such options can permit the trainees to exit the program to employment and reenter training to acquire skills for advancement beyond their present position. The employment spiral approach further provides a method of articulating secondary and post-secondary curricula.

A fresh dimension is offered by this handbook, in that the entire occupational curriculum is depicted within, and as an integral part of, a comprehensive careers cluster curriculum model. According to this model, preparation for work is the logical extension and capstone of career awareness, exploration, and orientation experiences. However, the handbook is equally useful to those not desiring the career education emphasis, because the entire employment curriculum development process may be pursued starting with the second chapter of the handbook.

Many curriculum developers will be pleased with the emphasis which is placed on the development of curriculum for individualized competency-based instruction. The handbook is very timely in meeting this growing need as competency-based instruction at all levels of instruction continues to grow. While the emphasis on competency-based instruction is evident throughout the handbook, users will find that curriculum developers can readily apply the steps and procedures to development of curricula for more traditional modes of instruction as well.

This handbook will make a significant and timely contribution in the area of occupational curriculum development, finding use by a broad range of vocational, technical, and business and industry educators.

James B. Hamilton
Senior Research Specialist
The National Center for Research
in Vocational Education

Preface

The purpose of this handbook is to assist those responsible for guiding prospective and in-service occupational teachers, guidance counselors, occupational teacher educators, on-the-job training directors, and employers to develop curricula that are realistic, relevant, current, and, above all, concerned with the needs of those enrolled in them.

The relationship of vocational, occupation, or work preparation education (three terms which this author views as synonomous) to career education is most succinctly put by Miller (1972, p. 12):

> Career education is not a synonym for vocational education, but vocational education is an integral and important part of a total career education system.
>
> It is through vocational education programs that employment skills can be delivered. In career education a student is guided toward a better understanding of himself, his interests, abilities and aptitudes. He is made aware of career opportunities consistent with his aspirations. He is provided a wide range of explorations which should assist him in career direction setting decisions. These decisions ultimately culminate in some kind of specific training for employment.

Any employment-oriented curriculum must, therefore, exist within an educational framework that promotes career awareness and career orientation. We can then be confident that the direction and occupational choice or choices of the individual are based in knowledge through experience, rather than in happenstance or tradition.

The handbook is comprised of two parts: Part One, *A Theory of Organization* and Part Two, *Implementing the Occupational Curriculum Development Theory*. The philosophical and organizational concepts of the book are discussed in Part One.

Part Two is divided into five sections. Each section focuses on and discusses a major step in the occupational curriculum development process.

The five sections are: *Gathering and Organizing Occupational Data, Converting Occupational Organization and Data to Work Preparation*

Curriculum, Organizing the Occupational Curriculum, Writing Occupational Program, Course, and Unit Descriptions, and *Preparing Occupational Learning Materials.* The information in Sections One through Three systematically guides the reader through a number of different curriculum development worksheets, to the completion of the long-range occupational employment-curriculum plan for organizing the work preparation phase of the comprehensive model discussed in Part One. The chapters of the remaining two sections deal more specifically with the preparation and packaging of learning materials.

The *Appendixes* are complete examples of the three major curriculum products that result from the completion of the process discussed and described in the preceding chapters in Part Two of the handbook. Included is a sample copy of an *Occupational Curriculum Development Worksheet Series,* a *Curriculum Guide,* and an informational and activities *Resource Guide* that would be developed for and included in a learning activities package.

These three items are included to give the reader a better idea of the outcome of the occupational curriculum development process, and to provide him or her with examples for planning work preparation curricula and preparing and organizing the necessary materials to implement them.

Acknowledgments

In preparing any manuscript an author quickly comes to realize the importance of other peoples' contributions to the completed work. Such is the case here. A special thank-you to Ms. Maria Butz and Ms. Beverly Faunce for their efforts in writing the materials, which, with some changes and additions, became the model presented herein. Their knowledge of the field of tellering, together with their preciseness and attention to detail, will be appreciated by all who use the book. Also, a special thank-you to Ms. Elizabeth Atteberry for her advice and technical assistance regarding the details of selling traveller's checks and her time and patience with an author very naive to the ways of banking. Thanks is also due Ms. Bobbie Ragan, University Bank of Carbondale, for her help in guiding the author in identifying various informational resources and the time she spent in discussing with him their importance to the activity. Also remembered is Ms. Carol Schultz who provided the various secretarial examples presented in the book.

Three other people who made significant contributions to the work were Ms. Linda Kuecker, Ms. Lois Carrier, and Mr. Jim Marshall. Lois' editorial review and comment greatly assisted in the organization and presentation of the first part of the manuscript. Linda's ability as a typist cannot be questioned or exceeded, but were it not for her grasp of the concept as a whole, her knowledge of the relationships of the materials that bring the concept to life, and her keen eye for detail, the manuscript would not have attained the standard it has. Also, I want to thank Jim Marshall. Only until you know him, realize his many and varied talents, and view his unsurpassed ability to keep innumerable irons in the fire, while at the same time, stoking it to a fevered pitch, can he be fully appreciated. Jim, my continued thanks for your help, humor, and friendship.

Lastly, I want to thank the group of people who turned the hand-written copy into a well organized and appealing typed copy. I can only hope that each of them understands the importance of their efforts and that I truly appreciate their contribution to the final work. Beginning with the typing of the first draft in Hamilton, New Zealand to final completion of the final manuscript, a special thank-you to Mss. Ina Derrick, Rachael Barlett, Jeanne McCarville, Mary Armstrong, and Melody Thomas. Their typing skill, and, perhaps more important, humor and patience with the author, in the end made this work a reality.

To anyone who reads this book and at some time in the future authors his or her own may you be so fortunate as to have as gifted a group of people to work with as I did.

R. F. B.

PART ONE

A Theory of Organization

Adolescence is seen as a period in which young people explore the
world in which they live, the subculture of which they are to become a
part, the roles they may be expected to play and their opportunities
to play roles which suit their personalities, interests, and aptitudes.

Jean Paul Jordaan

In early Western philosophic thought the world was seen as a remote on-going process to be studied, mused over, and intellectually dissected. As time passed, however, philosophers gradually turned from the "furniture of the mind" and began to re-evaluate and interact more with the world around them. Eventually some found answers to their questions about the nature of reality, truth, and goodness in experience and choice.

A similar progression can be seen in Western educational philosophy. Formal education traditionally sought to "liberate the spirit" and "unlock the minds" of a privileged few. A look at current educational practice reveals that many contemporary educators still wholly support the philosophies espoused by their Graeco-Latin predecessors, but that a movement away from traditional thought and practice is growing. Disciplines of classic origin are receiving proportionately less emphasis as curricula change to favor the needs, choices, and experiences of the individual. In essence, the emphasis is shifting from a concern for mastery of subject matter to a concern for the needs of people.

A growing number of contemporary writers, philosophers, theoreticians, and practitioners, from the fields of education, guidance, psychology, government, and philosophy, have rallied to extend and support this more recent approach to education. As the social, cultural, economic, ethnic, religious, and political backgrounds of students change it becomes more and more apparent that the traditional liberal arts curriculum is irrelevant to many students, particularly at this time in their lives. No longer is education a privilege of the select few. It is rapidly becoming a right and, in many cases, a necessity for all. If the slogan "education for all" is the educational hallmark of the time, then those responsible for developing curricula have but one alternative: to develop curricula which assist people in meeting their needs. Education must become a means to attaining a perceived goal rather than being an end in and for itself.

The school is charged by society with the responsibility of preparing youth for adulthood, and a part of its mission is to provide young people with experiences that will help them make crucial decisions throughout their lives. One of the most important of these decisions concerns career or occupation.

While the nature and characteristics of work can and do change over time, two factors remain constant: the individual's need to make employment and work decisions, and society's need for specific goods and services. The ebb and flow of demand for particular occupations, increasing numbers of different occupations from which to choose, the constant evolution of occupations, specialization of activity, and increasing prerequisities for entering many occupations and career pursuits makes choice of occupation considerably more complex and difficult (Toffler, 1970).

Assisting people in matching personal assets and liabilities with occupational interests, opportunity, and direction requires an appreciation and understanding of the problem and an ability to overcome it. Career education is a response to this need.

Definition and Purpose

Career education is that aspect of the total school curriculum designed to acquaint the individual learner with the world of work, and, through a gradual and systematic exploration of and orientation to the employment community, to bring the learner to a point where he or she can make a choice of career and begin preparation for it.

The focus of an established and successful career education program is on the knowledge, attitudes, and skills of the learner as they relate to concepts of self, community, and occupation. The long-range goal of a comprehensive career education program, which begins in elementary school, is to assist each individual to better understand the employment structure of the community in which he or she lives, and to guide him or her in selecting, preparing for, and advancing in an occupation or family of occupations.

The concepts of self, community, and career develop with involvement with various career and occupation-related learning activities, activities that parallel and complement the predictable stages of human growth, development, and maturation. Once the learner becomes aware of a concept, he or she begins a more in-depth study of families of occupations, and of the conditions which direct, limit, and influence them. The learning activities experienced during this first nine or ten year discovery period are varied. The learner can, for example, take part in various occupational and work-related games and simulated situations, assume roles in different types of learning enterprises, take field trips and make visits to various community businesses, industries, and agencies, discuss the pros and cons of various occupations with people employed in them, compile occupationally related diaries, and study growth patterns of various occupations and organizations. In sum, the focus of the learner's experience is self and the work community. The end goal is an integrated individual who, through understanding and experience, can begin preparation for work in a career family of occupations which best suits his or her abilities, interests, and temperament.

Curriculum Model

The *Comprehensive Careers Cluster Curriculum Model* discussed in the following chapter is a guide to developing and organizing a total career education program. It is a frame of reference in which the curriculum designer contrives and develops ideas, not a prescription for classroom/

learning laboratory activities. The chapter describes the position, intentions, and limitations of the various components of the model. If developed and implemented, the organizational plan would move learners gradually from the school to the community, through phases of career awareness, exploration, orientation and, finally, preparation for employment in a single occupation or family of occupations.

A detailed discussion of the rationale, organization, and application of the curriculum development plan appears in Chapter 1.

CHAPTER 1

The Comprehensive Careers
Cluster Curriculum Model

A cursory look at the typical adult's life shows that most adults spend fifty or sixty percent or more of their waking hours in work and work-related activities. Yet the contemporary public school curriculum makes little effort to assist learners in identifying and choosing an occupation which complements their interests and abilities. This chapter suggests an organizational plan which focuses on careers and career opportunities and provides the learner with experiences that move him or her from an initial awareness of the world of work through preparation for, entrance into, and progression in the employment community.

The *Comprehensive Careers Cluster Curriculum Model* is an organizational concept to be used by curriculum designers, teachers, and school administrators to plan and implement curricula that focus on personal growth and maturation and relate them to career development. The model provides an organizational structure and frame of reference for defining curriculum ideas and sequencing them to parallel and complement the needs and interests of the various age groups of individuals being served. The model does not define the activities or content that would be included within each of its modules.

The curriculum theory on which the model is based recognizes four phases of career development: career awareness, exploration, orientation, and occupational preparation. The model groups all of the career and occupational education offerings around a central theme of career education, and coordinates the four phases with the grade levels of the school. With a comprehensive career and occupational guidance program the various courses and units of learning comprise the total career education offering.

General Configuration of the Model

Figure 1.1 is an illustration of the Comprehensive Careers Cluster Curriculum Model, which is comprised of five career cluster axes. Each axis is, in turn, made up of five developmental modules, beginning with the central module common to all axes and working out to the last modules showing the stylized cloverleafs. Each module represents a stage in the progression from a beginning career awareness to occupational competence in one or more occupations in a specific occupational cluster. Typical occupational clusters represented by individual axes would be health occupations, industrial occupations, communications occupations, public service occupations. In addition, each axis has two auxiliary modules that influence and add perspective to the developmental modules. All of the modules will presently be explained more fully.

As shown in Figure 1.1, the model is designed to accommodate five major categories of occupations. With slight modification, however, it

Figure 1.1 *A Three-Dimensional View of the Comprehensive Careers Cluster Curriculum Model*

could be restructured to reflect other existing or yet-to-be-developed occupational classification systems.

The Developmental Modules

Each developmental module of the curriculum model contains a variety of activities at a particular grade level. The activities guide the learner's career education experience. The developmental activities systematically aid the learner in selecting and preparing for employment in an occupation or family of occupations that complements his or her occupational interest and capabilities. For convenience in identifying, labeling, and discussing the modular components a two-dimensional sketch of a single career axis is presented in Figure 1.2. The grade level for which each of the modules is designed is also included.

The proposed career education program begins in the early childhood years and continues throughout the educational life of the individual. While each developmental module is unique in its own right, the modules also share a number of traits. Each module makes provision for modifying, adapting and/or relating traditional subject matter to the central theme of career education. All the modules offer the learner the opportunity to experience the types of learning activities that will be required when he or she elects to prepare for employment in a particular occupation or group of occupations. The learning activities parallel the developmental life stages of the individual. Constant effort is also made to insure that the learner receives continuous, relevant, and up-to-date career and occupational guidance information, regardless of the module in which he or she is working.

Each of the stages represented by the developmental component modules focuses on two areas of learning: selfhood and reality. No study of the world of work (reality) can be very meaningful unless the individual can relate to it in some manner. To fully accommodate both selfhood and reality the modules take into account both directed and non-directed (synergistic) learning. Directed learning is often expressed in terms of learning objectives. For example, a student might be directed to learn the occupational titles of fifteen health occupations not requiring preparation beyond high school. The non-directed part of the learning process is by nature more subjective and qualitative. One objective of non-directed learning would be that the individual come to recognize his or her own feelings of security or insecurity, of interest or disinterest, in those fifteen occupations.

People learn more than they are taught. This concept must not only be recognized, but capitalized upon and used to enhance the directed learning process. The degree to which a child has developed the psychological security to stand by his or her own convictions without being narrow-minded may not be readily measurable or predictable. However, the child's level of self-understanding must be considered and be an

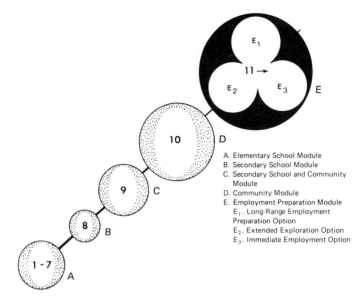

Figure 1.2 *A Single Career Cluster Axis With Its Developmental Modules*

integral part in the formation of the learning experience to which he or she is exposed. Non-directed learning complements and enriches directed learning.

The proposed curriculum model parallels the developmental life stages defined by Super (1957) and reflects the classification of behaviors as defined by Krathwohl (1964), Bloom (1956), Gagné (1965), and others. The learning activities assigned to the Elementary School, Secondary School, Secondary School and Community, and Community Career Component Modules (grades 1–10) emphasize the development, modification, and/or enhancement of the cognitive and affective behavior of the learners.

Beyond grade ten, the emphasis changes and the career-related learning activities defined in the Employment Preparation Module focus on the acquisition of knowledge and the development of attitudes and skills necessary for employment. (See Figure 1.3.) While individuals are continually learning about the work community, reassessing it, and changing their values with regard to it, there is an identifiable change in emphasis from the pre-occupational learning experiences to those that prepare a person for work.

Elementary School Module

The Elementary School Module (1–7) provides the learner with an initial awareness of the world of work. Bailey (1971) best summarizes the essence of elementary school career education:

. . . the interests of the child in early elementary school are largely centered around himself, his family and his immediate environment. Since vocational maturity involves both knowledge of self and the world of work the early grades of school can use the natural self-interest tendencies of the child to build a foundation of information about both areas. He can begin to learn about himself as a person distinct from other children in the class, defined in part by his environment — his unique family, his unique home. At the same time, he can be exposed to broad concepts about the world of work in the context of his self-centered world — occupational roles of members of his family, or workers who come to his home, or people who serve him. As the child explores home, school, and community, the importance and inter-dependence of workers can be stressed. Youngsters should also be helped to develop positive attitudes toward the world of work and the value of each individual's contribution. By increasing the awareness of self and the world of work, children begin to see a positive relationship between the two. Finally, it is central at this level to cause students to consider and evaluate their occupational "Fantasy Preferences." Such preferences can serve as a base of knowledge from which to develop more realistic attitudes and under-standing. . .

. . . in the latter part of elementary school the child becomes increasingly responsive to the demands of his teachers and parents and pressures to per-form well in school become acute. This stage appears right for introducing basic concepts of career development. Students should be made aware of the longitudinal, integrated, and dynamic nature of vocational behavior. Self appraisal, knowledge of the world of work and perhaps school work as a whole, may become more meaningful as the student's attention is turned toward the future and his role in preparing for it. At this level the study and understanding of work roles are extended to include the concepts of job families and interest-area families. Self appraisal becomes more meaningful as individuals are caused to think about changes due to maturation and learning, and understanding that certain self elements are related to various occupa-tional roles. An attitude of "planfulness" should be prompted by assisting students in making decisions and outlining future actions. Concrete expe-rience continues to be an important part of the program with much more responsibility attached to role playing and reality testing.

The Secondary School Module

The learner who has moved into the Secondary School Module continues to strive for an understanding of himself or herself and of the employment community in which he or she lives. The Secondary School Module ex-tends learning activities into grade eight, but in a somewhat different man-ner than the Elementary School Module. Whereas the world of work was discussed, described, and classified in various ways in the Elementary School Module, in grade eight the learners are afforded a closer look at the cultural, social, economic, and personal implications of work in various distinct occupational groups. The learner becomes increasingly aware of the similarities and differences within and among such groups. The oppor-tunity to compare types of occupations and the many events that bear upon them benefits the learner in that it permits him or her to re-evaluate different types of employment.

The goals and rationale identified by Bailey and Stadt (1973) for the awareness phase (K-3) of their curriculum model can be appropriated for use in the Secondary School Module. The following statements from them contribute to understanding of the projected outcomes of the module:

Awareness of Self

In early childhood the individual begins the process of self-concept formation which continues throughout his life. Initially, the child gathers sensory impressions (i.e., "self-percepts") related to his physical configuration and his capabilities (Super, 1963). Gradually, he begins to organize his perceptions into higher-order generalizations and, finally, into simple self-concepts. That is, the impressions he receives from his activities and interpersonal relationships are combined to form mental pictures. Emphasis on self-awareness and differentiation of self from others helps the child develop a repertoire of self-percepts which become the foundation for more accurate and comprehensive self-concepts.

Awareness of Different Types of Occupational Roles

The young child perceives people performing different types of work activities, but is not able to conceptualize differences among them (Goodson, 1970, Zimmerman and Bailey, 1971). For example, the child does not distinguish between the work that his parents may do in an occupation outside the home from the "work" that is done within the home, and from hobby and/or volunteer activities done in addition to an occupation. This goal is closely related to the fourth goal which is designed, in part, to help the child develop skills to make such distinctions.

Awareness of Individual Responsibility for Own Actions

This goal is related to the first goal in which the child begins to recognize his own uniqueness, and to the second goal in which he becomes more aware of the types of roles that he and others perform. These perceptions provide the basis for the child's understanding that (1) he is responsible for his activities and (2) controls them by choosing from available alternatives. The child's development of a sense of control is seen as a prerequisite to his later acceptance of responsibility for career planning.

Development of the Rudiments of Classification and Decision-Making Skills

This goal includes the development of two types of fundamental behaviors: (1) classification abilities and (2) practice in making decisions. With respect to the first type of behavior, research on the nature of concept formation has demonstrated that categorization ability is intimately related to children's cognitive development. Formanek and Morine (1972, p. 154) conclude that "Developing concepts such as 'group,' 'role,' or 'sanction' in the social sciences demands a skill in identifying similarities and differences in human behavior. Consequently, a child's ability to categorize would seem to bear some relation to his ability to understand much of the modern elementary school curriculum." The implications for the understanding of occupational groups are self-evident.

The emphasis on practice in decision-making is designed to acquaint the child with the "logic" of choosing from among alternatives. While most children may not be able to conceptualize decision-making as a process, they will be able to apply such methods to the choosing of alternate courses of action, alternate behaviors, and alternate modes of expression. "From early childhood through adulthood the skills and motives needed for making wise decisions are essential elements in the equipment of the maturing person" (Hill and Luckey, 1969, p. 14).

Learning Cooperative Social Behavior

Like previous goals, the need for effective working relationships is a fundamental behavior of childhood that continues throughout life. As Havighurst (1953, p. 31) notes, ". . . the nine or ten-year old clearly shows what he will be like, socially, at fifty." The technique of behavior modification notwithstanding. Havighurst's observation is well taken in that social relationships constitute a foundation element in later adaptions to life and its demands. Effective working relationships with his peers is not some frosting on the educational cake that is desirable if it were to come about incidentally. Rather, it is an essential ingredient of the cake itself (Hill and Luckey, 1969).

Development of Respect for Others and the Work That They Do

Probably at no other time does the individual have as high a regard for work as he does in early childhood. The tendency for children to play at work is well-known. Kabach (1966, p. 167) notes that ". . . the younger the child the greater the interest in the actual job performance itself. Most children are natural born actors; they want to act out in order to understand what it feels like to be a carpenter or a ball player." The question is not one of should attitudes toward work be taught in early elementary school. Students do, in fact, possess work attitudes. Generally, these are favorable. Rather, at issue is how to preserve positive attitudes so they may be used as foundation for more realistic attitudes and understandings (Herr, 1970).

The Secondary School and Community Module

A typical Secondary School and Community Module activity is the school-based learning enterprise. A learning enterprise in this sense is an activity which simulates business conditions in the working world. By having learners work in a realistic setting that permits the assuming of work roles, it helps them choose satisfying occupations.

Various approaches can be used to conduct a learning enterprise. One is to set up the learning enterprise as an already existing, ongoing activity, with the learner assuming the role of prospective employee. In this role, the learner would be expected to make application for work, be interviewed, hired, receive training, work at an assigned activity for a period of time, and lastly, go through the formal process of resigning from an occupation.

A modification of this approach is to have the learners develop their own enterprise. They would be required to establish a business appropriate to and reflecting a particular category of occupations, conduct business for a given period of time, and liquidate the operation in an acceptable and businesslike manner. Instead of assuming the role of employees, here the learners accept total responsibility for the creation and direction of a functioning business.

Either alternative provides the learners with an opportunity to orient themselves to the many aspects of work. They experience, to varying degrees, the feeling of being working members of a viable enterprise. They experience what it feels like to work in a specific type of occupation with its related personalities, tools, and environment. The learners also gain an appreciation of the time and effort required to maintain an ongoing business. Since the process is basic to our economic system, gaining familiarity with it has educational merit in itself.

Up to this point (the end of grade nine), *all* participants have received equal educational fare. At the completion of grade nine each individual learner is asked: "Based on your knowledge and experience to date, which category of occupations most appeals to you?" The learner's response adds direction and scope to his or her occupational and educational future and determines the focus of the orientation experience in grade ten.

Community Module

The Community Module is centered in the employment community and focuses on the work activities of employees in various enterprises. In some respects, the community-based offering closely resembles a work-study or cooperative education experience in that it relies on the work community for its content. There is, however, a significant difference. Whereas work-study and cooperative occupational education programs assist learners in acquiring work skills, the community-based career component module emphasizes career exploration, study, and involvement, with no emphasis on the acquisition of marketable skills.

The main purpose of the community-based module is to provide the learner with an opportunity for involvement with people working in a functionally related category of occupations. This module gives the learner a chance to directly observe people performing typical tasks in actual work settings.

The experience will conclude the awareness, exploration, and orientation phases of the Comprehensive Careers Cluster Curriculum Model and mark the beginning of preparation for employment.

The Employment Preparation Module

The Employment Preparation Module is the last in the series of five developmental modules. Learners who have progressed through the pre-specialized portion of the model are now ready to acquire specific knowledge, attitudes, and skills needed to become employable in a selected group of occupations. The cloverleaf within the module reflects the module's unique contribution, namely, the three employment options. These options offer alternatives to learners with differing occupational and educational needs. (For review, see Figures 1.1 and 1.2.)

The three options are designed to meet the needs of three classes of learners. Option One, the Long-Range Employment Preparation Option, is for those who are sure of their occupational choice and wish to begin preparing for it. Option Two, the Extended Exploration Option, is designed for those learners who wish additional career exploration before making an occupational choice. Option Three, the Immediate Employment Preparation Option, is for those individuals who have need for immediate employment. While the purpose, means of implementation, and outcome of the options differ, they all have one feature in common. Regardless of the option selected, each individual begins acquiring entry-level skills and knowledge in one or more occupational specialties or sub-specialties in an occupational group of his or her choosing. The plan also provides for maximum vertical and horizontal mobility for individuals who are active in it, as we will see.

The *Long-Range Employment Preparation Option* has a threefold purpose. First, it provides the individual who has a perceived occupational goal with a program that gets him or her moving in the desired direction; secondly, it prepares him or her for employment in a number of en route (related) occupational specialties and sub-specialties in case he or she should leave the preparatory program prior to attainment of his or her occupational goal. And thirdly, it adds long-range potential to the extended exploration and immediate employment options of the module should it be needed by a learner who initially opted for one of these other two options.

The main tool to be used by the curriculum designer in developing this option is the dual employment-curriculum spiral. Such a spiral is developed for each functionally related group of occupations, and provides a hierarchy of occupations through which a learner can move until he or she reaches his or her occupational goal. An example of an employment-curriculum spiral appears in Chapter 2. If the Comprehensive Careers Cluster Curriculum Model outlined in this chapter were adopted on a wide scale, a dual spiral would have to be developed for each of the occupational groups that make up the total labor force. But on a more modest scale, the curriculum designer or teacher could develop very effective spirals for the various occupational groups with which he or she is or will be working.

The *Extended Exploration Option* is for the person who has expressed an interest in a specific occupational category, for example, library science occupations, transportation occupations, agricultural occupations, but who needs more time to explore and evaluate the various occupations within the category.

A spiral configuration is also used to depict the organizational plan of the Extended Exploration Option. While the long-range spiral moves the learner from an entry-level occupation to the technical, professional, research, and administrative occupations in a given field, the extended exploration spiral moves the learner from one entry-level occupation to another. The tasks and learning objectives of a given entry-level occupation on the extended exploration spiral are selected because of their uniqueness to that occupation. Rather than selecting activities common to most or all of the other entry-level occupations on the spiral, the activities which are performed specifically in one occupation will give the learner a more realistic view of that occupation and assist him or her in distinguishing it from the other entry-level occupations. As the learner experiences the various entering occupations, he or she formulates opinions as to which type of work is most appealing. Once the learner chooses an occupation or shows particular interest in a group of occupations, he or she is guided to the appropriate occupational program to continue preparation in the long-range option.

The *Immediate Employment Preparation Option* also serves the learner who has completed the kindergarten through grade ten portion of the comprehensive curriculum model and is ready to begin occupational preparation. But rather than help him or her develop toward a long-range occupational goal as do the other two options, this option assists the individual who must go to work immediately.

After establishing his or her employment needs the learner enrolls in an occupational program where he or she prepares for work in a particular entry-level occupation or one of its specialties or sub-specialties. On completion of the training program, he or she goes to work. If, however, after working for a period of time, the individual wishes to return to school for additional occupational preparation, he or she can do so. The person re-enters the curriculum spiral at a point of demonstrable competence. In many cases, the re-entry will be at a higher level on the spiral than the original point of exit due to the fact that the individual will have gained in ability and knowledge while in the workforce.

The Auxiliary Modules

The auxiliary modules that accompany each of the career cluster axes of the Comprehensive Careers Cluster Curriculum Model are supportive of the developmental modules. An illustration of a single career cluster axis with its developmental and auxiliary modules appears in Figure 1.3. The Career and Occupational Guidance Module provides guidance information and service to the learner throughout his or her formal career education. The Related Subject Matter Modules relate the academic offerings of the school to the career education of the individual.

The *Career and Occupational Guidance Module* is the communications link between the occupational education offerings of the school and the employment sector of the community. While the learner is moving through

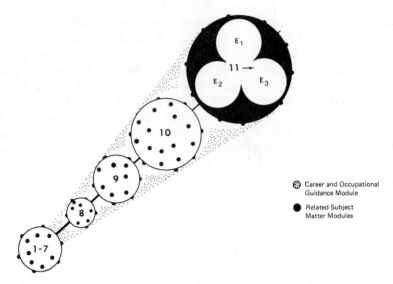

Figure 1.3 *A Single Career Cluster Axis With Its Developmental and Auxiliary Modules*

the program, he or she is gaining skills, experience, and knowledge. This auxiliary module provides counseling and guidance toward realistic goals, goals that clearly relate to the employment needs of the community. This module is a formal liaison between the school and the community and keeps track of the learner's progress toward an occupational goal.

The goals of the module are:

· Identify, gather, and maintain accounts of the immediate, short-range, and long-range employment needs of the community.
· Record the interests, capabilities, and preferences of the individual about his or her perceived short-range and long-range career plans.
· Assist the learner in acquiring information necessary for entering, receiving training, performing, and progressing in a selected occupation or group of occupations.
· Identify and make available home, school, and community career and occupational learning resources.
· Record the progress of the learner toward his or her career and occupational goals.
· Assist the individual, if and when the need arises, in the transition from the education setting to the community, or from the community to the school.

The *Related Subject Matter Modules* are academic courses that enhance the career education program. Examples of academic subjects that support the career and occupational education program include: economics, social studies, economic geography, psychology, and sociology. The work-related academic course offerings provide the learner with understanding of the influences of economic, social, and technical factors on the world of work. As might be expected, the subject matter objectives change to meet the informational needs of the learner as he or she progresses through the career model.

The learning activities of the subject matter components also expose the learner to the *types* of activities he or she could expect in preparing for a given occupation. For instance, a potential engineering technician should be introduced to the technical, scientific, and mathematical material that would be encountered if he or she pursued work in the engineering field. While he or she may be quite knowledgeable about the occupation itself, he or she may not expect the variety of courses that are required to prepare for employment in the field. The occupation may retain its original appeal, but the effort, expense, and/or time involved in attaining the end result should influence an individual's final decision if sound choices are to be made. In many cases, the effort required to reach an occupational end is a major factor in determining whether the end is ever realized. This fact dare not be overlooked in a comprehensive career education program.

Progression Through the Model

We have looked at all the components of the comprehensive curriculum model. Let us now look at the learner's progression through it. First, however, the four phases of growth through which a learner passes as he or she moves toward career and occupational maturity, awareness, exploration, orientation and preparation, must be considered. (See Figure 1.4.)

While the titles suggest that each of the four individual phases of involvement is distinct, the phases are actually a continuum of learning experiences in which a gradual, but constant change in emphasis occurs. As the individual learns he or she moves from an initial awareness of him or herself as a person in the economic world "out there" to a point in time at which he or she is prepared to become an important and contributing member of the workforce.

The four phases of the model are best discussed in terms of grade level. In the first seven years of school (grades one through seven), the learner's activities guide him or her toward an *awareness* of the world of work, the ways in which it is organized, the occupations of which it is made up, and the multitude of opportunities that exist in it. In grade eight, the learner continues in this phase of the model, but is now more involved in learning about the nature of work and types of occupations in specific occupational categories.

The learner moves into the *exploration* phase of the model at grade nine. In this second phase the learner is further oriented toward newly

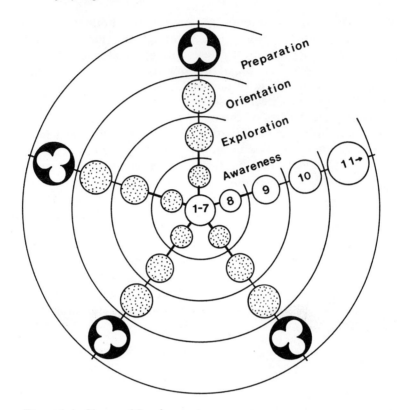

Figure 1.4 *Phases of Involvement*

found personal and career-related interests. Again all aspects of the world of work are studied, but now within the defined boundaries of the five occupational categories. The learner continues acquiring data that will be used in making occupational decisions.

Once the learner has compared various aspects of the many occupations in the five categories of the curriculum model he or she is asked to decide which occupational category is most appealing. When the decision is made, he or she moves into the *orientation* phase of the model at grade ten. The learner then becomes even more directly involved with people working in that particular category of occupations. Reflecting a gradual but constant movement away from school-based learning experiences, the orientation phase of the model takes the learner into various community-based enterprises in which he or she is particularly interested.

In the orientation phase the learner talks with people about their work. He or she experiences the actual work environment. Without actually assuming the occupational roles, he or she attempts to gain an understanding of them by watching, talking to, and vicariously sharing in the work experience.

The *preparation* phase of the curriculum model capstones the awareness, exploration, and orientation portion of the total career education offering. The preparation phase is, as its name implies, that portion of the curriculum model given over to preparing people for employment. It is the next logical step for the learners who have gained an experiential knowledge of the employment community, ordered their values according to their knowledge of its many options, and who are ready to prepare for work in a particular occupation or family of occupations.

If the comprehensive curriculum model were implemented in the education system, formal career education would begin with entry into elementary school and continue with varying degrees of involvement throughout productive adult life.

The Elementary School Module is common to all learners in a particular school. Once the elementary school-based career education program is complete, the learners enter the Secondary School Module at grade eight. Here, they are divided into groups by any convenient method and each group begins learning about occupations in one of the occupational categories. As the school year passes, the learners rotate at a prescribed rate among the five occupational clusters. (As mentioned before, the model can accommodate more than five axes or occupational clusters, if desired.) The rotation rate should be such that by the end of grade eight, all learners have had experiences in all of the categories. (See Figure 1.5.)

In the Secondary School and Community Module which begins with grade nine, the learners are again grouped and put into one of the courses

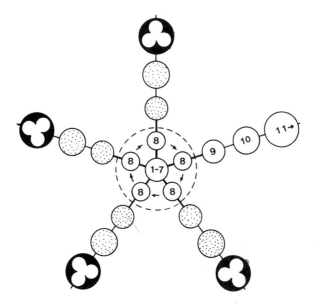

Figure 1.5 *Rotation of Learning Experiences at Grade Eight*

focusing on a single occupational category. A rotation system similar to that used in grade eight is used to move learners through the remaining categories. (See Figure 1.6.) Utilizing their already acquired knowledge and awareness of the world of work, and extending it to a more active involvement with the work process, the learners study the various categories of occupations in greater detail. One approach that might be used in the exploration phase of the model is that of the learning enterprise, which was discussed earlier. Whereas the learner's role during the awareness phase was that of an observer and questioner, during the exploratory phrase he or she is a more active participant in the process. The experiences afforded the learners in an activity such as a learning enterprise, coupled with other activities that support and add meaning to learning, comprise the ninth grade exploratory phase of the career education model.

The end of grade nine is the first point in the career education process at which the learners indicate a preference of category or categories of occupations. (See Figure 1.7.) Up to this point, the learners have all received the same educational fare. Assuming that they have all met the objectives of the preceding modules and have acquired some knowledge and ordering of values, they are now ready to respond to the question: "What category of occupations do you prefer?" Once a preference is stated, the learner enrolls in the appropriate community module at the tenth grade level to learn more about the occupations within that particular category.

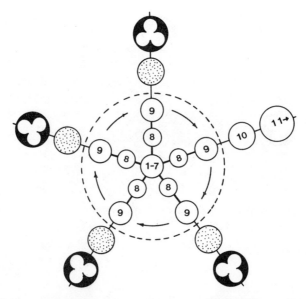

Figure 1.6 *Rotation of Learning Experiences at Grade Nine*

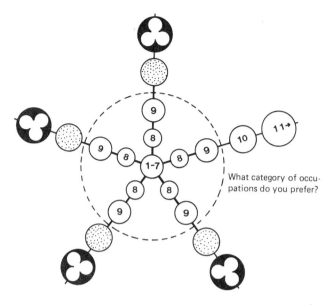

Figure 1.7 *Preference of Occupational Category at the End of Grade Nine*

Relying on the cooperation of the work community, the learner now becomes an observer of and interactor with members of that community. Like a work-study or co-operative education program, the learner in the community-based course leaves the school proper for a part of the school day and attends class in a community enterprise. If, for instance, the learner indicated an interest in health occupations, a part of each school day would be spent in businesses employing health occupations people. Such businesses include: hospitals, veterinary clinics, doctor's offices, funeral homes, and dentist offices. While on location, he or she would observe and interact with a particular work environment and learn what it is like to be a part of it. With this experience and other related assignments, the individual would, by the end of grade ten, be quite knowledgeable of both the common and the unique aspects of those occupations in which he is particularly interested.

Once the learner has completed the community-based career education course offering at grade ten, he or she is asked a second, more specific question: "For what *occupation* would you like to begin preparing?" (See Figure 1.8.) The learner's response sets in motion a customized but flexible occupational education option. This option is one of the three options represented by the cloverleaf of the Employment Preparation Module discussed previously. Curricular opportunities which provide for movement toward a long-range occupational goal, additional career exploration, or immediate employment in an entry-level occupation must now be made available.

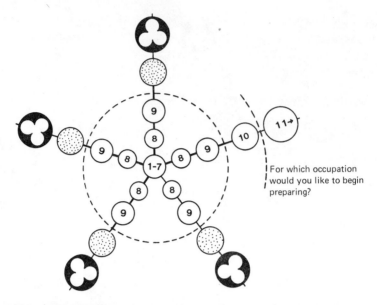

Figure 1.8 *Choice of Occupation or Career Alternative at the End of Grade Ten*

Philosophical Considerations

We have described the general configuration of the Comprehensive Careers Cluster Curriculum Model, related the components of the model to the traditional grade levels of the school system, and shown how the learner progresses through the model. In this section the philosophical assumptions which underlie the model and the provisions and limits of the model and its components are discussed.

The assumptions on which the model are based are:

- The individual ought to be the focus of all career education activity.
- Each individual differs, in varying degrees, in interests, needs, and abilities.
- Each individual can become qualified by virtue of these characteristics for a number of different occupations.
- Occupations are dynamic rather than static by nature.
- Occupations require a characteristic pattern of abilities, interests, and personality traits with tolerance great enough to allow both a variety of occupations for each individual and a variety of individuals for each occupation.
- Career education is a cumulative, lifelong, evolutionary process.
- Career education contributes to the establishment and complementary formation of the concepts of self, work, and occupation in the temporal context of human growth and maturation.

- An individual's career education, development, and maturation can be systematically influenced through personal involvement, inter-action, decision-making, and experience in simulated or actual career and occupationally related situations.

The provisions and limits of the model are:

- Continuous, lifelong career and occupational education and guid-ance, including career awareness, exploration, orientation, occupa-tional preparation and entry, advancement, and career and/or occupational change.
- Early career awareness, exploration, and orientation experiences that establish the basis for future occupational decision-making, preparation, entry, and advancement.
- Gradual and systematic progression in the learning environment from the school to the employment community.
- Gradual and systematic progression from a simulated to a real world learning situation.
- Relating academic subject matter to the career and occupationally oriented curriculum.
- Home, school, and community involvement and participation.
- Career and occupational education in each of a number of career clusters.
- Experiencing the *types* of learning and study necessary for prepara-tion for a given occupation or group of occupations.
- Relating the career and occupational activities common to two or more career groups.
- Meeting immediate occupational guidance and employment needs.
- Meeting extended career exploration and concurrent employment needs.
- Meeting long-range occupational preparation and employment needs.

The remainder of the book will deal with different aspects of the Employment Preparation Module, the module which contains the three options open to the learner who has progressed through the rest of the model.

Since the Long-Range Employment-Curriculum Spiral is the basic organizational plan for developing the Employment Preparation Option and the other two employment preparation options, an understanding of the spiral concept and the ability to apply this understanding to the occupational curriculum development process is essential. The following chapter discusses, at length, the dual employment-curriculum spiral and its use in developing and organizing the preparation phase of the Comprehen-sive Careers Cluster Curriculum Model.

In Review

1. The Comprehensive Careers Cluster Curriculum Model shown in Figure 1.1 is designed around five major occupational categories. What structural changes would have to be made to accommodate the occupational classification system of the Department of Labor? the Office of Education?

2. A single career axis of the total model represents one category of occupations. Using the single axis concept and, let us say, the occupational classification system of the Office of Education, could you design a curriculum model for a particular geographic area of the country? the central Midwest? the Pacific Northwest? the Great Lakes area?

3. The titles of the various developmental modules of the comprehensive model reflect an evolution beginning in the school and moving toward the community. Discuss the rationale for this movement from the school to the community in terms of awareness, exploration, orientation, etc.

4. The Employment Preparation Module is the last in the series of five developmental modules in the curriculum model. It is comprised of three program options. Name each option and discuss its purpose and rationale.

5. What is the purpose of the auxiliary Career and Occupational Guidance Module? Discuss its relationship to the developmental modules.

6. What is the purpose of the Related Subject Matter Modules? Discuss their relationship to the developmental modules.

7. The Comprehensive Careers Cluster Curriculum Model is based on four phases of career involvement. Discuss each phase in terms of types of activities that might be included, evolution of the learner's involvement, and rationale for the gradual increase in involvement as the learner progresses through the model.

8. Discuss the changes in emphasis that occur as the learner moves through the awareness, exploration, orientation, and preparation phases of the comprehensive curriculum model.

9. In part, the Comprehensive Careers Cluster Curriculum Model is described as a ". . . . frame of reference" for future development of career education offerings. In terms of the assumptions and provisions of the model, how can it be used in this sense to organize and develop career education curricula?

CHAPTER 2

The Long-Range
Employment-Curriculum Spiral

In the process of describing the Comprehensive Careers Cluster Curriculum Model from career awareness through occupational preparation, the three options that make up the Employment Preparation Module of the model were discussed. One of the alternatives in the preparatory module is the Long-Range Employment Preparation Option with its corresponding spiral. In this chapter the long-range employment-curriculum spiral concept for providing a structure for designing curriculum for this option is discussed. With minor modification, the dual employment-curriculum spiral is also the basis for developing the complementary Extended Exploration and Immediate Employment Options of the employment preparation module.

Characteristics of the Employment-Curriculum Spiral

The Long-Range Employment-Curriculum Spiral is the conceptual model used in developing and organizing work preparation curricula. A dual employment-curriculum spiral is created for each functionally related group of occupations within one of the occupational categories represented by a single axis of the comprehensive curriculum model. (See Figure 2.1.) Typical groups of occupations for which individual spirals might be developed are Automotive maintenance and service occupations, Clinical dental occupations, and Food service occupations.

A dual spiral is made up of two component spirals: a long-range *employment* spiral and a long-range *curriculum* spiral. In concert, these two produce characteristics which neither possesses independently; that is, there is a synergistic effect when the two function as a unit. Together, the

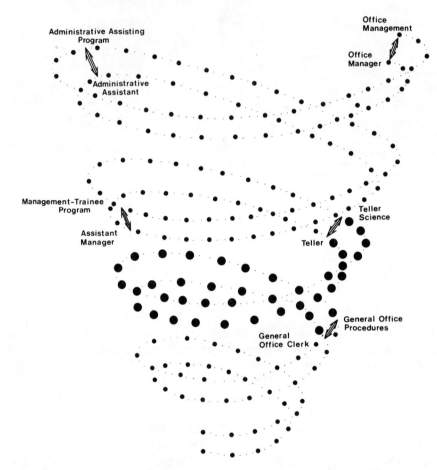

Figure 2.1 *A Long-Range Employment-Curriculum Spiral for Money Distribution and Management-Related Occupations*

two spirals provide the individual with a way to reach a particular occupational goal. At the same time a number of en route employment and educational options are made available in case they should be needed before the original goal is reached. The employment spiral is a hierarchical ordering of occupation, occupational specialty, and sub-specialty titles along a series of spirally arranged dots representing the tasks of the various occupations. The curriculum spiral is a *timeline* comprised of dots representing learning objectives of a total occupational curriculum.

The terms *category, division,* and *group* that appear throughout the handbook are not used indiscriminately. They should be viewed in the same context and with the same relationships to one another as in the *Dictionary of Occupational Titles.*

The Long-Range Employment Spiral

The Long-Range Employment Spiral is the conceptual model used to organize the occupations of a functionally related group of occupations. A sample employment spiral appears in Figure 2.2. The spiral assists the curriculum designer in establishing a hierarchy of occupations and in identifying the positions of the primary occupations with their occupational specialties and sub-specialties within the organizational plan. The employment spiral provides a conceptual basis for the future development of its companion long-range curriculum spiral. Together the two spirals provide the organization for the school/work concept, in which the school and the work community have active and interdependent roles.

The development of the employment spiral is the first step in the

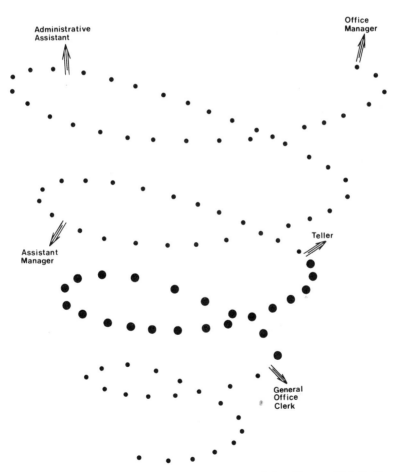

Figure 2.2　*A Long-Range Employment Spiral for Money Distribution and Management-Related Occupations*

implementation of the dual spiral theory. If the theory is extended to its logical conclusion, then each of the approximately 35,000 occupations, occupational specialties, and occupational sub-specialties that comprise the total labor force of the country are considered potential members of articulated hierarchies of functionally related occupational groups. When the need arises, these groups can be the basis for developing articulated employment training programs in the various occupational areas.

Components

Five primary occupational titles appear on any given employment spiral. A primary occupation is not a part of a larger occupation, but is made up of a number of occupational specialties and sub-specialties. The primary occupations for any employment spiral are: 1) an entry level occupation, 2) a technical occupation, 3) a professional occupation, 4) a research occupation, and 5) an administrative occupation. An example of a primary occupation with its components is the technical occupation of residential carpenter, with its specialties of rough carpenter and finish carpenter, with their respective sub-specialties of form builder, sheather, and roofer, and cabinet installer, hardwood flooring installer, and trim setter.

The five primary occupations establish the five major points on the spiral. Each point is marked by a triple-shafted arrow. The arcs of the spiral are in turn made up of a series of dots which represent the respective tasks of the five primary occupations. The *highlighted* dots represent the tasks of the *primary* occupation being analyzed. The title of the spiral is derived directly from the title of the occupational *group* for which the spiral is being constructed.

The occupational specialties and sub-specialties of each of the five primary occupational titles are implied on the spiral, although they are not shown. Each primary occupation has its particular occupational specialties and sub-specialties. The primary occupations with their lists of occupational specialties and sub-specialties, identified in the completed analysis, are used in determining occupational program, course, and unit titles of the occupational curriculum.

The Long-Range Curriculum Spiral

The Long-Range Occupational Curriculum Spiral for a particular group of occupations is the educational complement of the Long-Range Occupational Employment Spiral. (See Figure 2.3.) The curriculum spiral is an organizational concept that complements the employment spiral and adds educational dimension to it. Since the occupational curriculum is organized to complement the world of work, movement from work to education or education to work can occur with little or no penalty to the *worker-learner*. Vertical movement is also made easier by this employment-education organizational system.

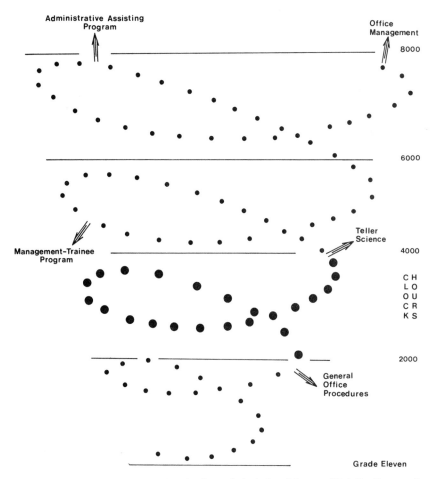

Figure 2.3 *A Long-Range Curriculum Spiral for Money Distribution and Management-Related Occupations*

Components

The curriculum spiral is comprised of five occupational programs. The titles of the programs are derived from and coincide with the five primary occupational titles listed on the employment spiral. The programs on the spiral in Figure 2.3 are: General Office Procedures (entry-level program); Teller Science (technical program); Management Trainee Program (professional program); Administrative Assistant Program (research program), and Office Management (administrative program).

The course and unit titles that make up each of the above occupational programs are implied on the curriculum spiral. The Teller Science program title on the curriculum spiral corresponds to the primary occupation of Teller on the employment spiral. The unlisted, but implied, course and unit titles of the program are derived from and correspond to the occupational specialty and sub-specialty titles of the teller occupation. This logic is extended to other programs, courses, and units that make up the total curriculum spiral.

Occupational Equity

Another important characteristic of the long-range employment-curriculum spiral concept is that it provides for *occupational equity*. Occupational equity is the resource of employment potential one builds through work and/or study and preparation for employment. As an individual invests time and effort in preparing for an occupation, actually working, or doing both activities, he or she is accruing educational and occupational benefits which are redeemable at a future time. The possibility exists when a learner is able to progress toward a long-range occupational goal and, at the same time, prepare for employment in a series of related specialties and sub-specialties of the larger occupation.

Included in the concept of occupational equity is the correspondence between progress on the curriculum spiral and on the employment spiral. A person on the employment spiral can achieve the same occupational goal as can a person on the curriculum spiral. The learner-worker on the curriculum spiral registers progress by learning objective attainment, while the worker-learner on the employment spiral marks his or her progress via mastery of tasks.

In the end, both individuals are doing the same thing, that is, mastering work activities and gaining information necessary to performance. The difference is in the situation in which learning and occupational advancement occur. The individual also has the alternative of beginning the learning process on one of the spirals and transferring to the companion spiral to continue working toward his or her occupational goal. This alternative might be more beneficial than staying on either of the two long-range spirals for an extended period of time.

The concept of occupational equity is a function of the approach used in designing and developing the occupational curriculum. It depends on the ordering of occupational programs, courses, and units in the school to reflect the hierarchical organization of the functionally related groups of occupations in the world of work. If the learning situation is designed so that the learner can acquire marketable skills and knowledge while he or she is preparing for future employment, then a realization of his or her investment in learning does not wholly rest on attaining a single, distant, occupational goal.

The following comparison of a traditional curriculum approach and the one advocated here demonstrates the benefits of the latter. The example can be adapted to other fields of endeavor. The traditional educational requirement for entering the profession of dentist is twelve years. The total includes four years of secondary school education, four years of undergraduate preparation, and four years of dental school. An individualized, performance-based approach that equaled or reduced the amount of time invested in schooling, and at the same time provided an occupational equity benefit, would be a viable alternative to the traditional method. Whereas the traditional aspirant to the occupation of dentist must meet all of the preparatory requirements before entering the occupational field, the same person could, in the system being proposed, attain the occupational goal and be qualified in a variety of related en route occupational specialties and sub-specialties. As the individual invests time and effort in acquiring the skills and knowledge of the occupation, he or she could, if the situation so demanded, delay work toward his or her long-range career goal and capitalize on the en route occupational opportunities accrued.

If the aspirant does not want to become a dental aide, or dental hygienist he or she would also have the option of *not exiting* the curriculum spiral and continuing in the clinical dental program.

The en route occupations are intended neither to impede nor enhance progress toward a selected occupational goal. Rather, they are there to provide related occupational alternatives should such alternatives ever be needed. A person might be happier, more productive, and more content working in an occupation or group of occupations that reflects an occupational preference even though the particular occupation might not be his or her first choice. Having to abandon one's chosen area of employment altogether and enter another not of one's choosing is a far from desirable alternative.

Benefits

Now that the reader has a better idea as to how the employment and curriculum spirals work together to form the long-range employment-curriculum spiral concept, it is time to discuss and clarify the benefits of the dual approach. The Long-Range Employment-Curriculum Spiral:

Creates an Individualized, Performance-Based Curriculum Plan. The curriculum that results from the implementation of the long-range employment-curriculum spiral concept is comprised of a series of learning activities packages. The individual completes the packages as he or she moves through the units and courses of the occupational program. An individual learning activities package is prepared for each learning objective in the curriculum. Each learning objective is derived from a single task identified in the analysis of the occupation. The relationship between the tasks and learning objectives creates a curriculum which is based on the organization and performance activities of workers in occupations for which the curriculum was developed.

Creates a Multiple-Option Curriculum Plan. Another of the benefits of the proposed plan is the number of employment and educational options offered the learner en route to his or her occupational goal. Unlike the traditional curriculum in which the learner is provided only a single employment option, the one offered at the time of graduation, the proposed concept is such that the learner enjoys the option of drawing on his or her investment of time in terms of employment options should the need arise. This option, labeled *occupational equity* and discussed earlier, is a built-in benefit of the long-range employment-curriculum spiral concept. The multiple-option plan can be viewed as a form of occupational insurance for the individual as he or she prepares for employment. The insurance increases in potential as the individual works toward a career goal.

Presents a Plan Which Articulates the Occupational Education Offerings of the High School, Community College, and University. Articulation of the three levels of schooling is achieved by ordering the occupational titles within a functionally related group of occupations to reflect the number of years of preparation for employment in those occupations. These occupational titles then serve as the basis for naming and ordering the programs, courses, and units in the performance-based curriculum. The occupational education offerings can then be arranged by level and adapted by the appropriate educational institution. Development and articulation of performance-based curriculum in this manner would accomplish the following: reduce duplication of offerings by educational institutions, eliminate curricular gaps within and between levels of schooling, and permit a smooth and continuous progression through the curriculum.

Develops a Plan that Coordinates the Educational and Employment Potentials of the Community. In developing the long-range employment-curriculum spiral, the employment preparation offerings of the school are coordinated with the structure, activities, and content of the employment community. If a relationship between school and work is established the needs of the individual, be they educational or work-related, can be met by either the school, employment community, or both. If the school's occupational curriculum were organized in terms of and complementary to the world of work, horizontal movement from school to work or work to school could occur with little or no penalty to the *learner-worker.*

Creates an Employment Preparation System Which Can be Used in Total or in Part to Assist the Individual in Attaining His or Her Long-Range Occupational Goal. If the school can be defined as a social enterprise established by the community at large to assist its members in meeting a particular set of needs, then its curriculum must be designed to meet the needs of those enrolled. The employment curriculum spiral concept is a curricular approach that can be used either as a total system or its components can be isolated and individualized to assist an individual in meeting his or her employment needs.

The dual concept can guide the learner who is ready to begin preparation for employment within a particular family of occupations toward his or her occupational goal. For the learner who finds employment in an occupational specialty or sub-specialty, but who needs training prior to entry, the appropriate group of objectives within the total curriculum can be identified and isolated. With these objectives in mind the learner can prepare for employment within the constraints of his training. Both alternatives are practical applications of the dual spiral concept and do not impede or restrict each other.

Provides for Vertical Mobility.   In the dual curriculum theory, vertical mobility is defined as opportunity or potential for movement in an upward or downward direction along either of the component spirals. The spiral concept offers the individual a means of attaining his occupational goal in a formal school setting, at work, or through a combination of the two. Equally important is the ability to move in a downward direction. This might occur when an individual moves from a current position on a spiral to seek employment or additional preparation in an occupation or learning situation that precedes his current level of attainment on the spiral.

Provides Horizontal Mobility.   Horizontal mobility, as it is applied to the long-range occupational curriculum theory, is movement between employment and curriculum opportunities that correspond on the component spirals. The *points of passage* between the spirals are based on the number of occupational specialties and sub-specialties of the five primary occupations and of the courses, units, and programs derived from them, and are the corresponding employment and educational options. The two sets of options provide for those who either elect or are required by circumstance to leave their educational pursuits for employment, who return to school from the work force, or who desire to combine schooling and work in pursuit of educational and career goals.

Reduces the Number of Dead-End Occupations.   The problem of dead-end employment situations is significantly reduced by the long-range employment-curriculum spiral concept. Based on the assumption that most occupations can be grouped into functionally related families and organized within each family, work preparation curricula can be developed to reflect the organizational structure and relationships of the individual occupational groups. Occupations in which there currently is no opportunity for advancement could be joined with other related occupations to increase attainable employment goals. For example, grouping and organizing occupations related to the maintenance and servicing of automobiles and developing a curriculum that would reflect this organization, would allow a person to move from the entry-level occupation of service station manager to automotive technician, automotive engineer, research engineer, and farther. An individual's progress within the curriculum is a function of desire and ability, but this structure would at least offer opportunity for advancement.

Related to the issue of dead-end employment is the person who changes career plans and permanently leaves the occupational program or area of work for some heretofore unforeseen goal. The decision to stay in or leave a particular program remains the prerogative of the individual.

If, however, at a later time the individual elected to return to the occupational program and/or area of work, his or her point of re-entry would be determined by several factors. If the period of absence had not been too long, the person could re-enter at the point at which he had exited and continue the learning process from there. However, if a significant amount of time had lapsed, the individual's ability to meet expected requirements would have to be determined. Re-familiarization, performance-testing, and retraining, or a combination of these might be necessary to assist the individual in returning to his previously attained level of performance.

The Occupational Curriculum Development Process

We have looked at the configuration of the Comprehensive Careers Curriculum Model in general, and the specifics of each module, particularly the last module with its three options. We are now ready to proceed to the development process. The remainder of the book will deal with the implementation of the ideas discussed so far. A brief introduction to each of the major steps begins here with an outline of the entire process.

I.   Gathering and Organizing Occupational Data

    A.   Develop the component Long-Range *Employment* Spiral

        1.   Determine the group title and list of primary occupations for the functionally related group of occupations.

        2.   Determine the occupational specialties and sub-specialties of the primary occupational title.

        3.   Write task listing sheets.

        4.   Write task detailing sheets.

      *5.   Write performance step detailing sheets.

      *6.   Write related occupational information topics.

II. Converting Occupational Organization and Data to Work Preparation Curriculum

    A.   Write task objective sheets.

---

*These two activities are not steps in the occupational development process. However, the data contained in each of the two worksheets are essential later in the development, preparation, and writing of the occupational learning materials.

III. Organizing the Occupational Curriculum

   A. Develop the component Long-Range *Curriculum* Spiral

      1. Determine the occupational program, course, and unit titles.

      2. Write an outline of the program, course, unit, and learning objective titles.

      3. Write unit learning modules.

IV. Writing Occupational Program, Course, and Unit Descriptions

   A. Write an Occupational Program Description.

   B. Write an Occupational Course Outline.

   C. Write an Occupational Unit Guide.

V. Preparing Occupational Learning Materials

   A. Prepare knowledge-related and performance-related learning materials.

   B. Prepare individualized learning activities packages (LAPS).

Gathering and Organizing Occupational Data

The first three major steps in the occupational curriculum development process deal specifically with the development of the long-range employment curriculum spiral. The last two steps, while necessary in implementing the process are not crucial to the theoretical and organizational development of the spiral concept.

The activities that comprise the first step, *gathering and organizing occupational data*, center on the development of the component long-range employment spiral and entail writing a series of worksheets. These worksheets establish the organizational structure within the group of occupations, determine the title of a functionally related group of occupations, and assist in identifying the five primary occupations used on the spiral. They also assist in listing the occupational specialties and subspecialties of the primary occupations, including the tasks, performance steps, and performance step details of the various occupational components. Lastly, they identify the technical, and career and occupational guidance information topics. Completion of the worksheets is the development of the employment phase of the dual spiral. The completed worksheets also provide the list of tasks which is used in the conversion of employment-related activities and information to occupational education objectives and informational resources.

Converting Occupational Data to Work Preparation Curriculum

The second major step in developing the dual employment-curriculum spiral is to convert the various occupational activities and related information topics to occupational curriculum. The term *occupational activities* includes all of the tasks identified in the occupational analysis together with their performance steps and performance step details. However, only the tasks themselves are essential to the conversion process. The activities implied in the individual task titles become the essence of the learning objectives. The related performance steps, step details, and occupational information topics are extended to the newly formed learning objectives.

The conversion of tasks to learning objectives is the intermediate step in developing the dual Long-Range Employment-Curriculum Spiral. With the employment spiral established, the ranking and ordering of the primary occupations, occupational specialties, and occupational sub-specialties completed, and the tasks of the respective primary occupations identified and listed, the creation of the complementary curriculum spiral is a matter of writing, in performance terms, each identified task in the occupational analysis, specifying the conditions under which performance will occur and the acceptable level of performance.

The worksheet called the *task objective sheet* guides the curriculum designer in establishing the performance conditions for a particular objective, and the criteria for performance evaluation. Detailed instruction for writing task objective sheets appears in Chapter 9.

The hierarchical organization that was established in ordering the occupational specialty and sub-specialty titles is maintained throughout the conversion process. Although the organizational structure does not play a crucial role in the transition process, it becomes significant in the organization of the occupational curriculum, and in identifying, naming, and ordering the various programs, courses, and units.

Organizing the Occupational Curriculum

The third and final step in development of the theoretical model is the organization of the occupational curriculum in terms of the Long-Range Curriculum Spiral. The curriculum spiral is the educational counterpart of the Long-Range Employment Spiral. The employment spiral, by itself, is an organizational concept for the ranking and ordering of a functionally related group of occupations. The curriculum spiral is a paralleling organizational concept that gives the employment spiral educational dimension.

The curriculum spiral illustrates the organizational concept for developing an articulated, performance-based, multiple option, work preparation curriculum.

Writing Occupational Program, Course, and Unit Descriptions

As mentioned earlier, the last two major steps in the occupational curriculum development process do not directly affect development of the organizational model. They are, however, crucial in that they guide in the preparation and development of learning materials needed to implement the concept. The results of the completed fourth step are: a written description of the occupational program, an outline for one of the applied courses in the program, a unit guide for one of the units within the course, and various corresponding record forms and achievement awards.

Preparing Occupational Learning Materials

This last step in the curriculum development process focuses on the planning, writing, and packaging of learning materials for use in the occupational program, course, and unit offerings. Initially, a plan is prepared that assists the individual in developing the materials that will be used in implementing the process. This includes reviewing and/or writing the various knowledge and performance-related learning materials, e.g., instruction sheets, presentation outlines, pencil-paper tests, demonstration outlines, practice supervision guides, and performance tests. Lastly, suggestions are made for readying the prepared learning materials for use in an individualized learning activities package.

In Review

1. What is the major purpose of the Long-Range Employment-Curriculum Spiral concept?

2. A dual spiral is made up of two component long-range spirals. What is the purpose of each of the two spirals? List some of the qualities of the combined spirals.

3. The dual spiral is an attempt to coordinate the employment aspects of the community and the work preparation offerings of the school. Discuss how this coordination takes place in the development and organization of the employment spiral, establishment of the curriculum spiral, and the points of passage between them.

4. Basically, how does the long-range *employment* spiral concept assist the curriculum designer in developing a long-range occupational curriculum?

5. In the process of designing the employment spiral, five primary occupations are identified. What are the five different types of primary occupations and how do they later serve in articulating the high school, community college, and university programs in a specific group of occupations?

6. Discuss the concept of *occupational equity*. What is its primary benefit to the learner?

Implementing the Occupational Curriculum Development Theory

The second part of the handbook focuses on the development of a Long-Range Employment-Curriculum Spiral. To review, the employment-curriculum spiral is a conceptual model used in developing and organizing the preparational phase of the Comprehensive Careers Cluster Curriculum Model of which it is a part. The employment-curriculum spiral is comprised of two component spirals: a long-range *employment* spiral and a long-range *curriculum* spiral. The purpose of the occupational employment-curriculum spiral concept is to create an individualized, performance-based, multiple option plan that coordinates the employment and work-related educational aspects of the community, and articulates the occupational preparation offerings of the high school, community college, and university.

The process for developing and implementing the employment-curriculum spiral includes gathering and organizing the occupational data, converting the organization and data to work preparation curriculum, organizing the occupational curriculum, writing program, course, and unit guides, and preparing the necessary learning materials.

The Development Process

The various worksheets and other learning materials used in the development of the dual employment-curriculum spiral are the tools used to make the idea a reality. Each worksheet has its own purpose and function in the total curriculum development process and as the sheets are serially completed, the process moves step-by-step toward completion.

I Gathering and Organizing Occupational Data

Most people, if you describe a train of events to them, will tell you what the result will be. They can put those events together in their minds, and argue from them that something will come to pass. There are few people, however, who, if you told them a result, would be able to evolve from their own inner consciousness what the steps were which lead up to that result. This power is what I mean when I talk of reasoning backwards, or analytically.

Sherlock Holmes — *A Study in Scarlett*
by Sir Arthur Conan Doyle

Gathering and organizing occupational data is the first step in the development of the dual *employment-curriculum* spiral. The development of the component *employment* spiral entails identifying the list of primary occupations for a functionally related occupational group, determining the occupational specialties and sub-specialties of the particular occupation being analyzed, identifying the tasks performed in the various specialties and sub-specialties of the primary occupation, listing the performance steps and performance step details of the tasks, and lastly, listing the information topics as they pertain to the individual tasks and the occupation as a whole. This listing identifies the work activities and informational content of an occupation and organizes the resultant data in terms of the occupational specialties and sub-specialties. The completed analysis, a compilation of the data, is a data bank and organizational model for the future development of curricula in the particular occupational area.

The user of this section of the Handbook will get more meaning from it if he or she assumes the role of an objective observer, or analyst, whose responsibility it is to observe, record, and organize the details of an occupation from which he or she is personally removed. The analyst is often analyzing an occupation in which he or she is also a practitioner, and the assumption of a detached role will add necessary objectiveness to the analysis. A subjective process is less reliable as a data resource. Ideally, a group of practitioners from the same occupation should contribute to the completion of the analysis. The greater the number of experienced and knowledgeable contributors the less chance there is for serious error due to short-sightedness, occupational bias, or limited knowledge from lack of occupational experience.

The development of curriculum materials for *one* particular primary occupation will be used as an example throughout the Handbook. The concepts and strategies used for that occupation will have general application to the development of curriculum materials for any other primary occupations regardless of their hierarchical location.

For a review of the Long-Range Employment Spiral, see Chapter 2.

CHAPTER 3

The Employment Spiral: Identifying the Group Title and Primary Occupations

The first step in developing an employment spiral is to determine the title of the functionally related *group* of occupations for which the spiral is being developed and to identify the five primary occupations that appear on it. The worksheet, entitled *Determining the Group Title and List of Primary Occupations for Developing a Long-Range Employment Spiral,* is used to classify functionally related occupations and identify the primary occupations within a particular occupational group. The completed worksheet, in Example 3.1, was written for a group of money distribution and management-related occupations. The title of this occupational group will be used directly in naming both the Long-Range Occupational Employment Spiral and later, the companion curriculum spiral. The primary occupational titles will appear verbatim on the illustrated employment spiral (Figure 3.1) and will later be used to name the five corresponding occupational programs on the yet-to-be-developed long-range occupational curriculum spiral.

Determining the Group Title

The first step in writing the above-mentioned worksheet is to state, in general terms, the occupational area of interest. In the example the general area is banking-related occupations. Having specified the occupational area, the designer will focus on only those categories, divisions, and groups which are relevant to his or her particular situation as he or she completes the remainder of the worksheet.

Following this step, and depending on the particular occupational

---

Example 3.1
Determining the Group Title and List of Primary
Occupations for Developing a Long-Range Employment
Spiral for Money Distribution and Management-Related
Occupations

I. *Occupational Area of Interest:* Banking-Related Occupations

II. *Occupational Category:* Clerical and Sales-Related Occupations

III. *Functional Divisions:*

    A. Stenography, Typing, and Filing-Related Occupations

   *B. Computing and Account Recording-Related Occupations

    C. Material and Production Recording-Related Occupations

    D. Information and Message Distribution-Related Occupations

    E. Miscellaneous Clerical Occupations

    F. Service Sales-Related Occupations

    G. Commodities Sales-Related Occupations

    H. Merchandising-Related Occupations (other than sales)

IV. *Functional Groups:*

    A. *Functional Division:* Computing and Account Recording-Related Occupations

      *1. Money Distribution and Management-Related Occupations

      2. Cashier-Related Occupations

      3. Bookkeeper-Related Occupations

      4. Automatic Data Processing Equipment Operator-Related Occupations

      5. Billing-Machine Operator-Related Occupations

      6. Bookkeeping-Machine Operator-Related Occupations

      7. Computing-Machine Operator-Related Occupations

      8. Account-Recording-Machine Operator-Related Occupations

      9. Computing and Account-Recording-Related Occupations

V. *Occupational Titles:*

    A. *Functional Division:* Computing and Account Recording-Related Occupations

    B. *Functional Group:* Money Distribution and Management-Related Occupations

---

*We assume that the curriculum designer already has an idea of the particular occupational group or individual occupation for which he or she wishes to develop curricula. The initial steps in writing this worksheet guide the designer to a category of occupations that is workable in a real world situation.

Example 3.1 continued

C. *Random List of Primary, Occupational Specialty and Occupational Sub-specialty Titles:*

**1. Teller
   2. General Teller
   3. Mail Credit Teller
   4. Paying and Receiving Teller
   5. Payroll Teller
   6. Return Items Teller
   7. Savings Teller
   8. Special Deposits Teller
   9. Collection and Exchange Teller
  10. Bond Teller
  11. Contract Collections Teller
  12. Domestic Exchange Teller
  13. Foreign Exchange Teller
  14. Note Teller
  15. Collateral Teller
  16. Commercial Note Teller
  17. Discount Teller
  18. Real Estate Loan Teller
  19. Utility Teller
  20. Head Teller
 *21. Assistant Manager
 *22. Administrative Assistant
  23. Business Office Machine Operator
 *24. Office Manager
 *25. General Office Clerk

classification source used (e.g. *Dictionary of Occupational Titles, Occupational Outlook Handbook*, personal experience), the occupational *category*, *division*, and *group* of the area of interest is specified on the sheet. The functional *divisions* in the example make up the occupational category of Clerical and Sales-Related Occupations and the functional *groups* make up a particular division (in this case, that of Computing and Account Recording Occupations). Once the various functional groups have been listed, the one that is most closely related to the occupational area of interest is selected and its title, with the addition of the prefacing phrase: A Long-Range Occupational Employment Spiral for. . . , becomes the title of the employment spiral. The title selected for the spiral should describe collectively the occupations that will be a part of the spiral and should not refer to only one or two of them. For instance, an employment spiral which includes only veterinary related occupations might appropriately be entitled "A Long-Range Occupational Employment Spiral for Veterinary Science-Related Occupations." The title identifies the spiral and indicates the group of functionally related occupations for which it was developed.

The categorizing of a larger, more diverse occupational population into component and sub-component groupings that is done in this worksheet is required if an articulated occupational curriculum is to be realized. As the various divisions and groups within categories are identified the functional relationships between occupations within each component become more clear. This organizational technique provides the greatest potential for preparing curriculum that will articulate the secondary school, community/junior college, and university offerings in a particular area of endeavor.

Identifying the Primary Occupations

The final step in completing the worksheet is listing the various occupations, occupational specialties, and sub-specialties of the occupational group. The list of titles is ordered randomly (no particular order is needed at this time) and includes all titles that are considered to be a logical part of the group, including, of course, the five primary occupational titles.

From this list the five primary occupations, entry level, technical, professional, research, and administrative, are selected and identified. The entry-level occupation is that occupation in which the skills and knowledge needed can be acquired by or about the time of graduation from high school or age eighteen. The technical occupation requires preparation beyond high school, but does not require baccalaureate preparation. The professional occupation requires additional preparation and training, and a baccalaureate degree. Formal preparation in research and development techniques applicable to the particular occupational area is needed for the research occupation. Lastly, the administrative occupation requires that the individual possess the essential administrative and supervisory skills and knowledge to function in a leadership capacity.

The five primary occupations are included in the total list of occupational titles of the particular group. The one primary occupation that is to receive major attention is marked with a double asterisk (**)*. The

*A note of caution is also appropriate here. Both the titles of the primary occupations just discussed and those of the occupational specialties and sub-specialties will eventually be used in developing the long-range occupational employment spiral concept. The occupational titles used must correspond to those found in the world of work and bear the same relationships to each other. At no time should occupational titles be fabricated. If, for instance, a title should be conjured up and no real-world occupation or occupational component by that name exists, then the system will fail in meeting one of its intended purposes, providing individuals multiple opportunities to move between work and education.

development process discussed here is restricted, for purposes of example, to organizing ideas and preparing materials as they relate to *one primary occupation* in the total curriculum development process. The development concepts and skill, once mastered can be applied in the future to developing the other aspects of the employment-curriculum plan.

Contribution to the Organizational Concept

Completion of the worksheet *Determining the Group Title and List of Primary Occupations for* . . . marks the end of the first step in transforming the long-range occupational employment spiral concept from a latent state to an organizational plan for developing occupational curriculum. (See Figure 3.1.)

The title of the spiral in Figure 3.1 is derived from the title of the

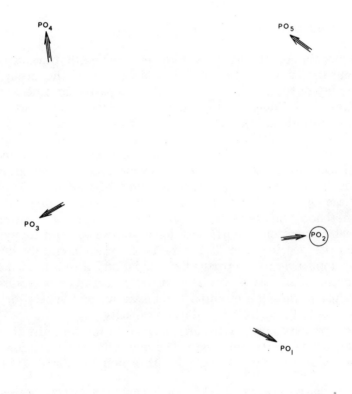

A Long-Range Employment Spiral
for   -Related Occupations

Figure 3.1 *The Development of the Employment Spiral Concept*

group of occupations, and the titles of the five primary occupations identified and selected from the total list of occupations, occupational specialties and sub-specialties that comprise the group. The position of each primary occupation is represented by a triple-shafted arrow along the yet-to-be-identified series of tasks that will eventually form the employment spiral. The remainder of the employment spiral is still in the latent state and will be developed as other worksheets are completed. The circle around PO_2 indicates that this is the primary occupation for which the remaining occupational curriculum development worksheets and other learning materials will be developed and prepared.

In Review

1. How does the worksheet *Determining the Group Title and List of Primary Occupations for. . .* , assist in developing the employment spiral concept?

2. How is the title of the occupational group used in developing the employment spiral?

3. How are the five primary occupational titles identified during the development of the employment spiral used in the later development of the curriculum spiral?

CHAPTER 4

The Employment Spiral:
Identifying the Occupational
Specialties and Sub-specialties

The second step in developing the employment component of the dual
Long-Range Occupational Employment-Curriculum Spiral for a particular
group of occupations is to identify the occupational specialty and sub-
specialty titles of the selected primary occupation. The occupational
specialties and sub-specialties are levels of specialization within the primary occupation being analyzed. The various titles establish the scope of
responsibility and imply the duties to be performed. The worksheet
entitled *Determining the Occupational Specialties and Sub-specialties
of the Primary Occupation of Teller* (Example 4.1) shows the analysis
of the occupation of teller with respect to its various occupational
components.

Listing the specialization titles of the primary occupation provides a
basis for the development of a multiple-option occupational program.
To develop the program the curriculum designer will need the various
specialization titles to establish points of passage between the employment
and curriculum components of the dual organizational employment-
curriculum plan. The titles of the occupational specialties and sub-
specialties will also serve in naming components on the yet-to-be-developed
Long-Range Occupational Curriculum Spiral. The title of the primary
occupation serves as the basis for naming an eventual occupational program, while the titles of the specialty and sub-specialty occupations will
be the basis from which the titles of occupational courses and units
respectively are derived.

Example 4.1
Determining the Occupational Specialties and
Sub-specialties of the Primary Occupation of Teller

I. Primary Occupation (PO):   Teller

II. Occupational Specialties (OS):

   A. General Teller

   B. Collection and Exchange Teller

   C. Note Teller

   D. Utility Teller

III. Occupational Sub-specialties (OSS):

   A. Occupational Specialty: A — General Teller

      1. Mail Credit Teller

      2. Paying and Receiving Teller

      3. Payroll Teller

      4. Return Items Teller

      5. Savings Teller

      6. Special Deposits Teller

   B. Occupational Specialty: B — Collection and Exchange Teller

      1. Bond Teller

      2. Domestic Exchange Teller

      3. Foreign Exchange Teller

   C. Occupational Specialty: C — Note Teller

      1. Collateral Teller

      2. Commercial Note Teller

      3. Discount Teller

   D. Occupational Specialty: D — Utility Teller

      (None)

Determining the Occupational Specializations

Writing the worksheet involves, first, analyzing the primary occupation with respect to its occupational specialties, and second, analyzing each specialty with respect to its various occupational sub-specialties. One or a combination of the following approaches is most often used for analysis. If experienced in the occupation the individual curriculum designer utilizes his or her experience to list the various specialization titles. Various people experienced in the occupational area are identified and used as resources in listing the various titles. Or government/business/

industry literature that categorizes occupations in terms of their specialty components are referred to.

While each approach has its merits and limitations, a combination of the three provides the best results in terms of overall title identification, relationship, and organization. The best way to insure the appropriateness of the occupational list is to seek the input of as many experienced practitioners as possible and use this input to come to a consensus. If the worksheet organization and data do not parallel those of the employment place, then the occupational curriculum materials eventually derived from the worksheet will have questionable value.

Contribution to the Organizational Concept

As mentioned in the preceding chapter, the purpose of each of the occupational development worksheets discussed in this section is to guide the curriculum designer in systematically developing the employment spiral concept. The purpose still holds with the worksheet *Determining the Occupational Specialties and Sub-specialties of the Primary Occupation*, but with a slight difference. Although not actually depicted on the employment spiral, the occupational specialty and sub-specialty titles of the primary occupation being analyzed are *implied*. Without the physical constraints of the illustration of the spiral itself and the space available on a page, the depiction of respective positions along the various arcs would be possible. As it is, however, the specialization titles are not presented on the completed illustration, but are shown in Figure 4.1 as they would appear if it were not for the aforementioned difficulties.

The figure includes a single primary occupational title with its list of occupational specialties and sub-specialties distributed along the yet-to-be-identified series of tasks. The primary occupation is indicated by a triple-shafted arrow and the positions of the specialty and sub-specialty titles

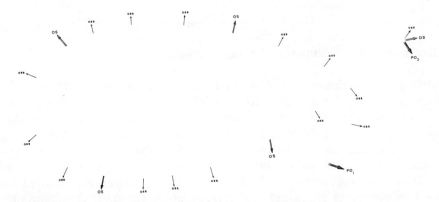

Figure 4.1 *Contribution of the Worksheet to the Development of the Employment Spiral Concept*

marked respectively by double and single-shafted arrows. Later, when the component *curriculum spiral* is developed, these locations mark points of passage between employment and school and school and employment, and are the basis for naming corresponding occupational programs, courses, and units.

The worksheet also assists the curriculum designer in writing task listing sheets, the next step in the process. The relationship of this worksheet to the task listing sheet will be discussed later.

In Review

1. What role does the worksheet, *Determining the Occupational Specialties and Sub-specialties of the Primary Occupations*, play in developing the occupational curriculum spiral concept?

2. Discuss how the occupational specialties and sub-specialties serve later on in developing a multiple-option curriculum.

3. Why is it desirable to have as many existing occupational specialty and sub-specialty titles as possible?

4. What is the danger of fabricating occupational specialty and sub-specialty titles?

CHAPTER 5

The Employment Spiral:
Writing Task Listing Sheets

With the title of the employment spiral now determined, the entry-level, technical, professional, research, and administrative occupations known, and the primary occupation with its specialties and sub-specialties identified and ordered, the next step in the development of the employment spiral concept is writing a set of task listing sheets.

A set of *task listing sheets* includes all of the tasks that comprise the primary occupation. (See Appended Item A, The Occupational Curriculum Development Worksheet Series.) The set is made up of individual task listing sheets, each of which is a worksheet used in ordering and listing the tasks of one of the occupational specialties being analyzed. (See Example 5.1.) The data on the task listing sheet will be used in organizing and preparing occupational curriculum materials, as a basis for determining the learning objectives of the yet-to-be-written program, course, and unit guides, and in planning and writing career and occupational guidance materials.

Criteria

The organizational format of the task listing sheet has five components. These are: the title of the worksheet itself, Task Listing Sheet, the title of the primary occupation, the title of *one* of the occupational specialties, the titles of *all* of its occupational sub-specialties, and the lists of tasks.

The task listing sheet is an extension of the worksheet, *Determining the Occupational Specialties and Sub-specialties of the Primary Occupation*. It uses the occupational specialty and sub-specialty titles on the

54

Example 5.1
Task Listing Sheet

Primary Occupation (PO): Teller

Occupational Specialty (OS): General Teller

Occupational Sub-specialty (OSS): Mail Credit Teller
  Tasks:
- Opening Envelopes
- Receiving Checks for Deposit
- Examining Checks for Endorsements
- Verifying Deposits
- Entering Deposit in Depositors Passbook or Checking Account
- Issuing Receipts

Occupational Sub-specialty: Paying and Receiving Teller
  Tasks:
- Counting Currency
- Cashing Checks
- Handling Check Deposits
- Handling Cash Deposits
- Receiving Personal Loan Payments
- Receiving Christmas Club Payments
- Issuing Treasurer's Checks
- Selling Money Orders
- Withdrawing Funds From No Passbook Savings Accounts
- Ordering the Daily Cash Supply
- Selling Domestic Traveler's Checks
- Balancing the Cash Drawer and Settlement
- Accepting Night Depository Deposits

Occupational Sub-specialty: Payroll Teller
  Tasks:
- Receiving Payroll Requests from Depositors
- Preparing Cash in Requested Denominations
- Verifying Totals
- Accepting Debit to Offset Payroll
- Assuring Funds are Available
- Computing Service Charges

Occupational Sub-specialty: Return Items Teller
  Tasks:
- Returning Item to Cashing Tellers for Collection
- Debiting Checking Accounts for Deposited Items

sheet, and adds to it the listings of tasks of the various specialty titles of the primary occupation.

Writing Task Titles

Tasks are those activities which a person performs during the course of the work day. A task might be best defined as:

> ". . . a complex unit of cognitive, affective and psychomotor behavior possessing an observable beginning and end and resulting in a salable product or service; a complete unit of work made up of a series of performance steps, e.g., procedural steps serially performed in completion of the task."

To complement the written definition, a list of sample task titles selected from various occupations appears in Example 5.2. Note that in each instance, the task has a logical beginning and end, and defines a complete unit of work of the particular occupation.

Example 5.2

Occupation: Dental Hygienist
   Tasks:

   Taking Dental X-Rays
   Administering Topical Fluoride
   Taking Patient's History
   Sanitizing the Dental Unit
   Making Appointments for Patients

Occupation: Construction Plumber
   Tasks:

   Repairing Faucet
   Installing Water Heater
   Installing Water Service Line
   Thawing Frozen Water Pipes

Occupation: Night Manager
   Tasks:

   Securing Perimeter
   Touring Functioning Building Area
   Reporting Maintenance Work
   Inspecting Vending Machines
   Directing Janitorial Work Assignments

Format

The suggested format for writing task titles is: the verb, written as a gerund, and the object of the verb. The task titles in the above list are typical of those written in the suggested form.

Written in this manner, the title assists the analyst in two ways. First, the format assists in differentiating between performance steps and performance step details of the tasks once they are written and the tasks themselves. Confusion can occur because the performance steps and performance step details also include verbs and objects. While other factors can and do distinguish tasks from performance steps and performance step details (as will be clear once the two are discussed) in some instances, the best single discriminator is the form in which the title of each is written. Secondly, when written as suggested the titles convert easily into the titles of learning objectives. When written in the gerund form, *the task title is used, without change, as the objective title.* This will have more meaning and importance once you get into converting tasks to learning objectives later in the curriculum development process.

Another important factor in writing task titles is the selection, number, and use of verbs. All verbs describe action or state of being. However, some also have implied characteristics and associations, making them excellent descriptors of events. For instance, such words as operate, perform, use, and do are verbs which provide no mental picture of the activity taking place. In contrast, a few descriptive verbs alone can convey a description of an activity. The following example, which uses only five descriptive verbs, provides the reader with enough data to immediately identify the occupation being described.

Drives _____ . Ropes _____ . Rustles _____ .
Herds _____ . Brands _____ .

Who else but a cowboy?

The point is obvious. When you are writing task titles consider carefully the verb used in each. If it is not a good descriptor of the action, attempt to replace it with one that is. As an example, the task title Cleaning Cars does not define for the reader whether the car is being swept out or vacuumed, washed or wiped off. The title Washing Cars more specifically describes the activity. The only replacement verb that is not appropriate is one which is not a term commonly used in the occupation. In this case, you must resort to the less descriptive verb.

The number of verbs needed in a task title is another important consideration. One verb is ideal in that it denotes only the one activity. Sometimes, however, there is a tendency to use two or, in some instances, three verbs in naming the task. This should be avoided. In most situations where this occurs, the writer has selected verbs from the list of performance steps of the task rather than selecting a term that encompasses all of the procedural activities.

Frequency of Performance

Frequency of performance is an entry that is commonly discussed in the listing of tasks of an occupation (Mager, 1967; Fine, 1974; Bartel, 1978). Defined as the number of times a task is performed over a given period of time, it is used by various authors to indicate the frequency with which tasks occur in an occupation. This information is intended to assist the curriculum designer or teacher confronted with time constraints and needing to make a selection of tasks for inclusion. This is a valid and important consideration. However, when tasks are listed by specialties and sub-specialties of a primary occupation, rather than in terms of a single primary occupation, the need for ranking by frequency loses importance. When the curriculum is such that the learner is occupationally prepared via small groupings of tasks and his or her success in the specialization is contingent on being able to perform *all* of the tasks within the grouping, the effect of ranking by frequency is negated.

On the other hand, if the reader still feels very strongly about including frequency as one of the entries on the task listing sheet, then he or she should do so.

Contribution to the Organizational Concept

The writing of the set of task listing sheets completes the development of the long-range occupational employment spiral concept. The title of the spiral has been determined, the five primary occupations identified and positioned, one of the primary occupations selected and its occupational specialties and sub-specialties determined, and lastly the tasks, as symbolized by the dots that give the spiral form and substance, identified and listed. (See Figure 5.1.) The particular arc being emphasized is highlighted to emphasize the portion of the spiral being given attention. Later, this same arc will serve as the basis for developing a parallel occupational program on the component long-range occupational *curriculum* spiral.

In Review

1. What is the major purpose of the *task listing sheets* in the development of the employment spiral concept?

2. In what respect is the *task listing sheet* an extension of the previously developed *Determining the Occupational Specialties and Sub-specialties* worksheet?

3. Discuss why, in almost all cases, a task is a combination of cognitive, affective, and psychomotor behavior.

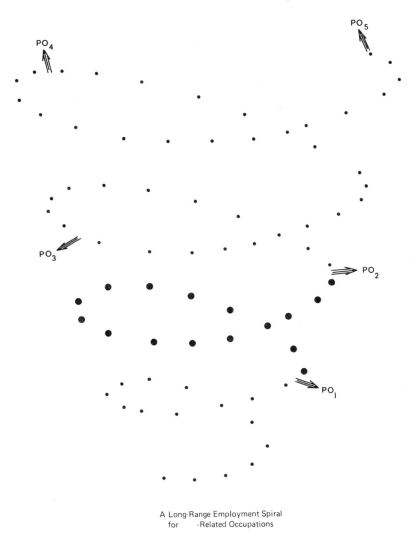

A Long-Range Employment Spiral
for   -Related Occupations

Figure 5.1 *Contribution of the Worksheet to the Development of the Employment Spiral Concept*

4. In each of the preceding worksheets, various items served as the basis from which components of the yet-to-be-developed curriculum spiral were derived. What components on the curriculum spiral are derived from the tasks on the employment spiral?

5. What is the rationale for not including a *Frequency of Performance* entry on the task listing sheet?

CHAPTER 6

The Employment Spiral: Writing Task Detailing Sheets

The *task detailing sheet* is a worksheet that assists the analyst in identifying and listing the performance steps of a given task, the standards of performance of each step, and the technical occupational information topics related to the task being analyzed. Example 6.1 is a completed worksheet.

The development and writing of the task detailing sheets are intregal parts in the development of the long-range employment spiral concept. The technical occupational information topics outline the knowledge needed to perform the given task.

The purpose of the task detailing sheet is to guide the curriculum designer and occupational analyst in listing the performance steps of the task being analyzed, establishing the criteria (standards of performance) of the performance steps of the task, and identifying the types of information or knowledge needed by the worker for its satisfactory completion. The criteria for writing the various entries found in a task detailing sheet follow.

Criteria

Heading. The heading of the worksheet includes the title "Task Detailing Sheet," titles of the "Primary Occupation," "Occupational Specialty," "Occupational Sub-specialty," and the "Task." The heading is designed to assist the reader in identifying the exact location of the task being analyzed with reference to occupation, occupational specialty, and occupational sub-specialty. The data for each entry is taken directly from the set of task listing sheets.

Example 6.1
Task Detailing Sheet

Primary Occupation (PO): Teller

Occupational Specialty (OS): General Teller

Occupational Sub-specialty (OSS): Paying and Receiving Teller

Task: Selling Money Orders

Performance Steps	*Standards of Performance*
1. Ascertain amount of check to be issued and accept payment.	The accepted payment is equal to the amount of the check to be issued.
2. Prepare the money order.	The money order is "cut" for the exact predetermined amount, and the current date appears on the check portion.
3. Process the money order.	The original is given to the customer. The credit copy is "cashed in" on the reverse side for the exact amount of the check and placed in the appropriate bin for transit pickup. The office copy is filed numerically, chronologically and by date in the appropriate file drawer.
4. Collect the commission.	Fifty percent commission is collected from the customer.

Technical Occupational Information Topics

1. Other Services
2. Protectograph Machine
3. Burrough's Teller Machine
4. Definition of Terms
5. Alphabetic, Numeric Filing Procedures

Performance Steps. Performance steps are the individual steps performed in sequence in the completion of a task. Much like the steps in a recipe, they add up to the completion of the defined unit of work.

A performance step contains a verb, written in the second person singular, present tense, and an object. Like the verbs used in writing task titles, they should be as descriptive as possible, but yet remain common to the terminology of the occupation being analyzed. Examples of performance steps selected from various occupations appear in Example 6.2. Note the format and tense in which the various steps are written.

Example 6.2

Occupation: Library Technician
Task: Typing Card Sets
Performance Steps:

1. Type catalog cards.
2. Type analysis records.
3. Type holdings record.
4. Type order record.

Occupation: Preventive Medicine Technician
Task: Determining pH Value of Water
Performance Steps:

1. Put a pH color disc into the comparator.
2. Fill two clean cells with water.
3. Add phenol red to left cell of the comparator.
4. Hold the comparator at eye level and rotate the color disc.
5. Compare colors.
6. Read the results in the front window of the comparator.

Occupation: Air Conditioning Mechanic
Task: Installing Electric Motors
Performance Steps:

1. Remove the motor from the shipping container.
2. Compare the name plate data with the blueprint specifications.
3. Place the motor on the support mounts.
4. Align the motor with existing pulleys and/or couplings.
5. Tighten mounting bolts.
6. Re-check drive alignment.

The sequencing of the performance steps is also an important consideration. Since the individual lists of performance steps will eventually be used to develop and write demonstration outlines, task procedure sheets, checklists, etc. for classroom and laboratory instruction, the sequence of the individual steps is as important to the curriculum development process as is the listing of tasks. The ordering of the performance steps is consecutive and dictated by the procedure followed in the occupation.

Standards of Performance. A standard of performance is a quantitative or qualitative statement which establishes the minimum level of acceptable performance of a performance step. The standards of performance will guide the occupational student toward mastery of the tasks of the occupation or component occupations.

The following statements of standards of performance for two different performance steps illustrate the point. The first is a quantitative statement of minimum level of acceptable performance, the second qualitative.

Performance Step: Fill the tub with warm water.

Standard of Performance: The tub is filled to a point 10 inches below its top edge. The temperature of the water is 80° F plus or minus one degree.

Performance Step: Clean the windows.

Standard of Performance: The windows are clean and dry. There is no trace of an oil film, dirt, finger prints, etc. or lint on either surface of the glass. With the exception of the removal of the dirt and grime, the original condition of the window has not been changed.

The words "minimum level" are an important part of the definition of standards of performance. They identify the cut-off point between acceptable and unacceptable performance. They are relative, and can define a low level of acceptable performance or, equally as well, a high level. Depending on the circumstances, the point of acceptance for one performance step might be low. For yet another performance step, the minimum level of acceptable performance might be one hundred percent accuracy each time the step is done. The expression *minimum level* applies in both cases.

The final consideration in writing standards of performance is wording, particularly if the standard is qualitative. The standard of performance must make clear to the doer when he or she has equalled or exceeded the minimum level of occupational performance. Words such as right, proper, and correctly, unless also operationally defined in the statement, do not denote satisfactory or unsatisfactory performance.

Below are two examples of qualitatively stated standards of performance for a performance step in the occupational sub-specialty of Service Station Attendant. The first uses the term "right" as its criterion term and the second, in essence, defines what "right" is.

Task: Changing Engine Oil

Performance Step: Add oil

Example 1 — The right amount of oil is added to the engine.

Example 2 — The level of oil in the crankcase falls between the "minimum" and "maximum" indicator lines on the oil stick.

The first statement does not communicate when the performance step has been properly completed. The second statement establishes a standard by which the doer can measure his or her performance.

Technical Occupational Information Topics

The Technical Occupational Information Topics are listed on the individual task detailing sheets because they bear a special relationship to the task being analyzed. They specify the knowledge necessary for satisfactory completion of the task at hand. A thorough discussion of writing technical occupational information topics is included in Chapter 8 of this section.

Contribution to the Organizational Concept

Like the other worksheets the task detailing sheet contributes to the development of the long-range employment spiral concept. However, because of physical constraints the contributions of the task detailing sheet, like those of the worksheet *Determining the Occupational Specialties and Sub-specialties of the Primary Occupation*, do not actually appear on the employment spiral, but rather are implied.

The contribution of the task detailing sheet to the development of the employment spiral concept can, however, be shown in a view of a single segment of the total spiral. (See Figure 6.1.) The four tasks of a given occupational sub-specialty (the four solid dots) and the technical information topics (smaller circles) that are identified with and related to each task are shown. Collectively, they illustrate the skills and knowledge of a person working in the sub-specialty.

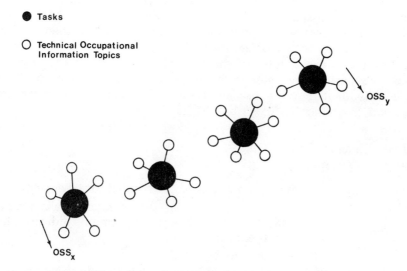

Figure 6.1 *Contribution of the Worksheet to the Development of the Employment Spiral Concept*

In Review

1. What is the purpose of the *task detailing sheet* in the occupational development process?

2. Discuss the relationship between a given task and its performance steps.

3. What is the purpose of the standard of performance statement that accompanies each performance step?

4. In terms of standards of performance, differentiate between qualitative and quantitative statements.

5. Define *technical occupational information.*

CHAPTER 7

The Employment Spiral: Writing Performance Step Detailing Sheets

The last step in analyzing the doing portion of the occupation is identifying and listing the performance step details in completing the various performance steps of a task. The *performance step detail sheet* is a worksheet (Example 7.1) used to itemize performance step details and their types and standards of performance.

Similar in purpose, organization, and format to the task detailing sheet, this worksheet carries the analysis process to a yet finer degree of detail. In some instances, this detail will not be necessary to the development of occupational curriculum materials. In other circumstances, however, it might be essential and the curriculum designer will be prepared for acquiring the data if the need does appear.

Criteria

Heading

The heading of the worksheet is the same as that of the task detailing sheet, but includes the name of the sheet itself and the number and title of performance step being analyzed. The components of the sheet are the title of the sheet, in this case, "Performance Step Detailing Sheet," "Occupation," "Occupational Specialty," "Occupational Sub-specialty," "Task," and the additional entry, "Performance Step" number and title.

Example 7.1
Performance Step Detailing Sheet

Primary Occupation: Teller

Occupational Specialty: General Teller

Occupational Sub-specialty: Paying and Receiving Teller

Task: Selling Money Orders

Performance Step #2: Prepare the money order

Performance Step Details	*Type of Performance*	*Standards of Performance*
1. Enter the dollar total amount on the money order form.	Recall/Manipulation	The total is stamped with the "Check Protector" in the designated space on the money order form. The total amount equals that specified by the customer.
2. Enter the data on the form.	Recall/Manipulation	The correct month, day and year are entered in the designated space on the money order form.
3. Initial the money order.	Recall/Manipulation	The initials of the teller making the sales transaction are entered in the upper right hand corner of the money order form.
4. Have the customer complete the remainder of the form.	Recall/Manipulation	The customer enters the name of the person to whom the check is payable, enters the name of the remitter (self), signs the form and enters his or her own address.

Performance Step Details

Performance step details are the most elemental steps found in the analysis of an occupational activity. The completion of a sequence of performance step details results in the completion of an individual performance step.

The components of a performance step detail are the same as those of a performance step: a verb, written in the second person singular, present tense, and the object of the verb. The verbs selected by the analyst should be as descriptive as possible, but still be typical of those used by people working in the occupation.

The sequence of performance step details is as important to the success-ful completion of the performance step as the sequence of performance steps is to the successful completion of a task. Because of their specificity performance step details are used in developing occupational curricula only in writing detailed instruction and performance sheets and in the development of detailed demonstration outlines.

The numbering of the step details is consecutive and determined by the performance sequence followed in the occupation.

Types of Performance

The phrase type of performance refers to the principal kind(s) of behavior exhibited by the learner in performing a performance step detail. The behaviors specified in the "Type of Performance" column on the perfor-mance step detailing sheet are used by the curriculum designer to make decisions concerning the development of learning materials. In concert with the type of performance data of other performance step details, an objective and accurate analysis of the behavioral nature of the tasks and the occupation itself can be made.

Several classification systems or taxonomies of human behavior have been developed in recent years. Of the better known are those written by Gagné (1965), Bloom (1956), Krathwohl (1964), and Simpson (1974). As would be expected, different interpretations occur. However, similarity and overlapping of findings is also evident. Whereas Gagné speaks of "signal," "stimulus-response," "chaining," "verbal association," "discrim-ination," "concept," "rule," and "problem-solving" types of learning, Bloom, Krathwohl, and Simpson refer respectively to "cognitive," "affec-tive," and "psychomotor" performance. Even a cursory study of the literature shows that the greatest differences are not as much in content and/or meaning as in terminology and categorical organization.

Mager and Beach (1967) incorporated a modification of Gagné's classification of human behavior in their text, *Developing Vocational Instruction.* Their list included five major types of performance: "recall", "problem solving", "discrimination", "manipulation", and "speech". This adapted classification of types of performance is used here with one exception. "Speech" has been expanded to include oral and written per-formance and has been renamed "communication". Whereas "speech" implies only spoken behavior, the term "communication" logically permits both oral and written expression.

A discussion of each type of performance follows;

Recall. Recall and *remember* are synonymous terms used to denote human behavior where a person's recognition of a given stimulus or set of stimuli and his or her response to them is primarily influenced, directed, and determined by personal knowledge. Examples of recall behavior abound. .From prior study and learning, the schoolchild recites the multi-plication tables; recalling his last oil change, the taxicab driver takes his taxi in for service; noting her activities for the day, the dentist suddenly recalls (it almost "slipped her mind") that she must have her assistant pick up the gold crown from the dental lab; a hotel receptionist offhandedly responds to a query as to the whereabouts of a certain room with "go up the stairs, turn right and it's the fourth door on your left."

In each of the above instances, the individuals have relied primarily on their personal knowledge to perform the respective activities. From a *type of performance* point of view, the important issue is not the conduct of the activities themselves, but the recalling of knowledge that prompted, influenced, and determined the individual's performance of those activities.

Several examples of various performance step details and their respective types of performance are listed in Example 7.2. For some of the steps, "recall" is singularly the most dominant type of performance. For others, "recall" plus another type of behavior best describes the step detail in performance terms. Recognizing that human performance is a conglomerate of behaviors, not a single, discreet behavioral event, the intent is to identify the one or two predominate types of performance "primarily associated with" (Mager and Beach, 1967) the step detail being performed.

Example 7.2

Note the relative position of the top splitring to the bottom splitring of the telescopic mount.	Recall
Select the appropriate drill for the root diameter of the screw.	Recall/Discrimination
Wash the wound.	Recall/Manipulation
Review the sequence of steps to be performed.	Recall
Check to see that the safety line is secure.	Recall/Discrimination
Set the blade height.	Recall/Discrimination
Fasten the ground wire to the (–) terminal of the battery.	Recall/Manipulation
Confirm the departure time of the plane.	Recall/Communication

The type of performance can generally be determined from the verb that introduces the performance statement. In each of the items in Example 7.2 where only "recall" was noted for the type of performance, the verb implied mental or cognitive behavior. "Note," "review," and "check" all describe covert or internal behavior. In the other step details however, the principal type of performance of "recall" is so closely allied with a second type that both are listed with primary type of behavior appearing first in the entry.

Problem Solving. Problem solving is that type of performance exhibited by an individual who, when confronted with a problem to which he or she has no ready solution, seeks out its cause(s) and remedies it. Recall behavior assumes that the doer already possesses the knowledge required to satisfactorily respond to a situation. Problem solving recognizes the person's lack of knowledge in dealing with a certain situation and stresses his or her ability to cope with the problem and, eventually, devise a solution. The uniqueness and effectiveness of the solution depend upon the individual's creativity.

Sample performance step details which require problem-solving behavior appear below. In some instances, the step detail is best described as solely a problem-solving activity, whereas other entries reflect both problem-solving behavior and a second type of performance.

Estimate the cost of repairs to the automobile.	Problem-solving/Recall
Estimate the time of arrival of the shipment.	Problem-solving
Diagnose the victim's condition.	Problem-solving/Recall
Predict the person's response to the situation.	Problem-solving/Discrimination
Identify alternative solutions to the design problem.	Problem-solving
List alternative routes to the destination.	Problem-solving/Manipulation

The introductory verb of the statement should be examined to determine the type(s) of performance of the performance step detail.

Discrimination. When a barber makes the last snip with his shears, gives the finishing touch with the comb, and says, "OK, you're done," he is demonstrating discriminating behavior. When the dentist selects one instrument over another in the process of filling a cavity, he or she also exhibits a discriminative type of performance. Likewise, when a chef cuts into a steak he is cooking, looks at it, and then removes it from the grill saying, "medium-rare T-bone, up" he also is discriminating in his behavior. In all three instances, the individuals are choosing between two or more alternatives, based on their knowledge of a particular situation. They are making a value judgment from a previously established criterion standard.

Based in knowledge and manifested as physical behavior, discrimination reflects the covert values of the individual as he or she distinguishes between objects and/or events in the environment. In the case of the barber, he, in essence, said to the customer, "this haircut now matches the one you described to me when you came in." The dentist selected the one instrument over the others in that he knew from experience (valued) that it would work best in the particular situation. The chef removed the steak from the grill when he saw that its color and texture matched his concept (knowledge) of medium rareness.

Examples of discriminative types of performance are shown in the following list of performance step details. Like the earlier examples, their verbs connote the types of performance of the individual step details. Some items are singularly discriminative in nature, whereas other items include discrimination and one other type of performance.

Note the different "feel" of the types of paper.	Discrimination
Point out the springwood and summerwood portions of the annual ring.	Discrimination/Recall
Check to see that no red warning lights are on.	Discrimination
Maintain the altitude of the aircraft.	Discrimination/Manipulation
Differentiate between the woof and warp of the material.	Discrimination/Recall
Tighten the nut fingertight.	Discrimination/Manipulation

Manipulation. Three examples of discriminative types of performance cited earlier involve a barber, a dentist, and a chef. Each was performing a task common to his or her particular occupation. The barber was cutting hair, the dentist filling a cavity, and the chef grilling a steak. Each of these tasks is an example of a manipulative type of performance associated with a particular occupation. In an occupational sense, manipulative behavior is the "doing" side of the occupation. In terms of "tasks," "performance steps," and "performance step details," manipulative behavior is the overt, observable activity of the occupation.

From the behavioral point of view, manipulative behavior is neuroskeletal-muscular performance. It is the physical interaction of the person with his or her environment. Unless instinctive, uncontrolled, or irrational, manipulative performance is prompted, influenced, shaped, and determined by the knowledge and attitudes or values of the doer. The barber's observable act of cutting hair was influenced primarily by three factors: the knowledge he had acquired from previous haircutting experience, the customer's instructions and expectations, and his ability to select "this" technique or "that" one (discrimination) in performing the task. Similarly, the dentist utilized knowledge gained from experience in selecting the tool and filling the patient's cavity. The chef retrieved the steak from the grill based on his concepts of "rare," "medium," and "well done" and "you won't believe this" continuum, and the ability to discern when the steak had reached the prescribed point on it.

This is an important consideration when selecting the verbs and types of performance of the performance step details in the analysis. If the analyst assumes a position similar to Miles and Robinson's, the use of the term "manipulation" in evaluating performance step details must be given due consideration. Depending on the analyst, manipulation could either always be included as a type of behavior for each performance step detail, or could be assumed present in all cases and not be included in the list. If the latter approach is adopted, the analyst should inform the reader of the assumption. Again, the decision to use or exclude the term manipulation in the evaluation of the performance step details is left to the discretion of the individual analyst.

Following is a list of performance step details. In some instances the activities are solely mechanical whereas, others are a combination of manipulative behavior and one other type of performance.

Drop the landing gear.	Manipulation
Mark the typographical errors on the card.	Manipulation/Recall
Knead the dough.	Manipulation
Set the rate of feed to twenty-five feet/minute.	Manipulation/Discrimination
Adjust the volume of the amplifier system.	Manipulation/Communication
Squeeze the trigger.	Manipulation

Communication. Communication is the term used to collectively describe written and oral types of performance. Like the other types of performance, writing and speaking are both manifest forms of behavior determined by the knowledge and attitudes of the communicator. In some instances, speech and writing are directly used in transmitting thoughts and ideas to others. Under other conditions, however, the acts of speaking and writing themselves become significant and occupationally relevant skills to be mastered.

Almost all occupations require some degree of communicative ability. Certain ones require speaking and/or writing abilities beyond those encountered in daily social discourse. Salespeople convince, coaches motivate and inspire, politicians promise, teachers clarify and guide, journalists inform, auctioneers appeal, sports broadcasters report, lawyers defend. The list goes on. In each instance, people are communicating as specialized parts of their work lives.

Since speaking and writing are such important aspects of a number of occupations, their mastery must be included in the eventual occupational courses and units. Several communication-related performance step details are listed below. The verb introducing each step detail identifies the type(s) of performance of the phrase.

Greet the customer.	Communication
Talk the student through the task.	Communication/Recall
Object to the prosecutor's line of questioning.	Communication/Problem-solving
Take the patient's history.	Communication/Manipulation
Ask the group to be seated.	Communication
Write the evaluation criteria for the objective.	Communication/Problem-solving

Standards of Performance

The criteria for writing standards of performance for performance step details are the same as those for writing performance standards for performance steps. Please refer back to Chapter 6 for a review of the material.

In Review

1. What is the major purpose of the *performance step detail sheet* in gathering occupational data?

2. In what ways would the data from the *performance step detail sheet* be used in developing occupational curriculum materials?

3. With regard to function and purpose, are the standard of performance statements on the *performance step detail sheet* any different than those found on the *task detailing sheet*?

4. Note the five types of behavior discussed in the chapter and list three different performance steps or performance step details for each type.

5. In listing the type of performance for a given performance step detail it often makes sense to assign two or three types of performance to a single activity. How can this be, particularly when the verb might so obviously be of one predominant type?

CHAPTER 8

The Employment Spiral:
Writing Related Occupational
Information Topics

As stated in the introduction, the purpose of Part Two, Gathering and Organizing Occupational Data, is, in part, "to identify the work activities and information content of an occupation." The list of occupational activities and informational content is the principal data resource for future curriculum development in a given occupational area.

The identification and listing of the tasks, performance steps, and performance step details of the occupation were done on the respective worksheets. The activity portion of the occupation has now been analyzed. Completing the analysis process involves identifying, gathering, and listing the related occupational information topics.

The emphasis of the analysis up to this point has been on what the person *does* in the occupation. This is prerequisite, since the tasks of the occupation must be known before the informational content (knowledge) can be identified and listed. For instance, if the analysis of a nurse's aide occupation reveals that the tasks performed by the aide require only selected bits of knowledge of anatomy, then only those selected portions should be included in the occupational program. In this case, any in-depth study (and hence, knowledge) of the interdependent relationships and functions of body systems and sub-systems which does not *relate directly to the tasks being performed* becomes, at best, irrelevant data.

The term *related occupational information* is used to refer collectively to two distinct types of occupational information: *technical occupational information*, and *career and occupational guidance information*. Writing the related occupational information topics identifies the information which is needed by the person performing the tasks of the occupation, and which will permit him or her successful entry, continuation, and advancement in the occupation.

Technical Occupational Information

Technical occupational information is that information which the worker *must* know to perform the individual tasks of the occupation in a satisfactory manner. The technical occupational information topics are directly related to the individual tasks themselves, rather than to the occupation as a whole.

Technical Occupational Information Topics is one section of the task detailing sheet. For convenience and review, a sample worksheet appears in Example 8.1. As was discussed earlier, the technical occupational information topics are initially identified in terms of tasks of the occupation. For that reason, they appear in the analysis in close proximity to the task to which they are related.

Sample technical information topics for various tasks of selected occupations appear below. In each instance, the topic specifies the types of information the person must possess if he or she is going to satisfactorily perform the given task.

Occupation: Business Programmer
    Task: Changing Input Formats
        Technical Occupational Information Topics
            Computer Systems Terminology
            System Flowchart Design
            Template Procedures
            Computer Configurations

Occupation: Emergency Room Nurse
    Task: Receiving Injured Patients
        Technical Occupational Information Topics
            Aseptic Technique
            Signs and Symptoms of Shock
            Signs and Symptoms of Skeletal Trauma
            Legal Rights of the Patient

Primary Occupation: Vocational Development Specialist
    Task: Gathering Information for the Client
        Technical Occupational Information Topics
            Admission Requirements
            Interviewing Techniques
            Methods of Recording Data
            Problem-centered Client Records

Example 8.1
Task Detailing Sheet

Primary Occupation (PO): Teller

Occupational Specialty (OS): General Teller

Occupational Sub-specialty (OSS): Paying and Receiving Teller

Task: Issuing Treasurer's Checks

Performance Steps	*Standards of Performance*
1. Ascertain amount of check to be issued and accept payment.	The accepted payment is equal to the amount of the check to be issued.
2. Prepare the Treasurer's check.	The Treasurer's check is "cut" for the exact predetermined amount. The current date, numeric amount, and the payee's name appear in the appropriate places on the check.
3. Have the Treasurer's check signed.	The check is signed by an authorized bank signer.
4. Process the Treasurer's check.	The original is given to the customer. The credit copy is "cashed in" on the reverse side for the exact amount of the check and placed in the appropriate bin for transit pickup. The office copy is filed numerically, chronologically and by date in the appropriate file drawer.

Technical Occupational Information Topics

1. Other Services
2. Protectograph Machine
3. Definition of Terms
4. Burrough's Teller Machine
5. Alphabetic, Numeric Filing Procedures

A complete list of technical information topics also includes all *safety* and *legal* types of information. Safety and legal information are as essential to the worker's continued performance in the occupation as is the information needed to complete the tasks.

Note the manner in which the topic titles are written. Closely resembling the titles of books, chapters, or section headings within a text, they quickly and precisely inform the reader of the type of information required to perform the individual tasks. This, of course, is their purpose.

One last point. It is very important that the analyst identifies *all* of the technical occupational information topics for *each* task, even if it means identifying topic titles common to a number of different tasks. The topics will eventually lead to the identification of other information sources, and/or the writing of various technical information sheets in the preparation of learning materials. Any oversight in identifying all of the necessary topics will seriously affect the quality of the forthcoming occupational learning materials. Moreover, there should be no attempt to avoid duplication of topic titles simply because they specify knowledge necessary for more than one task. Whereas a single technical information topic would probably require only a short discussion during a laboratory session, a number of related technical information titles for different tasks might justify the establishment of a complementary related subject matter course. The data provided by the analysis can be of assistance in making such decisions.

Career and Occupational Guidance Information

A brief review of the *Career and Occupational Guidance Module* of the *Comprehensive Careers Cluster Curriculum Model* will put occupational guidance information topics in context. The guidance module is the communications link between the people involved with the career and occupational education offerings of the school and the employment sector of the community. Those responsible for conducting the career and guidance program are liaisons between the school and community, and provide and maintain an open line of communication between the two groups.

The responsibilities of those in the guidance program vary according to the levels of attainment of the learners they serve. The nature of the guidance information necessary for those preparing for employment differs considerably from that required by individuals enrolled in the awareness, exploration, or orientation programs of the total career education curriculum. The two major responsibilities of the occupational guidance program to those preparing for employment or who are already employed are to keep all concerned abreast of the immediate, short-range and long-range needs of the work community, and provide information that will be of assistance to each individual in continuing and advancing in the occupation in which he or she is already employed.

Occupational guidance information is the information which provides the worker with greater insight into the trends, wage and fringe benefits, occupational hazards, health-care problems, advancement opportunities, etc. of the occupation in which he or she is or will be employed. It is necessary to occupational entry, growth, security, and advancement. A number of examples of selected career and occupational guidance information topics appear below. Unlike the titles of the technical occupational information which are directly related to a given task, career/occupation guidance topics are related to the occupation as a whole. Note also the topical format used in writing each topic title.

Occupation: Civil Engineering Draftsman
   Wages and Fringe Benefits
   Vertical Mobility
   Horizontal Mobility
   Societies and Unions
   Opportunities in Related Occupational Fields

Occupation: Receptionist
   Wage Scale
   Job Stability
   Sick-Leave Policy
   Overtime Practices
   Vacation Policy

Occupation: Flight Instructor
   Retirement Program
   Advancement Policies
   Resumé Writing Techniques
   Hours
   Wages and Fringe Benefits

Occupation: Business Programmer
   Working Conditions
   Career Opportunities
   Educational Advancement Programs
   Employment Agencies
   Retirement Benefits

The career and occupational guidance information topics appear as a single entry in the completed analysis. The sheet includes the title, Career and Occupational Guidance Information Topics, the title of the primary occupation, and the list of information topic titles. A sample list follows.

Career and Occupational Guidance Information Topics

Primary Occupation: Teller
   - Wage Scale
   - Working Conditions
   - Reasons for Discharge
   ∘ Vacation Benefits
   - Insurance Plans
   - Sick Pay Benefits
   - Workman's Compensation

- Continuing Education
- Civil Service
- Career Opportunities
- Retirement Program
- Horizontal Mobility
- Vertical Mobility
- Opportunities in Related Occupational Fields
- Wages and Fringe Benefits
- Sick-Leave Policy
- Vacation Policy
- Working Conditions
- Opportunities for Advancement

In Review

1. In the process of gathering occupational data, how has the emphasis changed in this chapter as compared to the preceding chapters?

2. Define *technical occupational information.*

3. Define *career and occupational guidance information.*

4. Make a sketch showing the relationships between an occupation sub-specialty and its tasks and technical occupational information topics. Also, depict how career and occupational guidance information topics relate to the occupation as a whole.

II Converting Occupational Organization and Data to Work Preparation Curriculum

> Having set up an educational goal, New-Fist proceeded to construct a curriculum for reaching that goal. "What things must we tribesmen know how to do in order to live with full bellies, warm backs and minds free from fear?" he asked himself.
>
> From *The Saber-Tooth Curriculum*
> by J. Abner Peddiwell. © 1939
> (McGraw-Hill Book Company)
> Used with permission of McGraw-Hill Book Company

The second major step in implementing the occupational curriculum development theory is to develop the component, long-range occupational curriculum spiral concept to complement the long-range employment spiral. This process will complete the development of the dual long-range employment-curriculum spiral. This section provides the rationale for the conversion of the spiral to an occupational curriculum, and the information, methods, and criteria necessary for implementation.

In review, the dual long-range employment-curriculum spiral is an organizational plan for coordinating the educational and employment opportunities for a group of occupations. The dual approach provides the person interested in preparing for work with a way to attain his or her perceived occupational goal and, at the same time, realize a number of en route employment and educational alternatives should he or she need them prior to reaching that goal.

The long-range occupational employment spiral discussed in Section I is the foundation for developing the dual employment-curriculum spiral. The completed long-range occupational employment spiral established:

. . . an organizational plan for organizing and ranking all of the occupational

80

titles and tasks of a single, functionally related group of occupations, e.g. library science-related occupations, dental-related occupations, poultry farming-related occupations, etc. and which, in turn provided a basis for the future development of work preparation work materials in a particular area of employment. . .

Now that we have established the employment spiral for the functionally related group of occupations, completed the ranking and ordering of the primary occupations, identified the occupational specialties and sub-specialties of one of the primary occupations, and listed the tasks of the occupational components, we can develop the component long-range occupational curriculum spiral.

The conversion is a relatively simple process, writing the individual tasks in performance terms or as learning objectives. Conversion of the employment spiral tasks to learning objectives is the essential step in the creation of both the component curriculum spiral and the total organizational concept of the dual employment-curriculum spiral.

The simple act of writing tasks in performance terms is the change agent and catalyst in the process. Prior to this act the employment spiral is a singular concept. Immediately following it, the spiral is an organizational plan which articulates the employment and educational aspects of society.

The conversion of tasks to learning objectives also creates a difference in the nature of the two spirals. Whereas the employment spiral is simply a hierarchical ordering of occupational titles (both actual and implied) along a series of spirally arranged dots, the curriculum spiral is a spirally configured *timeline* made up of individual learning objectives of a total occupational curriculum.

Only one chapter is included in Section II. Entitled "Writing Task Objective Sheets", it guides the reader through the process of writing tasks in performance terms to the creation of the curriculum and employment-curriculum spirals. The following section, Section III, will guide the reader in completing the development of the occupational curriculum development concept.

CHAPTER 9

Writing Task Objective Sheets

The *task objective sheet* is the worksheet used to convert the tasks identified in the occupational analysis into the learning objectives of an occupational program. A sample of a completed worksheet appears in Example 9.1. Its purpose is two-fold: to assist the curriculum designer in converting the tasks identified in the occupational analysis to the learning objectives of an occupational program, and to guide the designer in formulating the desired behavior of the learner, the conditions under which he or she will perform, and the criteria by which his or her performance will be evaluated.

Criteria

Heading. The worksheet is divided into two basic parts: the heading and the body of the sheet. The heading includes the title of the sheet itself, "Task Objective Sheet", and the titles of the "Occupation," "Occupational Specialty," "Occupational Sub-Specialty," and "Learning Objective." The heading is intended to assist the reader in identifying the exact location of the particular objective within the total curriculum.

Body. As stated earlier, one of the major purposes of the task objective sheet is to aid in the conversion of tasks of an occupation to learning objectives. This is done by writing each task in performance terms. The body of the sheet is made up of three major components: "Performance Conditions," "Desired Behavior," and "Evaluation Criteria." These three items together with the objective title comprise the complete statement of a learning objective.

A learning objective is a statement that specifies an act to be performed, the conditions under which the act will occur, and the standards to be achieved before it can be considered complete. A sample learning objective follows.

Example 9.1
Task Objective Sheet

I. *Primary Occupation:* Teller

II. *Occupational Specialty:* General Teller

III. *Occupational Sub-Specialty:* Paying and Receiving Teller

IV. *Learning Objective:* Selling Domestic Traveler's Checks

V. *Performance Conditions:* At a simulated bank teller's station in the classroom, given a cash drawer, supply of traveler's checks and purchase applications, desk calculator, inter-office general ledger tickets, and an assortment of wallets, and with no learning aids, but in the presence of an instructor,

VI. *Desired Behavior:* The learner will sell domestic traveler's checks.

VII. *Evaluation Criteria:* The domestic traveler's checks are prepared according to the underwriter's sales directions and the transaction verified by the instructor. The sequence of performance steps listed on the task procedure sheet given at the time of demonstration of the objective was followed exactly. The learner was able to explain the procedure he or she performed at the instructor's request. He or she demonstrated the complete procedure within a 10 minute time period. The task was repeated a minimum of four times distributed equally over a two-week time period.

Title: Washing Cars

Performance Conditions: In the carwash area of the school automotive laboratory, given a dirty car, sponge, chamois, pail, wheelbrush, washing detergent, hose, water, and a vacuum cleaner, a procedure sheet for performing the task, together with the help of a fellow student and in the presence of the instructor,

Desired Behavior: The student wash bay attendant will wash cars.

Evaluation Criteria: The outside and inside surfaces of the automobile are clean and dry. No damage or other conditional changes (other than the removal of the dirt) have resulted from the performance of the task. The sequence of performance steps listed on the procedure sheet was followed exactly. The learner was able to explain the procedure being performed at the instructor's request. The complete procedure was demonstrated within a 30 minute time period. The task was repeated a minimum of three times within a period of four weeks.

Components

Title. The *title* of a learning objective is a phrase that defines the activity to be performed. It gives the reader an encapsulated idea of the nature of the objective that follows.

The title of a learning objective contains a verb, written as a gerund, and an object of the verb, and is exactly the same as the title of the corresponding task in the analysis for which it is being written.

Several examples of objectives titles follow. Note how the format compares exactly with that used in writing the titles of tasks.

Dangling Patients
Installing Water Heaters
Baling Hay
Setting a Broken Arm
Giving Haircuts
Editing Films

Performance Conditions. *Performance conditions*, the second of four components used in writing learning objectives, describes the learning situation. A complete statement of performance conditions includes four sub-components: learning environment, equipment and materials (hardware), and learning aids (software), and miscellaneous.

Following is a statement of performance conditions. Parentheses have been included to assist the reader in defining the various sub-components.

Performance Conditions: (In the carwash area of the school automotive laboratory,) (given a dirty car, sponge, chamois, pail, wheelbrush, washing detergent, hose, water, and a vacuum cleaner,) (a procedure sheet for performing the task,) (together with the help of a fellow student and in the presence of the instructor),

The introductory phrase of the conditional statement describes the setting (environment) in which the student will learn the task. Particular attention must be given to the location, desirability, and availability of the learning site. If the student can attain a particular objective in an in-school setting, and perform the task at the level of expectancy desired once he or she becomes employed, then the school-based learning site is probably the preferred location. However, if the task is such that the work conditions play a major role in determining its outcome, and these conditions cannot be duplicated it would be preferable to place the learner at the actual work site for the learning experience. This alternative depends on the availability and cooperation of an employer, school policy, proximity of the school to the worksite, etc.

Desired Behavior. *Desired behavior* is singularly the most important entry in the total objective statement. It is the source from which the title of the objective is derived, and the performance conditions and evaluation criteria established. The statement of desired behavior is the educational extension of the specific tasks listed in the analysis of an occupation.

It is, by definition, written in the future tense, and defines a specific, observable, measurable activity.

Sample statements of desired behavior for various learning objectives follow. To assist the reader in better understanding the relationship between statements of desired behavior and objective titles, these examples correspond with the previous list of objective titles.

The student LPN will dangle patients.

The student plumber will install water heaters.

The student farmer will bale hay.

The student physician's assistant will set broken arms.

The student barber will give haircuts.

The student film editor will edit films.

The introductory phrase of the desired behavior statement identifies the learner, and gives the statement an orientation toward the future. The identification of the particular type of student adds a personal touch to the objective. The learner readily identifies his or her role in the educational scheme and begins formulating his or her eventual role in the work situation.

The essential act of converting tasks to learning objectives is writing each task in terms of the future, using the verb *will*. This transforms the tasks to learning objectives to be attained by students at some future point in time, and insures the relevancy of the objective to the prospective occupation.

The last part of the statement of desired behavior specifies exactly what the student must *do* to attain the objective. This activity remains the focus of the learner's efforts.

Evaluation Criteria. Evaluation criteria, the last of four major components of a learning objective, define the minimum level of acceptable performance for attainment of a given objective. A sample criteria statement appears below. Brackets have been used to differentiate between the sub-components of the example.

Evaluation Criteria: [The outside and inside surfaces of the automobile are clean and dry. No damage or other conditional changes (other than the removal of the dirt) have resulted from the performance of the task.] [The sequence of performance steps listed on the procedure sheet were followed exactly.] [The learner was able to explain the procedure he or she performed at the instructor's request.] [The complete procedure was demonstrated within a 30 minute period.] [The task was repeated a minimum of three times within a four week period.]

As stated above, the evaluation criteria statement defines the minimum level of acceptable performance. The phrase should not be interpreted as either low or high standard. It is intended to define a level or point at which performance will be considered acceptable. In an occupational education situation, the level is most often determined by the level of performance considered acceptable in the occupation.

Like Performance Conditions, the Evaluation Criteria statement is comprised of a series of sub-components that will assist the curriculum writer in specifying the various entries of the evaluative statement. The list includes criterion statements about the final outcome or *product* of the activity, the procedure or *process* followed in completing the activity, the *relationship* of the learner to the instructor during the learning of the objective, the amount of *time* given for performing the objective, and the *number of repetitions* over a period of time. Each criteria would have to be met before the objective could be considered learned.

The introductory sentence or sentences of the evaluation criteria statement describe the product or end result of the act being performed. Written in the present tense, they connote attainment of the objective and the corresponding ability on the part of the learner to perform the activity.

The second entry in the criterion statement deals with the evaluation of the process followed in completing the learning objective. In some instances, adherence to a given procedure is of little or no consequence in attaining the desired end. However, in other situations, the means to the end bears so heavily on the final outcome that it can almost be considered as important as the end itself. Whenever the inclusion of certain steps dictates the quality of the product, and/or when the sequence of performance steps influences its outcome, then attention must be given to evaluating the process in the completion of the act.

The third entry in the evaluation criteria statement describes the relationship of the learner to the instructor during the learning process. In most instances, it refers to the learner's ability to respond to questions concerning performance of the objective posed by the instructor.

The two remaining entries in the evaluation portion of the objective deal with allocation of time. The first specifies the amount of time the learner has to perform the learning objective at the time of final performance. The time can be stated either quantitatively (in 30 minutes . . . within a 40–50 minute period) or qualitatively (. . . within a reasonable amount of time).

The last factor in evaluating performance focuses on the learner's ability to repeat the objective over a given time period to the established level of performance. Once it is determined that the learner is consistent in his or her ability to perform the objective all of the criteria will have been met and the learning objective attained.

Contribution to the Organizational Concept

Writing tasks in performance terms makes three significant contributions to the development and organization of the employment-curriculum plan:

Figure 9.1 *Contribution of the Task Objective Sheet to the Employment-Curriculum Spiral Concept*

first, it establishes the tasks as the basis for determining and naming the learning objectives; secondly, it creates the curricular complement to the employment spiral; and thirdly, it moves the dual long-range employment-curriculum spiral concept one step closer to completion. (See Figure 9.1.) However, the individual component curriculum spiral and the dual employment-curriculum spiral are still not complete. The points of passage between the employment and curriculum components are established and marked with arrows. But the five occupational programs and their courses and units that comprise the occupational curriculum have yet to be identified. The courses, units, and list of learning activities for each individual learning objective are discussed in Chapters 10 to 12 in Section III.

In Review

1. Discuss how the writing of tasks in performance terms contributes to the creation of the curriculum spiral component of the dual long-range employment-curriculum spiral concept.

2. What is the major role of the *task objective sheet* in the total occupational curriculum development process?

3. Four major components comprise a *learning objective*. Briefly discuss the purpose and function of each.

4. Discuss the purpose of the four sub-components of a *performance condition* statement.

5. Discuss the purpose of the five sub-components of an *evaluation criteria* statement.

III Organizing the Occupational Curriculum

Order and simplification are the first steps toward mastery of a
subject. . .

Thomas Mann
From *The Magic Mountain* by
Thomas Mann. Translated by
H. T. Lowe-Porter. Copyright
1967 by Alfred A. Knopf Inc.

The organizational basis of the occupational curriculum is the long-range
occupational employment spiral concept, which is developed through
analysis of the organization of a particular group of functionally related
occupations, the selection of a particular occupation, and more detailed
analysis of its occupational specialties, sub-specialties and tasks. The organizational and functional aspects of a specific occupational group provide,
with only slight modification in most cases, the rationale and organization
for developing the work preparation portion of the school's total offering.

For a detailed review of the development of the long-range curriculum
spiral, see Chapter 2.

CHAPTER 10

The Curriculum Spiral: Determining the Occupational Program, Course, and Unit Titles

The organization of the long-range occupational employment spiral is the basis for organizing and developing the companion long-range occupational curriculum spiral. Determining the occupational program, course, and unit titles from the list of occupational specialties and sub-specialties of the primary occupation constitutes the first step in the conversion process.

A sample of the worksheet that serves as a guide in converting the various titles appears in Example 10.1.

Organization

The worksheet *Determining the Occupational Program, Course, and Unit Titles from the List of Occupational Specialties and Sub-specialties of the Primary Occupation* is comprised of two columns. The left column is a list of the primary occupation and its occupational specialties and sub-specialties. The right column is a list of program, course, and unit titles.

Before continuing with the discussion of the sheet however, another issue must be discussed that is crucial to the reader's understanding of how the curriculum is organized. There are a number of different ways the components can be ordered and named. The following organization is used for its widespread use and general acceptability, and its compatability with our occupational curriculum development theory.

The occupational curriculum, or the total occupational offering of the

Example 10.1
Determining the Occupational Program, Course and
Unit Titles from the List of Occupational Specialties
and Sub-specialties of the Primary Occupation

Occupation, Occupational Specialty and Sub-specialty Titles	*Program, Course, and Unit Titles*
I. *Primary Occupation (PO):*	I. *Occupational Program Title*
Teller	Teller Science
II. *Occupational Specialties (OS):*	II. *Occupational Course Titles:*
A. General Teller	A. General Tellering
B. Collection and Exchange Teller	B. Collection and Exchange Tellering
C. Note Teller	C. Note Tellering
D. Utility Teller	D. Utility Teller Procedures
III. *Occupational Sub-specialties (OSS):*	III. *Occupational Unit Titles:*
A. Occupational Specialty: General Teller	A. Course Title: General Tellering
1. Mail Credit Teller	1. Mail Deposits
2. Paying and Receiving Teller	2. Paying and Receiving
3. Payroll Teller	3. Payroll
4. Return Items Teller	4. Return Items
5. Savings Teller	5. Savings
6. Special Deposits Teller	6. Special Deposits
B. Occupational Specialty: Collection and Exchange Teller	B. Course Title: Collection and Exchange Tellering
1. Bond Teller	1. Bonds
2. Domestic Exchange Teller	2. Domestic Exchange
3. Foreign Exchange Teller	3. Foreign Exchange
C. Occupational Specialty: Note Teller	C. Course Title: Note Tellering
1. Collateral Teller	1. Collateral
2. Commercial Note Teller	2. Commercial Notes
3. Discount Teller	3. Discount
*D. Occupational Specialty: Utility Teller	D. Course Title: Utility Teller Procedures

*In the analysis, there were no occupational sub-specialties for the specialty of "Utility Teller". Hence, there are no unit titles for the course in "Utility Teller Procedures".

school, is comprised of occupational or work-preparation programs. For example, the curriculum for a School of Technical Occupations might include programs in the areas of Dental Hygiene, Computer Science, Library Technology, Poultry Husbandry, etc. In turn, the programs are comprised of applied and related subject matter courses which are then still further divided into occupational units of learning. For the reasons mentioned above, this is the categorization system used here.

Criteria for Writing the Worksheet

The data in the left-hand column of the worksheet are taken verbatim from the worksheet discussed in Section I, Chapter 5 — "The Employment Spiral: Identifying the Occupational Specialties and Sub-specialties". The entries in this column will be used to name the program, courses, and units that comprise the work preparation curriculum. The names of courses and units of the occupational program are found in the right-hand column.

In naming the various curricular components, the curriculum designer should keep the names of the program, courses, and units as close as possible to the occupational titles from which they are derived. This insures continuity of thought in the curriculum development process and keeps the occupational curriculum as representative as possible of the occupational group from which it was derived. An excellent example of the similarity of occupational and curriculum-related titles is shown in Example 10.1.

Contribution to the Organizational Concept

Completion of the worksheet, *Determining the Occupational Program, Course, and Unit Titles from the List of Occupational Specialties and Sub-specialties of the Primary Occupation*, results in the naming of the occupational program and its applied courses and units. The names of the entry-level, technical, professional, research, and administrative programs are the only titles that actually appear on the component curriculum spiral. Course and unit titles are not included, but are implied for the same reasons that the occupational specialty and sub-specialty titles are implied on the employment spiral.

Figure 10.1 is a portion of a total employment-curriculum spiral and shows how the course and unit titles would appear if the problem of limited space could be overcome.

The learning objectives for each unit of each course in the program are also depicted. The following chapter discusses, in greater detail, the organization of objectives into the various curricular components.

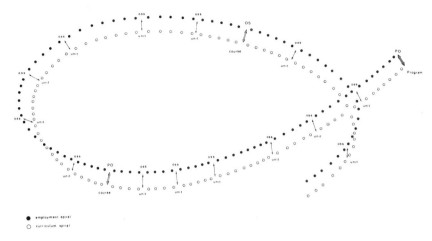

Figure 10.1   *Contribution of the Worksheet to the Curriculum Spiral Concept*

In Review

1. Discuss how the organizational hierarchy of occupational titles (the primary occupation with its occupational specialties and sub-specialties) influences and affects the organizational structure of the complementary occupational curriculum.

2. Why is it important that the organizational aspects of the school's occupational curriculum reflect the organization of the group of occupations?

CHAPTER 11

The Curriculum Spiral: Preparing an Outline of the Program, Course, Unit, and Learning Objective Titles

Once the titles of the occupational program and its courses and units have been determined (see Chapter 10), the only step needed to complete an outline of the program is to list the learning objectives, by units, for each of the applied occupational courses. Example 11.1 is a sample program outline (first page) for a program in Teller Science.

The worksheet for outlining the courses, units, and learning objectives of the occupational program closely resembles, in organization and appearance, the task listing sheets discussed in Section I, Chapter 5. The two worksheets differ in the titles of their various headings. The titles of the primary occupation, occupational specialties, and occupational subspecialties on the task listing sheet are now, respectively, the titles of the occupational program, courses, and units on the program outline.

The titles of the tasks and the learning objectives appear on both sheets without modification. This ensures that the tasks and related technical information topics found in the analysis of the occupations become the learning objectives and informational content in the corresponding occupational programs, courses, and units. Figure 10.1, in the preceding chapter, shows the relationships between the components of the employment spiral and those of the curriculum spiral.

Those who go through a learning experience developed and organized in this manner will be better prepared to leave the learning situation for one in the workplace which closely resembles it in both organization and activity. The transition will be made with relative ease because the indi-

Example 11.1
An Outline of the Teller Science-Related
Occupational Program with Course, Unit,
and Learning Objective Titles

Occupational Program: Teller Science

Course #1:   General Tellering

Unit #1:   Mail Deposits
  Learning Objectives:
- Opening Envelopes
- Receiving Checks for Deposit
- Examining Checks for Endorsements
- Verifying Deposits
- Entering Deposit in Depositor's Passbook or Checking Account
- Issuing Receipts

Unit #2:   Paying and Receiving

  Learning Objectives:
- Counting Currency
- Cashing Checks
- Handling Check Deposits
- Handling Cash Deposits
- Receiving Personal Loan Payments
- Receiving Christmas Club Payments
- Issuing Treasurer's Checks
- Selling Money Orders
- Withdrawing Funds From No Passbook Savings Accounts
- Ordering the Daily Cash Supply
- Selling Domestic Traveler's Checks
- Balancing the Cash Drawer and Settlement
- Accepting Night Depository Deposits

Unit #3:   Payroll

  Learning Objectives:
- Receiving Payroll Requests from Depositors
- Preparing Cash in Requested Denominations
- Verifying Totals
- Accepting Debit to Offset Payroll
- Assuring Funds are Available
- Computing Service Charge

vidual will already be familiar with conditions and activities in the workplace.

In Review

1. The *Outline of Program, Course, Unit, and Learning Objective Titles* closely resembles, in organization and content, the task listing sheet. What are the major differences?

2. Discuss the benefits of having an occupational program developed and arranged in this manner.

CHAPTER 12

The Curriculum Spiral: Writing Unit Learning Modules

The next and final step in the development of the occupational curriculum spiral is the identification and listing of learning activities needed to implement the individual learning objectives. The *unit learning module* (Example 12.1) is the worksheet developed for that purpose.

The *unit learning module* provides the form for presenting a learning objective, its representative list of learning activities, and other activities which complement the learning objective. The module guides the occupational curriculum designer in identifying and organizing the learning activities of a learning objective, establishing a basis for computing the time requirements for attaining the objective, and identifying and listing the audio-visual equipment and materials needed for completing the learning activities.

Criteria

Heading

The heading of the worksheet includes the title "Unit Learning Module", the names of the occupational program, course, and unit, and the title of the learning objective for which the module is written. The curriculum component titles that make up the heading inform the reader of the exact location of the learning objective within the occupational unit, course, and program.

Learning Objective

The learning objective that appears on a unit learning module is taken verbatim from the previously written task objective sheet. In brief review,

Example 12.1
Unit Learning Module

Occupational Program: Teller Science

Course #1: General Tellering

Unit #2: Paying and Receiving

Learning Objective #9: Withdrawing Funds from No Passbook Savings
Accounts

Performance Conditions: In the simulated bank teller station area of the classroom, given a Burrough's teller machine, Burrough's savings machine, Micro-
Fiche equipment, push button telephone, savings inquiry manual, receipts and
a cash drawer, given no instructional aids, and in the presence of the instructor,

Desired Behavior: The student will withdraw funds from no passbook savings
accounts.

Evaluation Criteria: The funds are withdrawn and paid to the customer after
standard established procedures, outlined and demonstrated in class, have been
accurately performed. The student was able to explain the procedure he or she
performed at the instructor's request. He or she demonstrated the complete procedure within a 5 minute time period. The task was repeated a minimum of four
times over a two week period.

Learning Activities:

1. Read section on "No Passbook Savings Accounts" in the Savings Fund
   Manual. (60 minutes)
2. Read chapter on "Signature Verification" in text. (60 minutes)
3. Read "Time Deposit Accounts Inquiry System." (60 minutes)
4. Answer questions on reading assignments. (60 minutes)
5. Participate in presentation/discussion on withdrawing funds from no
   passbook savings accounts. (120 minutes)
6. Take the Related Readings Test on "Withdrawing Funds from No Passbook Savings Accounts." (60 minutes)
7. Observe the demonstration of established procedures for withdrawing
   funds from no passbook savings accounts. (90 minutes)
8. Practice the activity. (180 minutes)
9. Take the final performance test. (5 minutes/each of four tests: 20
   minutes)

Estimated Time
11 hrs. 50 mins.

Complementary Learning Activities:

1. Tour Savings Fund Bookkeeping for lecture and discussion. (60 minutes)
2. Tour Information Center for a lecture and demonstration on information
   available from the computer. (60 minutes)

Equipment and Materials:

Equipment: Burrough's Teller machine, Burrough's savings machine, cash
drawer, coin machine

Materials: Teller's manual, Savings manual, handouts, currency, receipts, coin

---

the learning objective is a statement written in the future tense, that
defines a measurable act. It is comprised of four components: the *title*,
which identifies the objective; the *performance conditions* that describe
the learning environment and identify what equipment, materials, and
supplies, instructional aids, and other miscellaneous items the learner will
have at his or her disposal while performing the objective; the *desired
behavior* statement that specifies the activity the learner will perform; and
lastly, the *evaluation criteria* which establish the standards that must be
met before the learning objective can be considered attained.

For a complete review of writing learning objectives, read Section II,
Chapter 9, "Writing Task Objective Sheets."

Learning Activities

Learning activities are those activities performed by a learner en route to
attaining a particular learning objective. Ranging from reading a technical
information sheet, to taking a field trip, constructing a bulletin board,
viewing an illustrated presentation, taking a pencil-paper test, watching a
demonstration, practicing it, and taking a final performance test, they
guide and direct the learner from a point in time of not being able to perform a given objective to a point in time when he or she can perform the
stated act.

Learning activities can be categorized for use in an individualized
learning situation or in the more conventional teacher-directed classroom
arrangement. However, the development of the unit learning module and
the selection, listing, and ordering of learning activities discussed here are
intended for development of individualized learning activities packages
(LAPS).*

Approaches

Before beginning preparation of the learning materials, consider the situation in which they are to be used. A setting in which the individual initiative of the learner is sought would prompt a completely different approach
to the preparation process than would one in which the teacher is the
primary informational resource.

---

*A LAP is a self-contained package of learning materials with which the learner
assumes almost total responsibility for attaining the particular objective. The development of a learning activities package is discussed in Section Five, Chapter 24, "Preparing Individualized Learning Activities Packages."

Examples of learning activities and how they might differ in the two approaches are shown in Example 12.2.

Example 12.2 shows the similarities and differences in the individualized and teacher-involved approaches. The first list directs the learner to the various sources of information and techniques of performance and he or she completes the sequence of learning activities with little or no outside assistance. In contrast, the second list indicates considerable involvement on the part of the teacher in the learning process and attainment of the objective.

Careful selection of the verbs used in introducing the individual learning activities statements, and appropriate phrasing of the nature and scope of the statement are critical to the development of a particular approach. Judicious choice can make the approach wholly individualized, reflect significant amounts of teacher interaction and involvement, or demonstrate the desired combinations of both approaches. In the end, the approach is a function of the attitude and intent of the curriculum designer as he or she views the learner and the learning situation.

Example 12.2
Learning Objective: Preparing a Garden Plot

Individualized Approach	*Teacher-Involved Approach*
1. Read pages 7–21, Section 2, Chapter IX in the text. (20 mins)	1. Read pages 7–21, Section 2, Chapter IX in the text. (20 mins)
2. Read Information-Assignment Sheet "Tips on Planting" and complete the "Additional Study" section. (50 mins)	2. Read Information-Assignment Sheet "Tips on Planting" and complete the "Additional Study" section. (50 mins)
3. View the taped illustrated presentation "The Do's and Don'ts of Gardening." (30 mins)	3. Participate in the illustrated presentation-discussion "The Do's and Don'ts of Gardening." (50 mins)
4. Take the Related Information Test. (60 mins)	4. Take the Related Information Test. (60 mins)
5. Observe the slide series demonstration of "Preparing the Garden Plot." (60 mins)	5. Participate in the discussion of the test. (20 mins)
6. Practice preparing a garden plot. (120 mins)	6. Observe the demonstration of "Preparing the Garden Plot." (60 mins)
7. Take the final performance test of preparing a garden plot. (120 mins x 2)	7. Practice preparing a garden plot. (120 mins)
	8. Take the final performance test of preparing a garden plot. (120 mins x 2)

Writing Learning Activities

A properly stated learning activity identifies an action whose completion moves the learner one step closer to attaining the perceived objective. The learning activity statement is introduced by a verb that specifies what the learner will do, e.g., read, participate in, watch, practice. The next portion of the statement further identifies the existing resource in which information can be found or further clarifies the event to be performed. Following are several examples of various learning activity statements.

- Read Information Sheet #2, "Safety Practices for Taking Dental X-Rays." (20 minutes)
- Take the Related Readings Test on "Counting Currency." (30 minutes)
- View the video-taped presentation "Techniques and Materials for Casing Rough Door Openings." (60 minutes)

Grouping and Sequencing Learning Activities

The rationale and procedures for grouping and sequencing learning activities follows.

The list of learning activities is divided into two basic types: *knowledge-related* and *performance-related*. (See the sample list of learning activities in Example 12.3.)

Example 12.3
Learning Objective: Casing a Rough Opening
to Receive an Interior Door

Learning Activities:

Knowledge Related

1. Read Information Sheet "Grain Configuration, Color and Appearance." (30 minutes)
2. Read Information-Assignment Sheet "Types and Styles of Casing and Trim" and complete the study questions. (60 minutes)
3. Read Section #1, Chapter 7, "Finishing Rough Door Openings" in the text. (60 minutes)
4. Read Task Procedure Sheet "Casing the Standard Rough Opening for an Interior Door." (10 minutes)
5. View the taped illustrated presentation "Techniques and Materials for Casing Rough Openings." (60 minutes)
6. Complete the Related Information Test "Casing Rough Door Openings." (60 minutes)

Example 12.3 continued

Performance Related	7.	Observe the demonstration of "Casing a Rough Opening to Receive an Interior Door." (60 minutes)
	8.	Practise the activity. (480 minutes)
	9.	Take the final performance test of casing a rough interior door opening. (60 minutes)

There is no predetermined number of learning activities. In Example 12.3, however, the first six learning activities direct the learner in acquiring the knowledge he or she will need to perform the learning objective. The remaining three learning activities emphasize performance. Both types of learning activities, and the ordering and emphasis of each is essential if mastery of the skill implied in the title of the learning objective is to be realized by the learner.

Sequencing of Individual Learning Activities

The sequencing of individual learning activities in the knowledge- and performance-related groupings is also crucial to the individual's attainment of the learning objective. Basically, the knowledge-related learning activities are essential to performance in that they impart the information which regulates, influences, and directs the learner's judgement-forming and decision-making behavior during the actual performance of the objective.* The informational activities direct the learner to the various resources where he or she can acquire necessary technical information (books or portions thereof, journal articles, instruction sheets, guest presenter); guide him or her through an audio- or video-taped presentation that reviews, reiterates, and further clarifies the information presented in the preceding written materials or adds new knowledge to that already acquired; and assist him or her in determining, by means of a pencil-paper test, to what degree he or she has mastered the knowledge to perform the objective. When the informational learning activities are arranged in the suggested manner, the learner will know exactly what has to be done, how to go about it, and will always be assimilating new information from an established basis of knowledge and awareness.

The ordering of performance-related learning activities also follows a prescribed plan. With a basic knowledge acquired from the informational resources, the learner observes a demonstration of the objective to be performed, practices the activity until he or she has gained the skill and confidence needed to do it, and when he or she feels prepared, has his or her performance evaluated.

---

*The topics discussed in the various information-related learning activities were originally identified during the writing of the task detailing sheet of the task from which the learning objective was derived. See Part Two, Section I, Chapter 6, "The Employment Spiral: Writing Task Detailing Sheets."

The logic for ordering the performance-related learning activities is quite simple. In the best instructional manner, the learner is first shown that which he or she will later be expected to do. Next, he or she is given ample opportunity to practice the activity under the care and supervision of the instructor. And lastly, a measure is made of his or her performance to determine if he or she has successfully attained the defined objective. While other types of performance-related learning activities certainly can be included in the above-mentioned list, the "demonstration-practice-performance evaluation" sequence is fundamental to the ordering of performance-related learning activities.

Additional Learning Activities

There is no set number of types of knowledge-oriented or performance-oriented learning activities. Whereas the latter sequence involving the learner's observation, practice, performance, and evaluation of an objective is a tried and successful way of learning the doing aspects of a task, the kinds of activities that provide the learner with essential information are more varied. Activities such as those in the following list provide some idea of the many ways of imparting the needed technical occupational information to the learner.

Analysis of Current Events. Reports of events, or new findings from radio or TV newscasts, the daily newspaper, or a news magazine may provoke interesting discussion and help make tangible the concepts of occupational education.

Bulletin Boards. A bulletin board with a brief, compact message, prepared by the students themselves (with or without teacher help) constitutes a learning situation for both the group of pupils that composes the display and those who are attracted to it. Effective displays, filed in large manila folders, can be used over and over in a series constantly enriched by student ingenuity and teacher contribution.

Case-Study Problem. This technique allows a class to consider situations and events in relation to particular individuals (actual or fictional). The facts of the case, with an emphasis on background, are presented in written or oral form, and the discussion proceeds as in other problem-solving.

Collections. Individual or group collection projects, such as collections of occupational materials, the paraphernalia of an occupation or career — particularly when these are correlated with the gathering of information on the particular area of study — provide learning opportunities both for the collectors and for those that view the collection.

Commercial Films. The sound motion picture can both entertain and instruct. It can provide students with vicarious experiences and can provide them with images of things they could not otherwise see.

Debate. A debate would require four to eight participants, equally divided into two teams. The participants debate a single positive statement which begins, "Resolved: that. . ." One side argues the affirmative and the other argues the negative. Each has a chance to make a presentation plus a rebuttal to the opposing arguments. Means of judging as to which side presents the better argument may be considered. For best results the debate teams should have some time in which to prepare the arguments rather than be called upon for spontaneous performance.

Demonstrations. Well conducted demonstrations make verbal explanations more understandable. Models, live subjects, or equipment all have particular value in demonstration.

Educational Games. Because of their universal appeal to all age groups, educational games should be used more often by teachers for learning purposes. If properly conducted, the game creates a most favorable emotional atmosphere in the classroom for learning. Games are a means of securing widespread participation by pupils and can be highly motivating.

Evaluation of a TV or Radio Program. A particular program may be assigned as homework or heard or viewed by the class at school. Spontaneous, unassigned evaluation, including that of commercials involving the world of work, may also be encouraged.

Exhibits. The primary value of an exhibit as a learning experience may be for those who prepare it, but there is also some value for others who view the exhibit. This is especially true if the exhibit is of the audience participation type, where the spectator tests his or her knowledge of a given problem or manipulates some part of the exhibit in order to gain knowledge.

Field Trips. A planned and organized visit may be made by an individual, a small group, or a whole class to some business for the purpose of seeing it in operation and gaining firsthand knowledge about it.

Flannel Boards. The flannel board can be used in a variety of ways in a learning situation. It may be the core for illustrating certain facts, or it may be used as an adjunct to a self-test, a problem situation, a game, or another teaching technique. The board may be used by students to illustrate the characters, scenes, and other ingredients needed for a story they have written.

Guest Speaker. An outside resource person, preferably one whose work puts him or her in practical contact with the subject about which he or she is speaking, can enhance clsssroom learning. It is important, however, to ensure that the guest is an interesting and informative speaker.

Interview.   When the teacher wants to employ a guest authority, but wants to evoke answers to specific questions, he or she may use the interview technique. Questions are asked and answered (the guest is not expected to have a formal presentation). Students may be encouraged to use this technique also, inviting an authority and interviewing him or her in front of the class. A variation of this technique would be an interview with the authority by the teacher, an individual student, or a group of students outside the classroom. This interview may be taped and replayed for a class, or the results of the interview may be verbally presented by the interviewers.

Lecture.   This is the systematic presentation of facts and information, often a synthesis of many materials that the learner would be unable or unwilling to seek out on his or her own. It is theoretically efficient, but the learner plays a passive role in it. If learner motivation is high, the lecture can be very effective.

Lecture-Discussion.   In this approach, the lecturer retains control and direction of the class, but allows or encourages questions and other verbal responses from the learners.

Projects.   The construction of a project may be encouraged in the classroom, shop, home, or business establishment on an individual, family, or class-group basis. A continuing search by the students and the teacher for those skills essential to construction of various projects should be maintained. Getting families interested in such activities can be an effective means of parent education on many aspects of career development and guidance.

Panel Discussion.   The panel discussion brings together a group of four to eight people to talk on a chosen subject. Each of the participants should have some background and/or have done extensive preparatory work on the topic. An impartial moderator directs the panel, posing questions to certain members, regulating and limiting response, and often directing questions from the audience to panel members.

Pupil Surveys.   To answer the questions, "What are the facts?" or "What do people do?" or "What is really happening?" students may develop and conduct surveys of various kinds. The teacher must maintain control, however, checking topics, questions, and proposed survey methods and requiring students to have proper permission where this is appropriate and necessary.

Question Writing.   Students, individually or in groups, may write questions for an examination, an exercise that requires some grasp of the subject area. These may be used in actual examination or in an untabulated test. Question writers may be asked to score and grade the exams.

Records.   These may be used in the same general way as commercial tapes. Records often accompany color slide series or filmstrips, giving an audio explanation of the visual images or creating a background effect. Appropriate music and songs can often be used to introduce material, to create a general mood, or to supplement other media.

Reporting.   This is a rather spontaneous technique wherein students report to the class on occurrences they have actually observed or in which they have participated, such as a visit to the dentist, a person getting fired or commended, or a trip to the hospital.

Self-Test.   A test, of any sort, is given to students to show them what they know and do not know about a particular topic. Answers may be provided by the teacher, or the student may be expected to find them himself or herself. The test is not graded or the results recorded (for the individual), but students are encouraged to learn from what they demonstrably do not know. This technique may be used to introduce a topic or to check progress during a unit. Typically the administration of the test is followed by discussion.

Skit.   The skit is a rehearsed dramatization, and this is its essential difference from the sociodrama. It is a means of affecting attitudes as well as being an imparter of information. It typically invites or requires some discussion, interpretation, or analysis.

Small Group Discussion (or Buzz Session).   This approach often is an effective way to have students relate to controversial issues or questions. The class or audience is divided and each group, acting under a chairperson, advances its arguments for or against a proposal. After time for discussion, each chairperson reports on the views of his or her group in a succinct manner. The discussion promotes group interaction and provides an arena for airing and evaluating individual points of view.

Slides or Film Strips.   Although these, like movies, present visual images, they allow more flexibility, more explanation, and more discussion during the showing.

Sociodrama.   This is a largely spontaneous dramatization of some situation, usually involving different views of the same issue. Each participant is given a brief description of the character he or she is to portray; the drama or discussion begins and each reacts to what others say or do as his or her character would. The drama may have a logical ending or the teacher may stop it. Then discussion and analysis can proceed, with particular references to key statements by the various characters.

Symposium. The symposium is similar to the panel in being composed of authorities on a particular topic, but different in that it has no moderator and is, therefore, unstructured. To be successful, a symposium should be composed of individuals about equally willing to talk. The members ask questions of one another and let the discussion roam where it may (within the realm of the central discussion topic, of course).

Tape Recordings. Tapes can bring authorities or dramatizations to the classroom both through commercial tapes or student-prepared tapes (interviews, etc.). Classroom events (panels, symposia, etc.) can be taped and played later for other classes. A radio program or the sound track of a television documentary may be taped and played later for other classes and used as a basis for information and discussion.

Workshop Session. Workshop sessions on a particular problem such as the production of a bulletin board display, the binding of a class-prepared booklet, the preparation of a series of slides can be valuable learning situations. The workshop session typically results in the production of some tangible evidence of learning.

Estimating Time

An important entry on the unit learning module that will assist later in planning the occupational courses and units is the estimated time needed to complete individual learning objectives. For examples, see the completed unit learning module (Example 12.1) and the list of learning activities for Casing a Rough Opening to Receive an Interior Door shown on page 101–102.

The times for both the individual learning activities and learning objective can be stated in hours and/or minutes, depending on the preference of the curriculum designer.

Complementary Learning Activities

The complementary learning activities gain their name from their relationship with the learning activities discussed earlier in the chapter. Both types of learning activities move the learner closer to attaining a given objective. The learning activities discussed earlier are each considered essential or basic to the process of attaining the learning objective. In contrast, the complementary learning activities are not essential, and add to or enhance the basic list.

This complementary learning activities section can be considered a warehouse of learning activities. When a situation arises, the instructor can choose, if he or she so desires, one or more learning activities to add to the initial learning activities sequence. The complementary list is always in a state of flux. New learning activities are added by the curriculum designer or instructor. Established activities that remain relevant are retained, or, if their potential decreases, they are modified or dropped from the list. Regardless, the list is dynamic and the learning activities that comprise it are there to enhance the basic list of learning activities and not supplant it.

In determining the list of complementary learning activities, the curriculum writer reviews the basic list of learning activities and identifies other learning activities that complement and add to the instructional potential of the first list. The complementary learning activities are written in the same style as the basic learning activities. The following list is a series of complementary learning activities. After studying it, you will become aware that a student could not attain the particular objective of "mining coal" by completing the listed activities. Yet, it is also evident that these learning activities would benefit the learner and complement the activities that would actually prepare him or her for the activity.

- Take a field-trip to a shaft mine.
- Make a 3-dimensional model of an open-pit mine.
- Construct a bulletin board showing miners' equipment.
- Make a display of different types and grades of coal.
- Make a poster emphasizing one safety practice that should be followed in mining coal.

Equipment and Materials

In this section of the module the hardware and software items needed to complete the various learning activities of the particular learning objective are listed. For example, for the learning activity "Watch the illustrated-presentation 'Techniques and Safety Practices for Sterilizing Equipment'," on video tape cassette, the necessary equipment would be a cassette player and the cassette itself. Other items on the equipment and materials list for the learning objective would depend on the equipment and materials requirements of the other learning activities.

Contribution to the Organizational Concept

The planning and writing of the unit learning modules is the final step in the development of the long-range employment-curriculum spiral concept. The learning activities are the last components to be identified that move the spiral concept from its original latent state to that of becoming an organizational reality. For review, Figure 12.1 depicts a portion of an employment-curriculum spiral with the tasks of a given occupational sub-specialty comprising the employment component, and the corresponding occupational unit with its learning objectives and respective

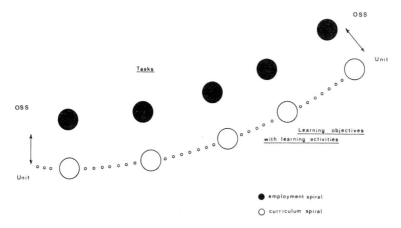

Figure 12.1 *Contribution of the Unit Learning Module to the Employment-Curriculum Spiral Concept*

series of learning activities making up the curriculum counterpart. The arc of the employment spiral is a serially arranged group of tasks that comprise the work activities of a particular occupational sub-specialty, the corresponding arc of the curriculum spiral represents a *timeline* along which the learning objectives and learning activities are distributed. The fulfillment of the objectives will prepare a person for employment, continuance in the occupational curriculum, or both.

A single learning objective with its learning activities is the smallest, self-contained, time-space segment of an occupational curriculum spiral that results in the attainment of a marketable skill. (See Figure 12.2). A group of learning objectives with their respective series of learning activities comprises a single occupational unit of a given course in a total occupational program.

Figure 12.2 illustrates the relationship of a learner to a learning objective and its learning activities. The dot marks the point that the learner currently occupies in *time* and *space prior* to beginning movement toward the learning objective. The learning objective, in turn, is the end to which the learner aspires and, barring difficulties, will attain at some time in the

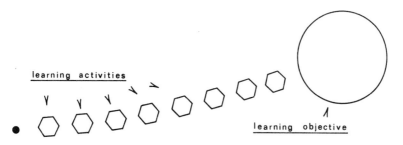

Figure 12.2 *A Learning Objective with its Learning Activities*

future. The learning activities are the en route activities that the learner must systematically complete, in the order they are presented, to attain the objective. Once the objective is mastered, the learner has added another skill to his or her occupational repertoire and is now ready to begin working toward the next objective in the series.

In Review

1. What is the purpose of the *unit learning module* in development of the Long-Range Occupational Curriculum Spiral?

2. Select any given learning activity and write it as it might appear for use in an individualized learning situation; in a teacher-led situation.

3. Discuss the rationale for having the knowledge-related learning activities appear before the performance-related learning activities in the total sequence of events.

4. Discuss the rationale for the ordering of the various learning activities *within* the knowledge-related series of activities; the performance-related activities.

5. What is the purpose of the *complementary learning activities* section of the unit learning module?

6. Illustrate how the unit learning module completes the long-range curriculum spiral concept. Include a point representing the position of the learner, the learning objective, and the learning activities that move the learner from his present position through time and space to the objective. Label each component.

IV Writing Occupational Program, Course, and Unit Descriptions

Curriculum is the stuff of the schools. Organized and labeled in a multitude of ways, in the end it should graduate people to meet the rigors of life with courage, enthusiasm, and preparedness.

Implementing the occupational curriculum development theory establishes the organizational basis and direction of the curriculum development process, provides substance to it, and readies the occupational curriculum designer to write the guides for the occupational programs, courses, and units.

Based on the organizational concepts established in the development of the long-range employment spiral and the identification and listing of the curriculum component titles, we have developed a complementary model for organizing and developing the occupational curriculum. The Long-Range Occupational Curriculum Spiral complements the parent Long-Range Occupational Employment Spiral and stimulates the writing of needed program descriptions, course outlines, and unit guides.

Section IV will provide the curriculum writer with the concepts and information for writing the various descriptions, outlines and guides, and guide him or her in actual preparation of the materials.

In preparing these materials it is very important that the writer remain interested, but *detached* from the curriculum being written. Many of the people using this book are practising occupational teachers or students preparing for work in that field, and have been and constantly are being conditioned to think more and more like teachers. In this particular instance, "teacher" may not be the most desirable role to assume. Many of these same people view the activity through the eyes of a person experienced in the particular occupation. This experience, while invaluable, must be kept in perspective if it is to have positive impact on the development of the curriculum.

History, tradition, and experience all bear on the final product. However, conscious effort must be made to ensure that their effects are positive and do not restrict or inhibit valuable new perspectives and concepts of curriculum, its purpose and its organization.

CHAPTER 13

Writing an Occupational Program Description

A *program description* outlines various aspects of a particular work-preparation program and includes the following entries: a title page, introductory statement, goals of the program, admission and retention requirements, a statement of costs and financial assistance, listing of applied and related subject matter course titles, career and employment opportunities, educational opportunities, and a source for additional information about the program. A program description is written for each program in an occupational curriculum. In the case of a long-range occupational curriculum spiral, five occupational program descriptions would have to be written to fully describe the total curriculum offering.

The description provides the reader with information about various aspects of the occupational program. In most instances, it appears as a catalog description, or in brochure or pamphlet form. The description assists the reader in understanding the intent and purpose of the occupational program, admission requirements, relationships among the various programs within the total occupational curriculum and between the program and the courses and units that comprise it, and occupational and educational opportunities once the program has been completed.

Criteria

Title Page

The two-fold purpose of the title page is to introduce the program description to the reader, and to locate it in context with the other programs on the curriculum spiral. In Example 13.1 the program description of the Teller Science occupational program is introduced and located as the

---

Example 13.1

A DESCRIPTION OF THE

TELLER SCIENCE

OCCUPATIONAL PROGRAM

by

Beverly Faunce

and

Maria Varano Butz

The second program in a series of five occupational
programs in the Money Distribution and Management-Related
Occupational Curriculum

---

second in a series of five occupational programs that comprise the Long-Range Occupational Curriculum Spiral for Money Distribution and Management-Related Occupations.

Introduction

The introductory portion of the program description gives the reader a basic understanding of the exact nature of the occupational program. With information in the other sections of the program description, the introduction informs the reader of the purpose, direction, and limits of the occupational program. It is suggested that the following items be included: a statement of purpose of the program, its nature and scope, and a statement justifying its presence. Also suggested, is a statement that defines what the completion of the program will bring — a certificate, diploma, degree, or qualification to work in a specific occupation, and occupational specialties and sub-specialties thereof. The introductory statement might also include a discussion of the employment and educational options afforded the "worker-learner" as he or she progresses through the program.

A sample introductory statement follows:

Although the rate of technological change is hard to measure, no one seems to argue that the useful life of technical training is growing ever shorter. The assumption that 10 percent of all technical knowledge becomes obsolete each year is generally accepted. Such obsolescence is likely to take one of two forms: inability to keep up to date with job requirements, or inability to maintain professional versatility.

Programs to combat labor obsolescence should be based on comprehensive manpower planning and curriculum design.

The program content has to be related to the individual's desire to acquire the new knowledge and techniques. The program may increase the effectiveness of the individual's performance or may serve to extend or enlarge his or her capabilities for a position in a higher level. No matter what the purpose, the program material must be relevant to the real world.

The Teller Science Program is the second in a series of five occupational programs that comprise the Long-Range Occupational Curriculum Spiral for Money Distribution and Management-Related Occupations. The two-fold purpose of the program is to prepare the student for work in any one of the occupational specialties or sub-specialties of the occupation of teller or to prepare him or her for entry into the Management Trainee Occupational Program. Completion of each of the applied courses in the program prepares the person for employment in one of the occupational specialties of the occupation of teller. Collectively, they prepare the individual for work as a general teller, collection and exchange teller, note teller and/or utility teller.

Goals

The introductory portion of the program description is followed by the list of goals of the occupational program. A goal is a statement that tells the reader the *direction* that the program is taking and the *boundaries* within which it will stay. Goal statements neither prompt nor demand qualitative nor quantitative evaluation.

Below is a statement of a goal. Let's analyze it in terms of the words that imply its direction and scope.

"To study American automobile manufacturers"

The goal statement in its entirety establishes the direction to be taken.

The reader knows that he or she will "study," and that the focus of the study will be "American automobile manufacturers." The statement is not an objective statement in that it is not, nor is it intended to be, measurable. The word "study" does not specify exactly enough the activity in which the person will be engaged.

The scope of the statement is implicit in the phrase "American automobile manufacturers". First, the study will not include any automobile manufacturer that is not American. The British, Japanese, or German automobile builders will not be studied, because they do not fall within the scope of the goal statement. Likewise, only American manufacturers of automobiles will gain attention. No emphasis will be given to those who build airplanes, motorcycles, push scooters, roller skates, or any other forms of transportation. And, in similar fashion, only the manufacturers of automobiles will be considered; not the people who sell them, but who make them.

The following examples of goal statements for various occupational programs are for your review.

- To develop an understanding of the relationship that exists between pre-occupational and occupational education and the individual and collective roles of each in the total career education scheme.
- To familiarize the students with a process of developing occupational curriculum and a theory of curriculum organization.
- To develop learning activities packages.

The inherent qualities of the goal statements themselves should also be considered. They may be written to include the total cognitive, affective, and psychomotor behavior of the learners. See the following example.

- Realize the need for an articulated, individualized, multiple option plan which coordinates the educational and employment aspects of society;
- Understand the process of developing such a plan; and
- Develop and implement curriculum materials which reflect the proposed organizational education-employment approach.

Using key words that imply particular types of behavior, the above three statements speak to having the learner "realize the need for" a particular type of curriculum (introduce new values, attitudes, priorities, or alter, adjust, or confirm existing ones), "understand the process" of writing the materials (gain the required cognitive knowledge and skills) and "develop and implement the needed curriculum materials" (now controlled by an existing set of values and newly acquired knowledge, the learner sets about performing the actual task at hand).

Again, goal statements can take on many forms and yet be workable. But when one is writing materials that encompass all aspects of human behavior, the goal statements should then also reflect total human performance.

Admission and Retention Requirements

This section of the occupational program description defines the requirements that individuals should have met prior to entering the occupational program. It also includes a statement of the standards and conditions that must be maintained for continuance in the program. A sample statement appears below.

Before enrolling in the secretarial program, the individual must first be officially admitted to the school. No previous work experience is needed in the secretarial field, but some background would prove beneficial. The student must be a high school graduate or its equivalent and must have a strong English background and a knowledge of basic math. The person must be pleasant to be around, tactful, dependable, have initiative, and work well with others. These traits are as important as skills such as typing and short-hand, since a secretary frequently meets the public and works in groups.

Retention in the program is dependent on the student's continuous attainment of the stated learning objectives.

The statement of admission requirements might contain some mention of the occupational, educational, and avocational experiences of the individual. Personal characteristics that are unique and must be possessed by people employed in the particular occupation should also be included as a part of the program's admissions' requirements.

The retention portion of the statement describes the conditions that must be maintained by the learner to continue in the program. The retention statement in the example reflects the performance- or competency-based approach.

Costs and Financial Assistance

This section of the program description provides the potential student with an estimate of the cost of completing the occupational program. Included also are lists of the names of sources of financial assistance, including scholarships, stipends, government, business or other sponsors, that would assist in meeting the costs of the program. A sample statement follows.

Costs of training will vary according to the school attended and may range from $1,000 to $2,000 for the program. Most large financial institutions have either a tuition advance or tuition reimbursement policy to assist the employee in his or her educational growth and development. There are also various state and federally funded programs which offer the student financial assistance.

Listing of Courses

The list of courses is prefaced by an introductory statement about the approximate amount of time required for completing the program, as well as the times required to complete the individual courses. A sample listing of courses for the Teller Science Program follows.

Clock Hours		*Clock Hours*	
Basic Mathematics	100	English Composition	90
*General Tellering	720	*Collection and Exchange Tellering	500
Business English	90	Basic Accounting	80
Principles of Loss Prevention	80	Interpersonal Communication	90
Subtotal	990	*Subtotal*	760

Clock Hours		Clock Hours	
*Utility Teller Procedures	80	*Note Tellering	120
Principles of Bank Operations	90	Principles of Data Processing	90
Principles of Economics	90	Money and Banking	100
Savings & Time Deposit Banking	90	Federal Reserve System	90
	Subtotal 350		Subtotal 400
			Grand Total 2,500

The clock hours listed may vary somewhat with each student in relation to his or her learning ability.

While all of the courses that comprise a program, occupationally oriented laboratory courses, related subject matter or theory courses, general studies courses, liberal arts courses, can appropriately be listed, it is equally appropriate to list only those that are occupational in nature. The decision what course titles to include in the program description is left to the discretion of the writer and the situation and needs of the people to be served.

In the example above, only the applied course titles (noted with an asterisk) and related theory courses are listed.

In the discussion of the development of the Long-Range Occupational Curriculum Spiral, the statement that "clock or learner contact hours" was the most desirable way to specify time requirements was made. This is the case because the curriculum spiral is, by definition, a timeline and, in essence, a total manifestation of its components. Time requirements can be adapted to the individual's needs and abilities.

The estimated amount of time needed to complete an occupational program, or any one of its courses or units, equals the total number of hours needed to complete the learning objectives contained in it. In turn, the time needed to complete a single objective is the sum of the amount of times required to complete the learning activities necessary for attainment of the learning objective. The objective, learning activities, and the times required for their completion appear on the previously discussed *unit learning module.* A detailed discussion of writing unit learning modules and estimating the time needed for attaining a given learning objective appears in Chapter 12.

Career and Employment Opportunities

In the admission and retention portion of the program description, the occupational and avocational prerequisites for *entry* into the program were listed. In contrast, this portion of the program description discusses the various career and employment opportunities open to the person who completes the occupational program. While the section deals primarily with opportunities afforded the graduate of the program, it may also include a discussion of the occupational specialty and sub-specialty options acquired by the person as he or she progresses through the program.

Such topics as places of employment, outlook for and trends within the occupation, probable and potential earning capabilities, working conditions, potential employers, geographic locations of employment, fringe benefits, are appropriately discussed in this section.

A sample statement of the career and employment opportunities for the occupation of secretary follows.

Career and Employment Opportunities

On successful completion of the two-year program, a student can locate employment in most any geographic location and in any size of firm. More than half of the secretaries and stenographers work for service, finance, insurance, real estate, and government organizations. Many work for professional people. A few — chiefly public stenographers and court and conference reporters — are self-employed.

Increased paperwork in modern business will tend to lead to a more rapid expansion of the number of secretaries and stenographers. Technological changes, per se, are not expected to greatly affect the number of people employed in the stenographic-related occupations.

In 1970, persons employed as general stenographers in metropolitan areas surveyed by the Bureau of Labor Statistics earned average salaries of $461 a month. Salaries earned by senior and technical stenographers working in metropolitan areas averaged $516 a month.

The salaries earned by individuals included in the survey varied considerably, partly because of differences in the location and industry where they were employed, but also because of differences in experiences. The earnings of reporting stenographers generally are considerably higher than those of other stenographic workers.

Salaries of secretaries to supervisors in small organizational units or non-supervisory staff specialists averaged $522 a month throughout the U.S., according to the same survey.

Secretaries to officers in small companies and to middle management executives in large companies earned average monthly salaries of $582 and $625 respectively. Secretaries having even greater responsibilities earned average salaries of $679 a month.

The entrance salary for beginning stenographers in the Federal Government in 1970 was $5,212 a year.

The office environment greatly depends on the size and nature of the business. A construction secretary may find himself or herself in an unattractive decor; whereas, a secretary to an investment firm often will find himself or herself in more plush surroundings. Various pieces of office equipment are used. Again, the type of equipment depends on the size and nature, as well as the procedures, of the business.

For those people who do not complete the Secretarial Science occupational program of study, employment opportunities in one or more of the above-mentioned occupational specialties are available. Because of the greater specialization, employment is generally limited to larger businesses and institutions. In the larger organizations, it is more common to find people working fulltime in a specialty occupation. In contrast, smaller organizations often cannot afford to keep people whose skills are limited to a particular specialty on their payrolls.

Pay for people working in a particular occupational specialty is com-
mensurately lower than for the person who is a fully qualified secretary.

Educational Opportunities

Together, the list of career and employment related opportunities and the
educational opportunities discussed in this section of the program description inform the student of the various opportunities open to him or her
once he or she completes the requirements of the occupational program.
The statements complement each other.

The statement of educational opportunities often refers to other programs that might be entered by the person once he or she has completed
the program in which he or she is currently enrolled. In the following
example reference to those occupational programs which "serially follow
the Secretarial Science program" is made.

On completion of the Secretarial Science program, the person may continue
his or her educational preparation for work in the Stenographic-Related
Occupational Curriculum. The programs which serially follow the Secretarial
Science program are Administrative Secretarial Science, Administrative
Assisting, and Office Management. The occupations for which the person
would be prepared on completion of these three programs would respectively
be, administrative secretary, administrative assistant, and office manager.
An individual stepping into any of these positions must have accumulated
work experience as a secretary.

Any entry that pertains to the educational opportunities that become
available on completion of the program should be included in the statement. These decisions are left to the discretion of the curriculum writer.

Additional Information

This portion of the program description tells the reader who he or she can
contact for further information about the program. As is shown in the
example, the name of the person to be contacted, his or her title, address,
and telephone number are the essential items in the statement.

> Mr. Noel Civil, Information Officer
> School of Business Occupations
> 34 Tudor Cresent
> Hamilton, Illinois 98714
> Telephone: 317-821-7369

In Review

1. What is the purpose of the *program description*?

2. Write for or otherwise obtain a number of program descriptions from various

educational institutions. Review them in terms of purpose, similarity of content, appearance, aesthetic design, etc.

3. Discuss how goals statements differ from learning objective statements.

4. In the listing of courses that comprise the program offering, times are included in terms of clock hours. Why is it desirable to note time in this manner?

5. Why is it important to include in the program description the Career and Employment Opportunities and Education Opportunities sections?

CHAPTER 14

Writing an Occupational Course Outline

In a typical curricular organization, the curriculum is comprised of programs, the programs are made up of courses, the courses of units, and the units of learning objectives. The purpose of the *course outline* is to put the particular course being described in context in the program, and establish its relationship with its companion courses and the units that comprise it. The course outline, like the program description, serves a particular purpose. Whereas the program description appears as a catalog description or in the form of a brochure or pamphlet to describe and promote the program, the course description contains those items that the practising teacher would include in a course outline or syllabus.

The course outline reflects the organizational logic of the Long-range Employment-curriculum Spiral discussed in Part I. The outline includes a title page, an introductory statement defining the purpose, scope, and intent of the course, the list of goals, admission and retention requirements, costs and financial assistance, list of unit titles, text and additional reference titles, text and additional reference titles used in the course, as well as career and employment, and educational opportunities available to course graduates. There also is a section listing the products of the course and source for additional information. The course outline and program description contain several entries that share the same title and appear very similar in content and organization. However, closer study will show that the content does differ in that it reflects the effects of the particular component's location in the system and its relationship to its supra- and sub-components.

Title Page

The title page of the course outline looks very much like the title page of the occupational program description. Parts of it, that is, the title itself and the context statement, have curricular importance in that they identify the course by name and locate it in time and establish its relationship to other courses in the program. A sample title page of a course outline appears in Example 14.1.

Example 14.1

AN OUTLINE OF THE

CLERICAL PROCEDURES

COURSE

by

Carol Schultz

The first in a series of four applied occupational
courses in the Teller Science Program in the
Money Distribution and Management-Related Occupational Curriculum

---

Introduction

The introduction of the course outline is similar in purpose to the introduction of the program description, in that both are intended to provide the reader with a basic knowledge and understanding of the nature and intent of the particular curricular component. The introductory statement of the course outline, while its content will vary somewhat depending on the background and orientation of the writer, might include a statement of the purpose, direction and scope of the occupational course, the reasons for such a course offering, and the various educational and employment options open to the learner as he or she progresses in and eventually finishes the course.

The introductory statement selected from the Clerical Procedures course outline follows.

The course, "Clerical Procedures", is the third in a series of five applied courses in the Secretarial Science occupational program. Its purpose and scope are derived from the analysis of the occupational specialty of office clerk. Once the requirements of the course are met, the learner will be qualified to work as an office clerk, or any one of the sub-specialties thereof, or continue his or her education in the occupational program.

The increased need for office clerks in many of the larger business organizations provides a ready market for people who possess the necessary occupational skill and knowledge. The purpose of this course is to prepare students for employment as office clerks, or provide them with the skills necessary for work in the related occupational sub-specialties of supply clerk, postal clerk, file clerk, purchasing clerk, forms clerk, or correspondence clerk. In either instance, the emphasis is on employment.

Once the requirements of the course are met, the individual will enjoy the options of being prepared for work as discussed above, or to continue his or her occupational education in one or more of the other courses in the program.

Goals

The goal statements of the course reflect its direction and scope. Not attempting to specify measurable human behavior, they define the expected limits of the course offering. A more detailed discussion and analysis of goal statements appears in the previous chapter.

The goal statements of a single course when viewed with the goals of the other courses fully support the goals of the program.

The goals of a course in Clerical Procedures follow. The statements are written to effectively include cognitive, affective, and psychomotor behavior, using key words that reflect the appropriate categories of behavior. Writing goals in this manner prompts the writer to consider all aspects of the learner's development.

The goals of the course are to:

- Provide the learner with an understanding of the purpose, role, and function of the office clerk in the business organization and with the information necessary to successfully perform in the occupational specialty.
- Cultivate attitudes, characteristics, and traits in the student that will benefit him or her in the business situation.
- Develop the skills necessary for employment as an office clerk or anyone of the occupational sub-specialties thereof.

Admission and Retention Requirements

The admission and retention requirements of an occupational course are the same in purpose and intent as are the admission and retention requirements for an occupational program. Both statements specify the requirements that must be met by the person prior to entering the particular course and the standards and conditions thereof to be maintained once entry is achieved. The admission and retention requirements for the course must reflect the work orientation of the applied course.

The admission and retention requirements of a given course might differ significantly from those of the program or of other courses in the program. Whereas the admission and retention requirements of the first applied course in the occupational program might coincide with those of the program, those of a subsequent course might differ considerably. An admissions and retention statement for a course in Clerical Procedures follows.

> The course is a requirement for all students enrolled in the Secretarial Science program. While there are no prerequisites, previous office experience would be beneficial. Success in the course is determined by the learner's continued attainment of the learning objectives. Consent of the instructor is required for those wishing to enroll but who are not in secretarial science.

Costs and Financial Assistance

As in the program description, this section of the course outline specifies the costs of the course and sources from which financial aid is available. Since the applied course is a part of the larger program, its costs are proportionally less then those incurred for the total program.

Units

The units of the course are listed by title and in the order of their occurrence in this section of the course outline. A sample list of unit titles taken from the Clerical Procedures course outline with the respective times for each unit follows.

> The units are as follows:
>
> Unit One — Supplies (28 hrs)
> Unit Two — Mail/Processing (18 hrs)
> Unit Three — Filing (27 hrs)
> Unit Four — Purchasing (32 hrs)
> Unit Five — Forms Design and Control (38 hrs)
> Unit Six — Office Communications (29 hrs)
>   Total: 172 hrs

The statement of time in the example includes both a total of the number of clock hours required to complete the course, and the amounts of time needed for completion of each of the occupational units. Since the individual units, like the programs and courses of which they are a part, are performance-based, the practice of unitizing time in clock hours or contact hours seems most appropriate. The more conventional and academic means of encapsulating time is not as well suited to a performance-based curricular system.

Text and Additional References

"Text" and "Additional References", although they appear separately in the occupational course outline, are discussed together here because both entries identify books that the learner will use in the course. The text and reference titles are the most important sources of information for the learning objectives of the occupational course.

In presenting the text and reference titles, use an accepted bibliographic style.

Career and Employment Opportunities

The end of the occupational course marks a point at which the learner is prepared for employment in a particular occupational specialty and number of occupational sub-specialties. The career and employment portion of the course outline alerts and reminds the learner of potential employment opportunities.

Topics discussed in the Career and Employment Opportunities portion of the program description are still very appropriate here. One caution however: To keep the topics relevant, they should be limited in scope to the particular occupational specialty and sub-specialties of the primary occupation. Trends, earning capabilities, opportunities for advancement, places of employment discussed in terms of the occupational specialty reflect the occupational assets and liabilities realized by a person making the career choice.

A statement of the career and employment opportunities open to a graduate of a course in clerical procedures follows.

On completion of this course, the person will be qualified for work as an office clerk or any of the clerical sub-specialties prepared for en route to completing this course. Because of the degree of specialization, most employment opportunities will be in larger businesses or other institutions where specialized clerical help is employed. With additional study, or experience gained while at work, the individual can acquire the necessary added skills to qualify for other stenographic-related occupations.

Salaries for inexperienced office clerks are usually similar to those of other office workers in the same organization. The work requires little heavy lifting, but usually involves some bending and reaching as well as some use of mechanized equipment.

Employment of office clerks is expected to rise rapidly through the 1970's as a result of the long-term growth of business and the need for more and better recordkeeping.

Educational Opportunities

The educational opportunities listed in the outline of a particular course specify the educational options available to the learner once he or she has completed the course. When the student has finished the course, he or she is expected to make some decisions about the future: to continue work preparation or to put skills into practice. The educational options open to the learner are stated in this section of the course outline.

A sample statement of the educational opportunities available to a person completing the course in Clerical Procedures follows.

As stated previously, upon completion of this course the student will have the basic skill and knowledge necessary to work as an office clerk. With additional preparation, the office clerk can eventually become qualified as a secretary or any of the other occupations in the stenographic field.

The list of educational opportunities included in a course description complements the list of career and employment opportunities of that same course. They collectively make known to the learner many of the options that are available. The individual can then make informed decisions about the future. When this type of data is available at the end of each program in the curriculum, at the end of each course in each program, and, as will be discussed in more detail in the next chapter, at the end of each unit within each course, the learner will enjoy an almost continuous input about the multitude of options from which he or she can choose. This, of course, is the intent of organizing curriculum in this manner.

Course Products

The optional "Course Products" section is included to provide a place to list the products of a given course if such a listing is essential. In courses from which tangible items result, it is appropriate and desirable to list the items for the benefit of the learners.

The course "Occupational Analysis and Curriculum Development" is one example of a course from which tangible products result. The list of course products is:

- · A Curriculum Development Worksheet Series
- · A Curriculum Guide
- · Learning Activities Package Resource Guide

Additional Information

This section of the course outline provides the name, address, and phone number of the person to be contacted for further information.

A program description would be written for each program within the occupational curriculum, and a course outline for each course in the occupational program. In like fashion, a description of each unit, entitled a *unit guide*, would be written for each unit within a given course. The following chapter deals with the writing and preparation of occupational unit guides.

In Review

1. What is the purpose of the *course outline* in terms of the program of which it is a part and the units and learning objectives which comprise it?

2. Whereas the program description appears in the form of a brochure or pamphlet and is used as a public relations tool in promoting the program, the course outline assumes a somewhat different role. What is its primary role and for what audience is it written.

3. How do the entries of the course outline differ in terms of purpose, direction, scope, etc. from those of the program description.

4. Career and Employment Opportunities and Educational Opportunities are sections that are included in the course outline as well as the program description. Why would they be needed by the learner at this point in his or her occupational preparation?

5. In what situation would a list of the products of the course be appropriate?

CHAPTER 15

Writing an Occupational Unit Guide

The *occupational unit guide* is, as its name implies, a guide to a particular unit of learning, and is written for each of the units that comprise an occupational course. The unit is the smallest grouping of learning objectives, whose attainment makes a person employable and, at the same time, offers him or her the option of continuing his or her occupational education.

The unit guide provides the learner with information concerning various aspects of the occupational unit. While the occupational program description and course outline assist the learner in understanding the various aspects and relationships that exist among the programs, courses, and units within a total curriculum system, the occupational unit guide serves as the focus of curriculum implementation and learning activity.

The unit guide includes the following entries: a title page, table of contents, introduction to the unit, goals, list of learning objectives, admission and retention requirements, titles of the text and additional references, costs and financial assistance, unit learning modules, career and employment opportunities, educational opportunities, and source of additional information. The organization and format of the program description and course outline are continued in the unit guide.

Title Page

Very similar in organization, appearance, and function to its program and course counterparts, the title page of the unit guide serves to introduce the unit and locate it in context within the occupational course and program.

A title page for an occupational unit in "Filing" appears in Example 15.1.

The title of the unit, "Filing," tells the reader the nature, direction, and scope of the unit. The context statement establishes the exact location of the unit.

Example 15.1

<u>A GUIDE TO THE</u>

<u>FILING OCCUPATIONAL</u>

<u>UNIT</u>

by

Carol Schultz

The third in a series of six occupational
units in the Clerical Procedures course in the
Secretarial Science Occupational
Program

Introduction

The opening statements of a unit guide should inform the learner of the nature and purpose of the occupational unit and should provide an idea of the direction and limits of the unit. A statement of justification, and a brief discussion of the relationship of the unit to its companion units and the total course itself might be included. Mention might also be made of the occupational sub-specialty for which the unit will prepare the learner.

A sample introductory statement follows. It was written for an occupational unit in filing.

> "Filing" is the third of six units in the course "Clerical Procedures." The two-fold purpose of the unit is to prepare students for employment as file clerks, or to further their occupational education toward employment in the stenographic-related occupational field. The unit title and the list of primary objectives are directly derived from the analysis of the occupational sub-specialty of the file clerk. En route to meeting the objectives of the unit, the student file clerk will acquire skills and knowledge needed to establish, maintain and dispose of records via accepted filing practices.
>
> The student will become familiar with the various rules for filing and retrieving filed documents commonly used in the most exacting business organization.

On a smaller scale, the unit, much like the program and course, provides the student with various employment and educational options. Once the learning objectives of the unit are realized, the student can then elect to enter the work force as a file clerk or any one of the other occupations, occupational specialties, or sub-specialties for which he or she has prepared. However, if the student wishes to continue occupational education he or she can then begin preparing for employment in one or more of the other stenographic-related occupations.

The author of the introductory statement should write for his or her particular group. The suggestions and examples are only given to guide the reader as he or she begins to prepare curriculum materials.

Goals

The goal statements of a unit determine its direction and establish its parameters. They confirm the direction established by the goals of the parent course and program, and are written to include the three major categories of human behavior (Bloom et al., 1956), namely cognitive, affective, and psychomotor. The verbs used in goal statements of an occupational unit reflect the appropriate category of behavior. However, the unit goals are more limited in scope than those of the parent course or program.

The following are the goal statements for an occupational unit in Filing. Note how they individually reflect cognitive, affective, or psychomotor behavior.

- Provide the learner with an understanding of the purpose, role, and function of the file clerk in an organization, and a knowledge of the various accepted methods and techniques for maintaining records.
- Create within the student a recognition and appreciation of the importance of an organized and ordered system of maintaining records.
- Develop the skills necessary for employment as a file clerk and for continuing in his or her occupational education.

Learning Objectives

The learning objective titles are derived directly from the list of task titles of the occupational sub-specialty for which the unit is named. The objectives of the occupational unit in "Filing", for example, are derived directly from the list of tasks of the occupational sub-specialty of file clerk.

The organizational theory discussed in Part One establishes the occupational unit as the smallest grouping of learning objectives which, once attained, prepares a person for employment or for continued occupational preparation in yet another occupational unit of study. While, in theory, learning objectives could appear in the program description and course outline, they actually appear only in the individual unit guides. Course objectives can be established simply by compiling the learning objectives of the units. A complete list of program objectives would require the compilation of the objectives of each of the courses of the program.

Only the titles of the learning objectives are listed in this section of the unit guide. The learning objectives appear in their entirety on the individual *unit learning modules* later in the unit guide.

The following is a list of learning objective titles as they might appear in a unit guide.

- Typing Business Letters
- Cleaning the Typewriter
- Changing the Typewriter Ribbon
- Ordering Typing Supplies
- Answering Routine Correspondence
- Maintaining a Correspondence File
- Maintaining Form Letter File
- Taking Dictation
- Checking Files
- Filing Documents
- Preparing Cross-Reference Cards
- Making New Files
- Pulling Outdated Files

Admission and Retention Requirements

The admission requirements are the occupational, educational, and personal prerequisites that must be met by the prospective learner. The occupational prerequisites spell out the type of work experience, if any, the learner must have to successfully attain the unit objectives. The educational prerequisites tell the student the minimum amounts and type of education necessary for entry into the unit. The personal prerequisites denote the personal traits and characteristics that are helpful for completion of the unit.

> While no specific occupational prerequisites exist for entry into this unit, any type of experience in organizing, categorizing, or ordering things would be beneficial. Such hobbies as stamp or coin collecting or any type of activity requiring a systematic, organized approach would complement the types of activities included here. Educational prerequisites include the ability to read, a working knowledge of the alphabet and the ability to count and serially order numbers. Personal traits include an attention to detail, orderliness, and a liking and understanding of structure and organization.
>
> Successful completion of the unit is dependent on the regular attainment of the learning objectives.

In some instances no specific requirements for a unit exist. In this case, rather than ignore the entry take a more positive approach. The first part of the above prerequisite statement demonstrates this approach.

The person determining admission requirements should be very much aware of their effects on the composition of the student group. If the occupation or specialty or sub-specialty thereof demands a very exact type of worker then, of course, prerequisites must be utilized to insure that only those types of people enter the preparatory educational program. On the other hand, most occupations do not have such exacting standards and the prerequisites should be written accordingly. In those cases where prerequisites are essential, they must be used. However, the number and type of prerequisites should be kept to an absolute minimum. The purpose of any occupational education offering is *not* to keep people out, but to prepare them for employment in an occupation of their choosing.

Admission requirements directly affect the number and kinds of people entering the occupational unit. Stringent requirements increase the homogeneity of the group. If prerequisites are kept to a minimum, the heterogeneity of the group becomes more evident.

Text and Additional References

The text and additional references contain information essential to the completion of the unit learning objectives. The text and other reference materials often coincide with those titles listed in the course outline.

As previously suggested, an accepted bibliographic style should be followed when writing the text and reference titles.

Costs and Financial Assistance

This section of the unit guide, like that of the program description and course outline, defines the cost of the unit to the learner. Also included are sources to which the learner could turn for financial assistance if necessary.

Career and Employment Opportunities

The career and employment opportunities section of the unit guide lists the employment opportunities for which the person is prepared once he or she has completed the occupational unit. Whereas the prerequisite statements discussed earlier in this section specify the requirements that must be met prior to entering the occupational unit, the career and employment opportunities section points out the various work-related options a person has once he or she leaves it.

The writer of the unit guide and particularly, of the career and employment opportunities portion thereof, has the responsibility to discuss both the assets and liabilities of opting in favor of employment over education once the unit is completed. This is particularly true if the unit being discussed appears early in the program of the curriculum. At this point in time, an individual would not have had the opportunity to establish an occupational basis from which to begin to seek other employment options. The skills and knowledge gained in a single unit do prepare a person for employment. However, the real problems encountered by a person with only a limited number of skills should also be recognized.

The following statement of the career and employment opportunities for a person who has completed an occupational unit in "Filing" is taken from a unit that appears in one of the first courses in a secretarial science occupational program. The example points out the employment opportunities enjoyed by the person completing the occupational unit, but also mentions what might be considered by some to be liabilities attached to the occupational sub-specialty of file clerk.

> Typically, employment for people prepared to be file clerks is found in large business corporations, some federal and/or state agencies, and in large college and university offices. Only such large organizations can accommodate people whose skills are so specialized.
>
> The file clerk generally receives the minimum hourly wage. Opportunities for advancement within the occupational sub-specialty are few. However, other opportunities are available with additional training in other secretarial-related occupations.

Educational Opportunities

The educational opportunities portion of a unit guide is a discussion of the educational options available to the learner once he or she has completed the learning objectives. Knowledge of educational opportunities coupled with knowledge of career and employment opportunities, allows the graduate of an occupational unit to decide upon a future plan of action: employment, additional work preparation, or both.

A statement of the educational opportunities of the occupational unit in "Filing" follows. Note how the author has listed the various educational choices that the graduate of the unit will have.

> Other occupational education opportunities exist within the Clerical Procedures course. Having completed the first three units in the course, and, hence, being prepared to work as a supply clerk, postal clerk or file clerk, the learner can continue his or her occupational education in the "Purchasing", "Forms Design and Control," or "Office Communications" units. By completing the remaining units, the learner will then be qualified to work as purchasing clerk, forms clerk or correspondence clerk. When all of the units of the course are completed, the person will be prepared to work in all aspects of the occupational specialty of office clerk.

Each program, course, or unit in the curriculum marks a point at which one must choose between work or education or a combination of both. This organization requires that the learner be fully informed of his or her options at all times. When a Long-range Employment-curriculum Spiral is developed for a group or family of occupations, the individual units on the component curriculum spiral are the basic and most vital "grouping of objectives." When the learner finally attains a unit's objectives, the acquired skills and knowledge make the person employable.

Additional Information

This section of the unit guide provides the user with the name and location of a contact for further information. A totally articulated, individualized curriculum plan requires that specific informational sources be identified for each element.

Unit Learning Modules

The unit learning modules are the last entry in the unit guide. Duplicates of the modules developed during the occupational curriculum development process, they guide the learner through the series of learning activities to final attainment of the learning objectives, and guide the curriculum designer in the development and preparation of the individualized learning activities packages that comprise the occupational unit.

For a review of the unit learning modules, see Chapter 12.

In Review

1. What is the purpose of the *unit guide*?

2. The occupational unit is the basic component in the total occupational curriculum concept. In terms of employment and educational potential, discuss why this "... smallest grouping of learning objectives" is basic to the concept.

3. Much like the program description and course outline, the unit guide also includes *Career and Employment Opportunities* and *Educational Opportunities* sections. Why is this important?

CHAPTER 16

Developing Performance Record Forms and Achievement Awards

The occupational programs, courses, and units with their learning objectives are points of passage between the occupational employment spiral and its counterpart, the occupational curriculum spiral. Having successfully completed a program, course, or unit, a person can leave the curriculum spiral to seek employment in one or more of the occupations, occupational specialties, or occupational sub-specialties for which he or she is prepared.

Because of this curriculum design, the records that mark the learner's progress and the awards presented at the completion of the units, courses, and programs must reflect the performance-based concept and organizational scheme of the occupational curriculum. This chapter is devoted to the development and preparation of such record and achievement forms.

The chapter is divided into two major parts; *record forms* and *achievement awards*. Each time a learner attains the learning objectives of a particular program, course, or unit his or her achievement becomes official record and he or she is awarded a credential noting the success.

Performance Records

There are three types of performance records: the *program transcript*, *learner's record booklet* and *course achievement record*. Each is designed to maintain a record of the learner's performance and attainment of learning objectives within the program, course, or unit.

Program Transcript. The program transcript is the official record, maintained by the school's administrative personnel, of the learner's progress in each unit of each course within the total occupational program.

The transcript contains the usual types of necessary biographic and demographic information, and notes the learning objectives the student has attained. The transcript is the property and official record of the credit awarding institution, and copies are made available at the student's request. A format for an abbreviated performance-based program transcript appears in Example 16.1.

The organization and listing of the courses, units, and learning objectives are taken from the program outline discussed in Section III, Chapter 12. The transcript provides for recording the learner's achievement in both the applied courses and the related subject matter or theory courses. The transcript should be dated and initialed upon completion of each unit and theory course.

Learner's Record Booklet. The learner's record booklet is an unofficial record maintained cooperatively by the learner and the instructor, and serves as both a guide and a progress chart. It has the same content as the official program transcript. Like the performance-based transcript, the booklet is divided into two sections: Applied Courses and Related Subject Courses. Individual course titles, together with the titles of the various units and learning objectives, are listed in the first part. The titles of the related subject matter courses are listed in the second. Provisions are made in both sections to evaluate and confirm the learner's attainment of the individual learning objectives of the applied courses and units and the related subject courses as a whole.

The booklet, together with the official program transcript and instructor's course records, is an up-to-date account of the skills and knowledge of the learner and indicates possible employment opportunities.

Course Achievement Record. The course achievement record is the official record of the learner's progress kept by the instructor. (See Example 16.2.)

The course achievement record is divided into three parts: the heading, the body, and the confirmation statement. The heading includes provision for the biographical data, e.g. name of the learner, address, telephone number, etc. needed for course records.

The body of the record sheet is a list of all of the units of the course and their respective learning objectives, with spaces for dating and initialing. A "Remarks" section for any additional comments regarding the learner's performance is also included.

The confirming portion of the record sheet is signed and dated by the instructor when the learner has attained the objectives of the course.

Achievement Awards

An achievement award is presented to the learner upon successful completion of an occupational program, course, or unit. The award highlights the accomplishments of the individual and marks his or her progress in the

Example 16.1

BLACK DIAMOND COMMUNITY COLLEGE

Teller Science Occupational

Program Transcript

I. *Performance Record of:*

Name: _____

Address: _____
         Street

_____
City   State   Zip

Telephone Number: ( ) _____

II. *Biographical Data:*

Date of Birth: _____

Place of Birth: _____

Social Security No.: _____

Date of Admission: _____

III. *Program:* Teller Science:

A. Applied Courses:

Course #1 — General Tellering

Unit #1 — Mail Deposits

Learning Objectives:

	Date	Initial
· Opening Envelopes	____	____
· Receiving Checks for Deposit	____	____
· Examining Checks for Endorsements	____	____
· Verifying Deposits	____	____
· Entering Deposit in Depositor's Passbook or Checking Account	____	____
· Issuing Receipts	____	____

Unit #2 — Paying and Receiving

Learning Objectives

	Date	Initial
· Counting Currency	____	____
· Cashing Checks	____	____
· Handling Check Deposits	____	____
· Handling Cash Deposits	____	____
· Receiving Personal Loan Payments	____	____
· Receiving Christmas Club Payments	____	____
· Issuing Treasurer's Checks	____	____
· Selling Money Orders	____	____
· Withdrawing Funds From No Passbook Savings Accounts	____	____

Unit #3 – Discount

Learning Objectives	*Date*	*Initial*
· Computing Interest		
· Posting Payments		
· Maintaining Ledgers		
· Issuing Receipts		
· Verifying Ledger Balances		

Course #4 – Utility Teller Procedures

Unit #1

Learning Objectives	*Date*	*Initial*
· Collecting Payments for Customers		
· Total Items on Bill Using Adding Machine		
· Recording Transactions		
· Issuing Receipts		
· Adjusting Bill Complaints		
· Handling Partial Payments of Bill		
· Crediting Utility Company Accounts		

B. *Related Subjects*

1. *Grading*

   S – Satisfactory
   U – Unsatisfactory

2. *Courses*   Grade   Initial

   · Basic Mathematics
   · Business English
   · Principles of Loss Prevention

2. *Courses* (cont'd)   Grade   Initial

   · Principles of Bank Operations
   · Principles of Economics
   · Savings and Time Deposit Banking
   · English Composition
   · Basic Accounting
   · Interpersonal Communication
   · Principles of Data Processing
   · Money and Banking
   · Federal Reserve System

Example 16.2
Course Achievement Record
General Tellering

I. *Performance Record of:*   II. *Student Data:*

Name: _____   Date of Entry: _____

Address: _____   Date of Completion: _____

_____

Telephone: (   ) _____

III. *Units with Learning Objectives:*

Unit #1 — Mail Deposits

Learning Objectives	*Date*	*Initial*
• Opening Envelopes	____	____
• Receiving Checks for Deposit	____	____
• Examining Checks for Endorsement	____	____
• Verifying Deposits	____	____
• Entering Deposit in Depositor's Passbook or Checking Account	____	____
• Issuing Receipts	____	____

Unit #2 — Paying and Receiving

Learning Objectives:	*Date*	*Initial*
• Counting Currency	____	____
• Cashing Checks	____	____
• Handling Check Deposits	____	____
• Handling Cash Deposits	____	____
• Receiving Personal Loan Payments	____	____
• Receiving Christmas Club Payments	____	____
• Issuing Treasurer's Checks	____	____
• Selling Money Orders	____	____
• Withdrawing Funds From No Passbook Savings Accounts	____	____
• Ordering the Daily Cash Supply	____	____
• Selling Domestic Traveler's Checks	____	____
• Balancing the Cash Drawer and Settlement	____	____
• Accepting Night Depository Deposits	____	____

Unit #3 — Payroll

Learning Objectives	*Date*	*Initial*
• Receiving Payroll Requests from Depositors	____	____
• Preparing Cash in Requested Denominations	____	____
• Verifying Totals	____	____
• Accepting Debit to Offset Payroll	____	____
• Assuring Funds are Available	____	____
• Computing Service Charge	____	____

Example 16.3

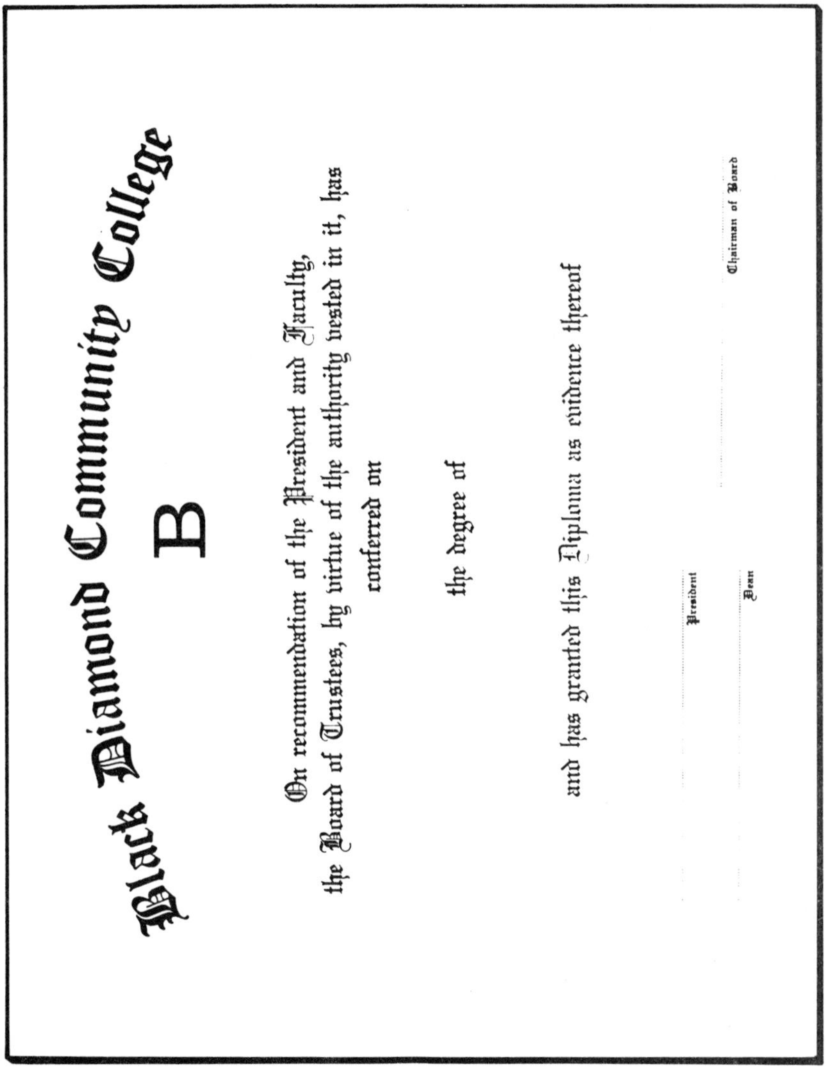

Black Diamond Community College

B

On recommendation of the President and Faculty,
the Board of Trustees, by virtue of the authority vested in it, has

conferred on

the degree of

and has granted this Diploma as evidence thereof

President

Dean

Chairman of Board

Example 16.4

Black Diamond Community College

Business Occupations

B

Certificate

This certifies that

has successfully

completed the course

given this _____ day of _____ 19____

_____
INSTRUCTOR

_____
CHAIRMAN

work preparation curriculum. Three types of awards are granted: a *program diploma, course certificate*, and an *objective attainment card.*

Program Diploma. The diploma is presented to the individual on graduation from the occupational program. The awarding of the diploma to the individual is the institution's way of recognizing the person's achievement and proclaiming his or her capabilities as a practitioner in a given occupation. Example 16.3 is a sample diploma.

A diploma typically includes the following entries: the name of the faculty, department, and institution awarding the diploma, the name of the recipient, the title of the program, a statement regarding the rights, privileges, and responsibilities that accompany the award, the signatures of the appropriate administrators, the date of issuance and the embossed seal of the institution. Depending on the institution however, the types and number of entries on a diploma may vary. Regardless of its final appearance, though, it is a document that publicly recognizes the accomplishments of the individual. In a performance-based program it marks a point of preparedness for entry into an occupation.

Course Certificate. The occupational course certificate, like the diploma, is an award that notes a person's progress in the occupational curriculum. An example of a course certificate appears in Example 16.4. The awarding of the certificate marks successful completion of the occupational course. At this point in time the person can choose to either continue occupational education, seek employment, or pursue a combination of both activities.

Although the number and types of entries on certificates may vary they are usually very similar to those on the diploma awarded at the completion of an occupational program. Commonly included on a course certificate are the name and seal of the awarding institution, the name of the recipient, the title of the successfully completed course, the date the certificate was awarded, and the signatures of the administrators in charge at the time of the award.

Objective Attainment Card. The objective attainment card is the last of three achievement awards used to recognize the progress of the learner in the occupational curriculum. The card is unique in that it serves as both a record of attainment and a visible mark of achievement. As an award, the card verifies the holder's accomplishments within a particular unit and indicates yet another point in time when the person has the option of choosing to continue in the occupational program, go to work, or do both.

Example 16.5 is an objective attainment card. On the front of the card is the name of the accrediting institution, the name of the person to whom the card is being issued, the title of the occupational unit, the date of issue, and the signature of the instructor. The back of the card shows the list of learning objectives for the occupational unit.

Example 16.5

BLACK DIAMOND COMMUNITY
COLLEGE

This is to certify that

_____

has attained the learning objectives of the Unit in

_____

* * * * * * * * * * * * * * * * * *

Date of Issue: _____

Signature of Instructor

Learning Objectives

- Counting Currency
- Cashing Checks
- Handling Check Deposits
- Handling Cash Deposits
- Receiving Personal Loans
- Receiving Christmas Club Payments
- Issuing Treasure's Checks
- Selling Money Orders
- Withdrawing Funds From No Passbook Savings Accounts
- Ordering the Daily Cash Supply
- Selling Domestic Traveler's Checks
- Balancing the Cash Drawer and Settlement
- Accepting Night Depository Deposits

An objective attainment card is awarded on completion of each unit within a course. If a particular course contains six units, the learner accumulates a total of six objective attainment cards by the end of the course.

In Review

1. List the three types of *performance records* and discuss the purpose of each. For whom is each of the records intended?

2. List the three types of *achievement awards* and discuss the purpose of each.

V Preparing Occupational Learning Materials

Individuality must be preserved in the emerging, highly organized, centralized, and technologically automated society. Although innovations (particularly those connected with technological advancements) hold great promise, they also pose the threat of undermining the potential and self-determination of individuals. Properly integrated, these innovations may provide the basis for a continuous progress curriculum which promotes individuality.

Kapfer and Ovard
Preparing and Using Individualized Learning Packages

The final step in the process of developing occupational curriculum is to prepare and package the learning materials or software needed to implement the learning activities of the various learning objectives. The learning activities for a particular objective are those knowledge and performance-related events that the learner must complete if the objective is to be realized. However, before the learner can begin work toward an objective, he or she must have prepared learning materials.

This section of the Handbook will assist the occupational curriculum designer in preparing the needed learning materials. In those cases where no relevant learning materials exist, new ones will have to be written, presentations readied, tests prepared, demonstrations filmed, and so on. In those cases where learning materials exist, they will still have to be reviewed, selected, coordinated, and otherwise adapted to the sequence of learning activities and attainment of the learning objective.

Secondly, this section will guide the curriculum designer in packaging the learning materials for use in an individualized learning situation. Materials must be organized in such a way that they become integral parts of a self-contained learning activities package. Individual instruction sheets should be ordered and bound in some type of informational resource booklet or guide. Portions of existing books that are used must be identified and labelled. Illustrated reviews of the informational resources must be video-taped for inclusion within the learning package. Likewise, the audio and visual portions of the demonstration of the objective must be put on video-tape or, if motion is not an important part of the activity, on narrated slides or film strip. All of the learning activities will be presented so that the individual learner can, with little or no outside assistance, work toward and attain a particular learning objective.

Derivations of Chapters

The chapters and activities in this last section of the Handbook are products of an analysis of a number of occupationally related learning activities' sequences, course outlines, lesson plans, etc. The activities discussed appeared most regularly in the above mentioned sources and include reading activities, listening to and viewing lectures and illustrated presentations, taking written tests, observing and practising demonstrations, and performing and being evaluated on the acquisition of various skills. All of the activities have the potential to be used in an individualized learning activities package, some with the incorporation of audio-visual techniques.

This section is not intended to limit or restrict the numbers or types of learning activities included in a learning package, but rather to add insight, reason, and direction to the development of activities common to many occupational learning situations. The following chapter, entitled "Writing the Learning Activities Development Sheet," while not directly concerned with the development or preparation of specific activities, does assist the curriculum designer in planning the packaging of the learning materials.

CHAPTER 17

Writing the Learning Activities Development Sheet

The *learning activities development sheet* is a planning guide used to prepare the learning materials necessary to implement the individual learning activities. A completed example of a learning activities development sheet appears in Example 17.1.

The guide has three basic parts: the heading, the body of the sheet, and the agreement section (optional). The heading includes the title of the sheet itself and the titles of the particular program, course, unit, and learning objective titles for which it is written. The heading, like those of the task listing sheets, task detailing sheets, task objective sheets, etc., informs the reader of the location of developmental activity in the total occupational curriculum development process, and prepares the reader for the information that follows.

The body of the planning guide contains the learning activities statements for the particular learning objective, and the sequences of procedural steps necessary to prepare learning materials for the various learning activities. Because the process for writing learning activity statements has been previously discussed, no further discussion is necessary here. However, the rationale and suggestions for writing the steps used in preparing materials for implementing the learning activities are pertinent and merit some explanation.

The procedural steps that appear under each learning activities' statement define exactly what has to be done to ready the various learning materials for the package. As in the statement of the first learning activity in Example 17.1, the procedural steps specify what must be done to prepare materials needed to implement the first learning activity. Systematic completion of the sequences of procedural steps of the remaining learning activities statements will result in the eventual completion of materials to be used by the learner in attaining a particular learning objective.

Example 17.1
Learning Activities Development Sheet

Occupational Program: Teller Science

Course #1: General Tellering

Unit #2: Paying and Receiving

Learning Objective #11: Selling Domestic Traveler's Checks

Learning Activities

1. Read the Information Sheet "Terms"
   A. Review the list of technical occupational information topics on the task detailing sheet "Selling Domestic Traveler's Checks."
   B. Research the topic to be discussed.
   C. Prepare the organization outline of the sheet.
   D. Write the information sheet.
   E. Proofread and make the necessary changes/corrections.
   F. Duplicate/assemble the sheets.

2. Read the Information-Assignment Sheet "Traveler's Checks."
   A. Review the list of technical occupational information topics on the task detailing sheet "Selling Domestic Traveler's Checks."
   B. Research the topic to be discussed.
   C. Prepare an organizational outline of the sheet.
   D. Write the information-assignment sheet.
      For the assignment portion of the sheet.
      1. Review the topic(s) discussed in the information portion of the information-assignment sheet.
      2. Pose probable questions and/or situational problems.
      3. Prepare an organizational outline of the assignment portion of the sheet.
      4. Write the assignment section.
      5. Proofread and make necessary changes/corrections.
      6. Complete the assignment section of the information-assignment sheet.
   E. Proofread and make the necessary changes/corrections.
   F. Duplicate/assemble the sheets.

3. Complete the assignment portion of the above information-assignment sheet.

4. Read pages 44–48 in the "Training Manual for Tellers", Fidelity Bank of Carbondale.
   A. Review the text materials.

    B.   Select the sections that are appropriate to the assignment.

    C.   Note section title and location.

5. Read the Task Procedure Sheet "Selling Domestic Traveler's Checks."

    A.   Review the list of performance steps and standards of performance on the task detailing sheet "Selling Domestic Traveler's Checks."

    B.   Prepare the organizational outline of the sheet.

    C.   Write the task performance sheet.

    D.   Proofread and make the necessary changes/corrections.

    E.   Duplicate/assemble the sheets.

6. View the video-taped illustrated presentation "Traveler's Checks — An Informational Review."

    A.   Review the information presented in the above sources.

    B.   Develop a set of presentation notes.

    C.   Develop a series of coordinated illustrations.

    D.   Practice the presentation.

    E.   Tape the presentation.

    F.   Review/edit the tape and make the necessary changes/corrections.

    G.   Ready the video-tape for the LAP.

7. Complete the related information test on traveler's checks.

    A.   Review the materials on which the test is based.

    B.   Select the types of questions to be used.

    C.   Prepare the organizational outline of the test.

    D.   Rough-state the questions and review same.

    E.   Write the final draft of questions.

    F.   Self-take the test.

    G.   Make the necessary changes/corrections.

    H.   Prepare the answer key.

8. Observe the narrated slide tape demonstration of "Selling Domestic Traveler's Checks."

    A.   Revew the list of performance steps and standards of performance on the task detailing sheet "Selling Domestic Traveler's Checks."

    B.   "Walk through" the activity to be demonstrated.

    C.   Prepare a demonstration outline sheet and card.

    D.   Proofread same.

    E.   Duplicate demonstration outline materials.

    F.   Prepare the picture guide.

    G.   Select the demonstration site.

    H.   "Shoot" the demonstration slide series.

    I.   Narrate the slide series.

Example 17.1 continued

    J.   Review the slide series/narration and make the necessary changes/corrections.

    K.   Ready the narrated slide series for the LAP.

9. Practise the activity.

    A.   Review the list of performance steps and standards of performance on the task detailing sheet "Selling Domestic Traveler's Checks."

    B.   Develop a performance checksheet and list of oral test questions.

    C.   Review/proofread checksheet/test questions and make necessary changes/corrections.

    D.   Ready checksheet for use.

10. Take the final performance test of selling domestic traveler's checks.

    A.   Review the list of performance steps and standards of performance on the task detailing sheet "Selling Domestic Traveler's Checks."

    B.   Identify events (performance steps and task itself) to be checked.

    C.   Specify oral questions to be asked (optional).

    D.   Prepare an organizational outline of the performance test.

    E.   Write the performance test instrument.

    F.   Proofread the test instrument and make necessary changes/corrections.

    G.   Field-test the instrument.

    H.   Make necessary final revisions.

Agreement

The signatures of the two parties involved in the development of the learning materials for the learning activities package "Selling Domestic Traveler's Checks" confirms an agreement that the developmental steps specified for each learning activity will be adhered to. Any changes that might be made in the established development process must be agreed to by both parties prior to the time of change.

_____	_____
Student	Date
_____	_____
Instructor	Date

    The agreement portion of the development sheet is an optional entry used primarily in a learning situation in an occupational curriculum development course. Its purpose is to formalize an agreement between the instructor and the learner as to how and what the latter will do in preparing and developing learning materials for a particular series of learning activities. By preparing a development plan and confirming it with the instructor the learner gains assurance and confidence as to what exactly is expected and the manner in which it will be achieved.

Used in this manner, the sheet is a performance contract between the instructor and learner, as well as a plan for completing the various learning materials. The contract is realized by the signatures of both parties involved.

The following chapters discuss in detail the preparation of learning materials for implementing a series of learning activities that are common to many performance-oriented learning situations. The last chapter guides the learner in packaging the prepared learning materials for use in an individualized learning situation.

In Review

1. What is the basic purpose of the *learning activities development sheet* in the preparation and development of learning activities packages?

2. How does the development sheet assist the curriculum designer or teacher in readying the learning package for use?

3. When does the *learning activities development sheet* become a contract in the development of a particular learning activities package?

CHAPTER 18

Writing/Compiling Related Reading Materials

The writing and/or compiling of related reading materials is an essential part of readying a learning activities package. A review of the various lists of learning activities discussed earlier, together with those shown on the sample learning activities development sheet in the preceding chapter, shows that many learning activities use some form of written material.

This chapter will discuss the different types of related information and instruction sheets that can be used in a LAP, and provide suggestions for writing them. In addition, the editing of existing written materials that will be used by the learner in the individualized learning situation is reviewed.

In review, a given list of learning activities is made up of two basic types of activities: knowledge or theory-oriented, and performance or application-oriented. The knowledge-oriented learning activities (of which related reading materials are a part) provide the learner with information (knowledge) he or she will need and later apply in observing, practising, and performing the activity specified in the learning objective statement. Related reading materials include existing textbooks or other such published materials, and/or several kinds of information sheets authored by the curriculum designer and/or instructor.

The *technical occupational information topics* specified in the various learning activities statements specify knowledge needed by the learner to perform that objective.

Writing Related Instruction Sheets

When the occupational curriculum designer or instructor begins preparing the reading-oriented learning materials he or she is immediately confronted with the problem of determining whether or not the particular reading materials exist. If they do not exist or are unavailable, he or she must set about writing the materials or have someone else author them.

The four types of instruction sheets discussed in this chapter will provide the curriculum writer with examples of and suggestions for preparing the written materials for use in the learning activities package. The four types of instruction sheets include an: *information sheet, information-assignment sheet, assignment sheet,* and a *task procedure sheet.* The four sheets either directly provide the learner with information, or refer him or her to other informational sources.

The rationale for and organization of each of the instruction sheets are discussed in detail in the following sections of this chapter. The discussion is only intended to establish the purpose of and necessity for the various sheets, and to offer suggestions for writing them. The individual curriculum writer must take license to use, alter and/or adapt the ideas presented here to best suit his or her particular purposes and needs. Information can be presented in a variety of ways. But, in the end, it is the responsibility of the author to gather and present the information so that it has both meaning for the learner and application to the objective.

Information Sheet

The *information sheet* provides the learner with the technical occupation information he or she will need to attain the learning objective. The information sheet is one way of providing information in the completed learning activities package. A sample information sheet appears in Example 18.1.

Example 18.1
Medical Records

Learning Objective

The following information is directly related to performing the objective of "Arranging the Medical Record."

Introduction

A medical record is a permanent report of an individual's illness or injury and is maintained primarily for the benefit of the patient. It also has scientific and legal value. The medical record is used to diagnose and treat illnesses, to plan for hospitals, to aid in public health, and to assist in research.

A medical record technician is a trained health professional working in the medical records department of a hospital. It is the responsibility of the medical record technician to prepare, analyze, and preserve health data required by patients, by doctors, by hospitals, and by the public.

The duties of a medical record technician include reviewing of medical

Example 18.1 continued

records for completeness and accuracy, coding of diseases and operations, transcribing of medical and surgical reports, compiling statistics, assisting the medical staff, and supervising the day-to-day operation of a medical records department.

A medical record is started on a patient as soon as he or she presents him- or herself at the admitting department of a hospital. Here pertinent information to positively identify the patient is taken along with sociological data. Then the patient is escorted to the nursing unit or ward where, once treatment is assessed and initiated, several more forms are added to the medical record. Each addition has its purpose and importance. The health team treating the patient is able to view and analyze this written information as needed and in the process, assure the patient of the best possible care.

Upon discharge of the patient from the hospital, the medical record is sent to the medical records department for analysis and permanent filing. The medical record is the property of the hospital and cannot be removed except by court order.

The information contained within the medical record is private and confidential. All persons dealing with the medical record have a moral and ethical obligation to maintain this confidentiality.

Arrangement of Medical Records

In order to ensure maximum efficiency for analysis and future use, the medical record must be arranged in an order that is both practical and effective.

The arrangement of medical records will vary from hospital to hospital. The decision regarding the arrangement is generally made by the Medical Records Committee of the hospital. There is, however, a standard or basic outline of arrangement that can be identified in most hospitals. This outline resembles a "storybook" format, that is, there is a chronological sequence of events, from admission to discharge.

This chronological sequence is very important when records are being analyzed or reviewed by members of the health team. They do not have to flip through the entire record to get a "picture" of what happened to the patient during his stay in the hospital or to ascertain the course of a particular treatment or test.

It should be noted that during the actual hospitalization of the patient, the medical record on the ward is maintained in a different type of arrangement. The forms which are being used daily are kept on top and those that require only periodic reference are kept on the bottom. For example, during the hospitalization of the patient the nursing and medical staff would primarily be concerned with the graphic or clinical chart (which records the patient's temperature, pulse, respirations and blood pressure), the physicians' orders (for medications, diet, laboratory tests, etc.) and the nurses' notes (which record the day-to-day observations and progress of the patient). The order of arrangement on the nursing unit then is a reverse chronological order.

Should a patient be re-admitted to hospital, a doctor can review the previous record very quickly and effectively if the record has been arranged correctly. This means less time and effort for the doctor and better care for the patient and, perhaps, even a shorter stay in hospital.

Doctors and nurses simply cannot be expected to remember everything about every patient and this is one of the main reasons why medical records are maintained and mandatory for hospitals.

The proper arrangement of the medical record is valuable to all members of the health team.

Quantitative Analysis

Once the record is arranged in order, it is ready for the Quantitative Analysis in which the record is scrutinized to ensure all the required forms have been completed and all signatures are present.

From the quantitative analysis, the record can go in two directions in the medical records department:

1. Incomplete medical records will be signed out to doctors' files in the medical records department for completion of the different items.
2. Complete medical records will be coded and indexed. Here the diseases and operations indicated on the Admission and Discharge Form are assigned numerical figures to denote particular diseases and operations. Subsequently, these records are indexed or posted under the particular disease or operation code number and these are used for research and retrieval purposes.

Once a medical record is coded and indexed, it is used for any statistical analysis and, lastly, it is filed in the permanent file area of the medical records department.

A medical record is not filed unless it has gone through the complete process.

Notes

References

1. Edna K. Huffman. *Medical Records Management.* Berwyn: Physician's Record Company, 1972.
2. Ernest D. Bassett et al. *Business Filing and Records Control.* Cincinnati: Southwestern, 1964.

Body. The body of the information sheet contains the knowledge that the learner must acquire to aptly perform the learning objective. The expansion and discussion of concepts, ideas, and theories can occur in any

Figure 18.1 *Flow Chart of Medical Record. The flow of the medical record through the Medical Records Department of a hospital can be represented diagrammatically as follows:*

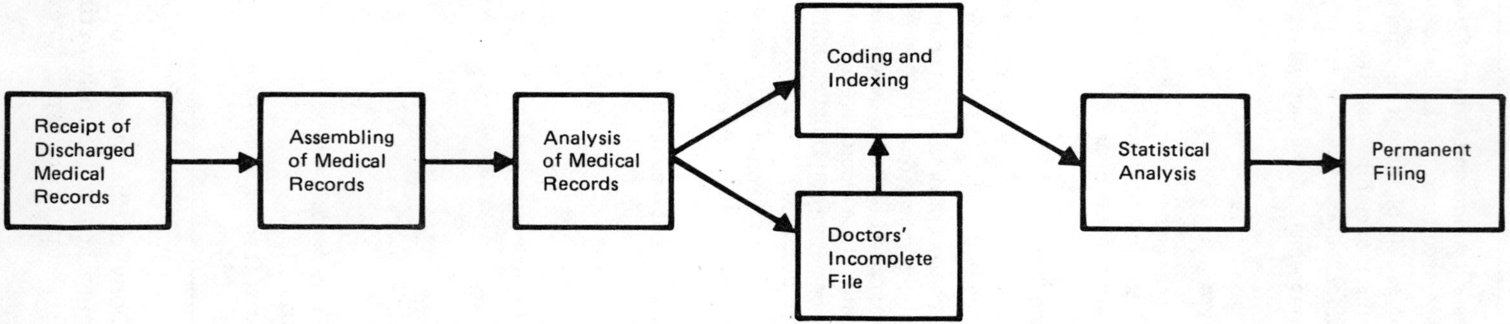

of several organizational formats and is often supplemented with pictures, drawings, graphs, diagrams, and other types of illustrations.

Printed matter, interspersed with illustrations, is a desirable organizational format for presenting information intended for practical application. The nature, amount, and scope of the information topics is determined by the writer and the parameters of the learning objective itself. Topics that do have general application include occupational health and safety practices, occupational hazards, legal implications of the performance of the objective, and suggestions as to the procedure to be followed in its performance.

Notes. Because the learner will often want to emphasize, clarify, or otherwise set apart some portion of the material he or she is reading, it is suggested that provision be made for reading notes. In Example 18.1, this was accomplished by heading a portion of each page "Notes."

If provision for reader's notes is made in printed materials which are included in a learning activities package, each LAP user will need a new copy of the reading materials. However, the benefit to the learner of keeping notes as he or she reads and studies offsets duplication costs.

References. The reference section of the information sheet is a listing of books and other printed materials to which the learner might refer for additional information on the topic(s) being discussed. The various references supplement the information contained in the information sheet.

A list of references appears in the sample information sheet (Example 18.1).

Information-Assignment Sheet

The *information-assignment sheet* is a modification of the information sheet. It includes a section of questions and/or statements that require the participation and response of the learner. A sample information-assignment sheet containing information on "Hand Saws" appears in Example 18.2.

Example 18.2
Hand Saws

Learning Objective

The following information and assignment are directly related to performing the objective of "Installing the Box Sill".

The Saw in History

Long before the dawn of history, saws were being used in every part of the inhabited world. The saw is one of man's most ancient tools, and antedates civilization by many thousands of years.

Example 18.2   continued

There are many different kinds of hand saws, and each is designed for a special purpose. They vary in weight, length, tooth points to the inch, character of steel, finish, pattern, and construction.

Handsaw Nomenclature

Whether the saw is a crosscut or a rip saw there are parts common to both. The figure below shows the profile of a handsaw, with the various parts indicated.

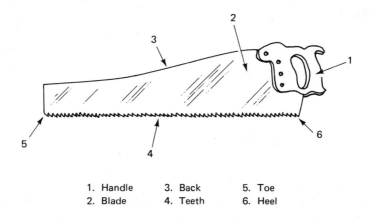

1. Handle	3. Back	5. Toe
2. Blade	4. Teeth	6. Heel

The Cross-Cut Saw

The cross-cut saw is used for cutting across the grain, and has a different cutting action from that of the rip saw. The teeth cut like sharp-pointed knives. There are more points to the inch on a cross-cut than on a rip saw.

The angle of a cross-cut saw tooth is $60°$, the same as that of a rip saw. The angle on front of the tooth is $15°$ from the perpendicular, while the angle on the back is $45°$.

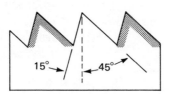

The teeth are usually filed with a bevel of about $24°$. The upper half of each tooth is set, alternately, one to the right, the next to the left, to assure clearance. The true taper grind of hand saws gives them additional clearance, and makes them run more easily and more accurately with less set than saws ground in the ordinary manner. The grind also helps to keep saws sharp for a longer time.

"Points per inch" is a term used to designate the size of teeth in a saw. The saw with a small number of tooth points to the inch, 7 points for example, will make a quick rough cut. Saws with more points, say 10 or more, will make smooth, even cuts, but will not cut as quickly as the coarse tooth saw.

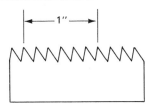

The amount of set given a saw is highly important because it determines the ease with which the saw runs; it insures accuracy of cutting; and it helps keep the saw sharp for a longer time.

The nature and character of the wood to be cut also must be considered. Green or wet wood requires a saw with coarse teeth and wide set, 7 points to the inch, while a 10 or 11 point saw with light set will work better in dry, well seasoned lumber. For ordinary cross-cutting, the user will find the 7 or 8 point most in demand.

The length of either rip or cross-cut hand saws is measured from point to butt on the cutting edge. Cross-cut saws are made in different lengths.

Some patterns of cross-cut saws are made with blades 20, 22, 24, and 26 inches. Saws 24 inches and shorter are known as panel saws. The 20 inch, 10 point cross-cut saw is most popular among the shorter saws.

The Rip Saw

The rip saw is used for cutting with the grain. Teeth differ from those of a cross-cut saw in size and shape. The rip saw has fewer teeth, or points, to the inch. The points are, therefore, larger. The angle of a rip tooth is 8° from the perpendicular on the front, and 52° on the back. The tooth resembles a small chisel, and its cutting action is much the same, each tooth chipping out a small portion

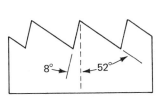

Example 18.2   continued

of the wood from the kerf. Cutting is done by the forward stroke. The upper half of each tooth is set alternately, one to the left and one to the right, to give clearance. This set, on each side, is equal to one-third or less the thickness of the blade. The size of the teeth in a saw is determined by points to the inch, as shown in the illustration.

An ordinary rip saw is made with 5 1/2 points to the inch in the 26-inch length. The teeth in this saw are one point finer at the point than at the butt. This permits easier starting in the cut.

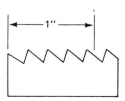

Blade lengths of both rip and cross-cut hand saws are measured from point to butt on the cutting edge. Rip saws are made 26 inches in length. Cross-cut saws are made in different lengths.

Use of a Handsaw

To use a handsaw most efficiently, follow these several hints:

1. Start the cut using a short, quick forward stroke. Do not let the entire weight of the blade rest on the work.
2. Cut with a smooth easy motion, using as much of the blade as possible.
3. Keep the saw at the correct angle in relation to the stock.
4. If possible, saw to the outside of the line.
5. When finishing a cut, take short, quick, light strokes to help avoid splintering.
6. Keep your saw in the best possible condition. Sharpen it when it gets dull; do not allow it to fall and damage the teeth; keep a light coat of paste wax on the blade to help prevent rusting and ease the cutting operation.

Assignment

1. Read and study the above section of this information-assignment sheet.
2. In your text, *Industrial Arts Woodworking,* read Section II, Unit 7, pp. 54–59.
3. Study page 19 in the *Stanley Tool Guide.*
4. Complete the work in the following section.

For Study and Discussion

Complete the following:

1. What is set? Is it used in only one of the two types of handsaws we studied?
2. What is the most common length of crosscut saw? Rip saw?
3. What is the name given to a crosscut saw that is 24" or shorter?
4. Sketch a crosscut tooth and show its hook angle with degrees. Repeat for a rip saw.

5. To what might you compare a row of crosscut teeth? Rip teeth?
6. If you were to look at the *end* of a row of saw teeth, how could you tell if it was a crosscut or a rip saw?
7. What single characteristic differentiates between a rip saw and a crosscut saw?
8. What saw would have the large teeth?

    A. a 6 pt. or a 14 pt.?   D. a 6 pt. or an 8 pt.?
    B. a 10 pt. or a 6 pt.?   E. a 5 pt. or a 5 1/2 pt.?
    C. a 7 pt. or an 8 pt.?

9. Sketch how the points are counted 1 inch for a 5 point rip saw; a 5 1/2 point rip saw.

References

Feirer, John Louis. *Industrial Arts Woodworking*. Peoria, Ill.: Charles A. Bennett, 1950.

Title. The title of the information sheet tells the reader, in brief, the nature, direction, and scope of the contents of the sheet. The title is derived from one or more of the technical occupational information topics noted on the task detailing sheets. The technical occupational information topics listed on the task detailing sheet were identified and listed as topics of information that a worker *must know* to perform the given task. Later, these same titles specified topics of information that a learner must acquire if he or she is to attain the learning objective. Depending on the intentions of the curriculum writer and the circumstances, the title of the instruction sheet might speak to only one topic, or encompass several. Regardless, the title connotes the contents of the sheet.

Learning Objective.   This entry on the information sheet serves two purposes. First, it reaffirms for the learner the importance of and need for the information in performing the learning objective. Secondly, it acts as a constant reminder to the curriculum writer in selecting and restricting the information being presented to the particular objective being sought. In both instances, the entry focuses the attention of the person involved on the intended purpose of the information sheet and re-emphasizes the purpose of the sheet.

In Example 18.2 the components — the title of the sheet, learning objective statement, body, provision for the reader's notes, and list of references — all serve the same function as those of the information sheet. As mentioned, the significant difference between the two information sheets is the inclusion of an assignment section in the information-assignment sheet.

In the assignment section of the sheet, the learner is expected to respond to a number of different types of items. These items are derived from the information presented in the body of the sheet. The learner's responses to the various items indicate his or her comprehension of the material and ability to apply it.

The individual items are presented in such a way that they require written response from the learner.

Assignment Sheet

The *assignment sheet*, as used in the learning activities package, serves primarily to guide the learner to those learning activities which cannot, for various reasons, be included in the LAP. (See example 18.3.) Such activities are taking field trips, practising the performance of a given task, conducting interviews, participating in role-playing situations, etc. Leonard, Fallon, and vonArx (1972) examined types of assignments and made the following distinctions: reading and answering questions, writing assignments, problem solving activities, and projects. Each type of assignment has its specific merits and limitations and these should be considered by the curriculum writer or instructor when preparing them as learning activities (assignments) in a learning package.

The assignment sheet can be used to direct the learner to new sources of information and/or to situations in which knowledge can be applied. A sample assignment sheet appears in Example 18.3. Although format can differ somewhat depending on the author, all assignment sheets have a common purpose; to direct the learner to an information or activity source from which he or she can acquire a specific type of knowledge or skill.

Example 18.3
Assignment Sheet

Learning Objective

The following assignment is directly related to performing the objective of *cutting hair.*

Introduction

The procedure for cutting hair can be learned in the hair cutting and styling area of the laboratory, but the learner will benefit from a visit to one or more beauty salons in the community to see the various settings in which hair stylists work, and to talk with them about the various things they do. The purpose of this assignment is to encourage you to visit a local beauty salon, tour the business, talk with the hair-stylists working there and, in general, become familiar with a work situation that resembles the one in which you will work once you graduate.

Assignment

1. List three beauty salons in the community that you would like to visit. Rank the salons in your order of preference. Submit the list to the instructor for review.

2. Once selected, make arrangements with the salon owner for your visit.

3. Prepare a list of questions that you might ask the owner and hairstylists during your visit. Review the questions with your instructor.

4. Write a three or more page report on what you learned and observed during the visit.

References

1. Elizabeth Atteberry. *Hints and Suggestions for Taking Fieldtrips.* Cutler: Racking Press, 1975.

The assignment sheet includes a title of the sheet itself, a learning objective statement, introduction, assignment section, and references. The title of the sheet informs the learner of the type of sheet, and specifies the type of material contained therein. The learning objective statement informs the reader of the particular learning objective to which the assignment pertains. The introductory statement includes a statement of the purpose of the assignment and the ways it will help the learner attain the given objective. The assignment section of the sheet specifies, in detail, exactly those things that the learner will do to complete the assignment. If, for instance, the assignment is to take a field trip to a local dairy farm,

Example 18.4
Procedure for Taking a Radial Pulse

Learning Objective: Taking a Radial Pulse

Introduction

The purpose of this task procedure sheet is to guide you through the process of *taking a radial pulse.* Taking the pulse is one method of counting the number of heartbeats of the patient. The pulse tells whether the heart is beating fast, normally or slowly (rate), weak or strong (volume) and if it is beating in a regular or irregular manner (rhythm). The pulse rate can be measured at several sites on the body, but the radial pulse is taken at the patient's wrist.

Equipment and Supplies

The following items are needed to complete the task:

- Watch with a sweep second hand or stopwatch
- Patient's record book or TPR chart
- Pencil or pen

References

Peters, H. Irene and Rich, Dorothy K. *Instructor's Guide for Teaching Nurses' Aides.* Concord, New Hampshire: State Department of Education, Division of Vocational Technical Education, 1969.

Knoedler, Evelyn L. *Manual for the Nurse's Aide.* Albany: Delmar Publishers Inc., 1968.

Performance Steps

The performance steps for taking the radial pulse are:

1. *Wash your hands.* Following accepted aseptic technique procedures, wash, rinse, and dry your hands before performing the activity. Make sure to wash the entire surfaces of your hands, but with special attention to areas between your fingers and around the fingernails.
2. *Tell the patient what you are going to do.* This is done to put the patient in a state of ease. The patient, particularly if he or she is inexperienced, might not know what you are going to do or why it needs to be done and become frightened or upset. By informing him or her, you will eliminate or reduce the chances of this problem occurring.
3. *Position the patient's hand and arm.* With the patient in a comfortable, relaxed position, place his or her hand and forearm either on the arm of a chair, the bed, a table or across his chest. (See Figure 1.) In the latter case, the patient should be resting in either a reclined or horizontal position. In this way, the weight of the arm and hand is supported by the body itself and not held up by the patient during the procedure.
4. *Locate the pulse site.* The pulse site is near the top of the inner side (thumb side) of the wrist between the tendons and wristbones. To locate the pulse exactly, place the tips of your first three fingers in this

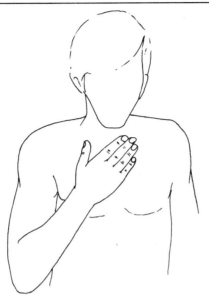

Figure 1

area. See Figure 2. Some slight repositioning of your fingertips on the patient's wrist might have to be made to locate the place where the pulse feels the strongest.

5. *Count the pulse rate.* Exerting a slight pressure on the pulse site, count the number of beats/minute. In some doctors' offices and hospitals, the practice of counting the beats for 15 seconds and multiplying by 4 or counting the beats for 30 seconds and multiplying by 2 is followed. As a learner it is suggested you base your count on a full minute (60 seconds) and, only after gaining experience, possibly adopt one of the other practices.

Figure 2

6. *Record your findings.* To complete the task, you must record your findings in the patient's record book or TPR chart. In addition to the patient's pulse *rate,* also record the relative *strength* of the pulse (weak, normal, or strong) and its rhythm, e.g., regular or irregular. If there seem to be any extreme characteristics, report them to your supervisor or the doctor immediately.

activities might include: keeping a record of the things and events seen, noting comments of the dairy workers, and writing a brief statement about the value of the field trip. The reference portion of the assignment sheet, much like those of the information and information-assignment sheets, is a list of supplementary materials.

Task Procedure Sheet

The *task procedure sheet* is one of the sheets contained in the learning activities package, and assists the learner in attaining the learning objective. It is basically a guide to the sequence of performance steps performed in the completion of the task, and to the standards of performance for each step in the procedure. As a learning resource, the task procedure sheet can be used in two ways. Its primary function is to guide the learner in the step-by-step performance of the objective. Secondly, it is an information sheet which gives the reader a preview of the total process to be performed and a detailed knowledge of the procedural steps of the task. A sample task procedure sheet appears in Example 18.4.

The components of a task procedure sheet are the title of the sheet, statement of the learning objective, introduction, equipment and materials, references, and procedure. All of the entries guide and direct the learner in performing the given objective. The title, learning objective statement, and introduction alert the reader to the purpose, direction, and scope of the sheet. The equipment and materials section, as the name implies, lists the various pieces of equipment the learner will have in performing the objective and the materials that he or she will need and use in the process. The references listed are those resource materials to which the learner can refer for additional information regarding the process. Lastly, the procedural section gives the learner the list of steps to be performed, their order of occurrence, and the standard or level of performance that must be attained before the step can be considered complete.

The data contained in a task performance sheet is derived from that contained in the corresponding task detailing sheet developed earlier in the occupational curriculum development process. (For review, see Chapter 7.) Note that the technical occupational information topics that appear on the task detailing sheet do not appear on the corresponding task procedure sheet. These topics, as you will recall, were adopted and expanded by the curriculum writer during the writing of the information and/or information-assignment sheets or, as will be discussed next, during the editing and compiling of existing written materials for use in the LAP.

Compiling Related Reading Materials

The first part of this chapter focused on the writing of learning materials for use in the learning activities package. However, in many instances, the original composition of reading materials is not needed because materials which provide the learner with the necessary information are already available.

The process of searching for information in existing sources is by no means a simple task. In fact, often writing the needed learning materials might be less trying. However, if resources do exist they are convenient and appropriate entries in the completed learning activities package.

Process

There are several steps in the process of readying existing reading materials for use in a LAP. With the particular learning objective in mind and the technical occupational information topic(s) needing development clearly stated, the curriculum writer sets about identifying possible informational resources — textbooks, journal articles, magazine articles, manufacturer's directions, owner's manuals, etc. This identification process involves reviewing the contents of the various publications to identify those sections or portions thereof that speak directly to the issue. With the topics identified and the appropriate sections in the publications noted, the reviewer can then take notes as to the exact location of the information in the resource material and begin preparing it for use in the learning package.

A word of caution. When using published materials, there is both an ethical and legal responsibility to request and obtain a written release from the publisher of the material before copying, or reprinting, or duplicating it for inclusion in a learning package. There is a great temptation to abuse the rights of the authors and publishers of their work, but this temptation should be resisted.

Once the written materials are prepared and incorporated into the learning activities package, a means for determining whether the learner has acquired the information has to be developed and also included in the package. The following chapter deals with the evaluation of acquired knowledge and the writing of testing devices.

In Review

1. What purpose do the various types of reading materials fulfill in a learning activities package?

2. List the four types of instruction sheets discussed in the chapter. Discuss the purpose of each and how each differs from the others.

3. What is the nature of the related information covered by the various types of instruction sheets and already published material in a learning activities package?

4. The information that is included in a learning activities package and directly related to performance of the learning objective is derived directly from what source?

5. What benefit is realized by the learner if the various instruction sheets include a *Reader's Notes* section?

6. What steps must be taken by the curriculum designer/teacher to avoid possible legal complications when using copyrighted or otherwise already existing published materials in a learning package?

CHAPTER 19

Writing an Illustrated Presentation Guide

The illustrated presentation is another in the series of learning activities in a total learning activities package. As a component of an individualized learning package, the illustrated presentation guides the learner in reviewing the reading-related learning materials and helps him or her clarify any of the informational content he or she might not have fully understood when he or she first read and studied the material.

To follow through the logic of organizing and developing individualized learning materials, the illustrated presentation is best recorded on video-tape and included in the learning activities package in that form. The illustrated presentation, then, has the same advantages and disadvantages as the traditional lecture. However, with careful planning and development on the part of the curriculum designer, and with transparencies, slide series, drawings, and the medium of the video-tape itself, the illustrated presentation will remain a valuable part of the complete learning package.

The position of the illustrated presentation in relation to the other learning activities in the series is crucial to the progress of the learner. As a part of the *knowledge-related* learning activities, the presentation immediately follows reading and writing assignments, and precedes the taking of the related information test. The presentation gives the learner opportunity to review the various concepts and other related informational content he or she has acquired, and refine his or her thinking on the pertinent technical information topics. Once the illustrated presentation has been viewed and the learner is satisfied with his or her mastery of the material, he or she then is ready to measure the success of his or her effort on the information test.

Characteristics of an Illustrated Presentation

The illustrated presentation, as stated earlier, closely resembles the traditional lecture in style. Because it is presented on video-tape no shared communication can occur between the person making the presentation and the learner who is viewing it. However, like the lecture, the illustrated presentation has certain characteristics that contribute considerably to learning the defined material, and, for that reason, is included as one of the essential learning activities. Characteristics of the illustrated presentation are:

Means of Review.   Once the learner has completed all of the reading and written assignments, a review of that material and a reiteration of the key points made in it are desirable. At this point in the series of learning activities, a review is needed to help insure that the learner has acquired the information he or she will need to meet the immediate goal, taking the related information test, and the longer range goal, performing the learning objective to which the information relates.

The illustrated presentation draws together the various thoughts and ideas presented in the reading materials. It helps clarify points of information that might not have been fully understood at the time they were first studied, and integrates them into a related whole. The illustrations used during a presentation add a visual dimension and assist the learner by depicting ideas and concepts that otherwise might have remained abstract.

Efficient Way of Presenting Material.   The illustrated presentation is an efficient and effective way of reviewing the information topics that will be included on the related information test and, later, applied in the performance of the learning objective. If the presenter carefully and critically reviews the materials found in the informational resources specified in the reading-related learning activities, plans the presentation in terms of his or her findings, makes use of illustrations that complement the presentation topics, and presents the information in an organized and thorough manner, the purpose of the illustrated presentation will have been met. Although significant amounts of time are used in organizing and preparing the presentation in the above manner, the time investment will be realized once the presentation is recorded and used by various learners to achieve the learning objective.

Directed Specifically to a Single Learning Objective.   The topics that are discussed in an illustrated presentation are directly related to a particular learning objective and applied by the learner in his or her performance of that objective. The information topics were originally identified in the occupational curriculum development process discussed in Part Two. There they appeared on a *task detailing sheet* as *technical occupational information topics* and were related to the task for which the sheet was written. By definition, technical occupational information is that information that the worker *must know* to perform a given task. Later, the information topics accompanied the task through its transition to a learning objective and the same topics, when expanded, became the informational content that the learner would have to know to perform the learning objective. Eventually, the information topics guided the curriculum designer in selecting and writing the informational resources to be included in the learning activities package for that objective, and in turn, provided a central point to be discussed in the illustrated presentation in that package.

Once you grasp the concept of the origin and evolution of the technical information topics, you will better understand their relationship to one particular learning objective.

Complements the Other Learning Activities and Instructional Techniques. The series of learning activities for a particular learning objective are systematically ordered by the curriculum designer to guide the learner toward the objective in as efficient a manner as possible. For instance, the illustrated presentation, as positioned in the sequence of knowledge-related learning activities, follows all of the activities from which the learner derives the needed technical information and precedes the administration of the related information test, where the learner is expected to divulge his or her knowledge of the informational topics. The illustrated presentation is positioned between the two types of learning activities to act as a buffer and provide the learner with one last opportunity to review the information and ready him or herself for the knowledge test.

Illustrated Presentation Guide

In preparing for an illustrated presentation, the presenter must first plan and write a guide to follow in conducting a review of the information topics covered in the learning activities package. A presentation guide can take many forms, but, in the end, it must help the learner review the information in a systematic and organized way. An example of a well planned guide appears in Example 19.1.

The sample presentation guide is made up of three basic parts: the learning objective statement, the listing of the topics to be presented, and the list of visual aids used to illustrate the presentation. The learning objective statement is included to tie the presentation to the learning activities package of which it is a part, and to re-emphasize the relationship of the presentation to the learning objective.

The presentation topics and their respective lists of key points, again, are derived from the technical occupational information covered in the reading-related learning activities that precede the presentation. The order in which the topics occur also reflects the arrangement of the parent learning activities.

Example 19.1
Presentation Guide

Learning Objective #11 — Selling Domestic Traveler's Checks

Presentation Topics

Terms	*Visual Aids*
1. Discuss various terms and meanings	T_1 — "Terms"

Traveler's Checks

1. Definition	
2. Brands	T_2 — Major brands
3. Physical make-up and appearance	T_3 — Single check
	T_4 — Parts of check
4. Denominations and packaging	Samples of various "loose" and "pre-packaged" checks
A. "Loose" and "pre-packaged"	
B. Advantages and disadvantages of each	T_5 — Denomination and value

Purchase Applications

1. Definition and purpose	Sample purchase application forms
2. Types	
A. Loose style checks	Sample — loose
1) Parts of form	
2) Customer's section	
3) Seller's section	
4) Precautions	
B. Pre-packaged style checks	Sample — pre-packaged
1) Parts of form	
2) Customer's section	
3) Seller's section	
4) Precautions	

Wallets	*Visual Aids*
1. Definition and purpose	
2. Types of wallets	Samples of various types of wallets
3. Advantages/disadvantages of various types	

In the example, the visual aids include both transparencies (indicated by a "T_n") and actual examples of various other related items. Any type of visual aid, be it two or three dimensional, that assists the learner in better understanding the information being reviewed can, and should, be used. As in Example 19.1, the list of aids is also coordinated with the list of topics and key points to make for a smoother presentation.

In Review

1. What is the purpose of the illustrated presentation in the sequence of learning activities of a particular learning objective?

2. In its assigned role and in accordance with good instructional technique, why is the illustrated presentation an essential learning activity?

3. Compare the illustrated presentation to the traditional lecture and presentation-discussion. Discuss its strengths and weaknesses with respect to each of these techniques.

4. What is the basic purpose of the illustrated presentation guide?

5. Discuss how the various presentation topics contained in a guide are determined.

CHAPTER 20

Writing a Related
Information Test

The related information test is a pencil-paper test designed to measure the extent of a learner's understanding of a given area of knowledge. The test, as used in the context of the occupational curriculum development theory, appears as one of the entries in a completed learning activities package. Like most other knowledge tests prepared for use in the classroom-laboratory situation, the related information test performs several functions. It indicates the knowledge the learner has of a particular area of information, stimulates interest and motivates the learner, marks progress in the learning process, and establishes the readiness of the learner for beginning the *performance-related* learning activities. As with any type of well-constructed knowledge test, it also points out those areas of information in which the learner is deficient and needs additional study and review.

The related information test has a number of advantages in the individualized situation. First, when properly used, it is invaluable in measuring the information the learner has retained and in guiding his or her progress in the learning situation. Also, the test is designed to measure only that information which the learner will need in attaining the particular learning objective. The length of the test and the point in time at which it appears in the sequence of learning activities are easily determined by the curriculum designer or instructor and are important considerations in developing the series of individualized learning resources.

As mentioned above, the related information test is one of a variety of different types of learning materials found in a learning activities package.

The test typically appears as the last entry in the series of learning activities that emphasize knowledge acquisition. (See Example 20.1.) Its

---

Example 20.1
Learning Objective: Preparing a Garden Plot

1. Read pages 7–21, Section 2, Chapter IX in the text (20 mins).

2. Read Information-Assignment Sheet "Tips on Planting" and complete the "Additional Study" section (50 mins).

3. View the taped illustrated presentation "The Do's and Dont's of Gardening" (30 mins).

4. Take the Related Information test (60 mins).

5. Observe the slide series demonstration of "Preparing the Garden Plot" (60 mins).

6. Practice preparing a garden plot (120 mins).

7. Take the final performance test of preparing a garden plot (120 mins × 2).

---

position and relationship to other learning activities in the sequence reflect the logic with which the series of learning activities was originally ordered.

In Example 20.1, as well as in those that appear elsewhere in the Handbook, the learner is first directed to various resource materials which provide him or her with the information needed to perform the learning objective. This information, derived from a previously established list of technical occupational information topics, is considered essential knowledge for the learner. During the course of performing the learning objective, the learner will draw on, apply, and use this knowledge as the situation demands. The information influences, directs, controls, and affects the learner's judgment-forming abilities as they relate to performance of the objective.

The importance of such information, as it pertains to the learner's performance, is obvious. However, simply because the learner has completed the various reading and other knowledge-oriented learning activities, it cannot be assumed that the information has been assimilated and retained. A measure of the individual's understanding and internalization of the information topics discussed must be made. Hence, the related information test. If the learner's knowledge of the material proves adequate he or she continues on to the next learning activity in the sequence. On the other hand, if his or her knowledge of the topics proves inadequate, he or she must then return to review and study further those materials which contain the necessary information.

To measure the learner's understanding of the topics discussed in the informational learning materials, the related information test must be well designed and constructed. This chapter will assist the reader in preparing a well constructed pencil-paper test. The related information test discussed here is designed to be used in an individualized learning situation. However, with little or no modification, the same test could be successfully used by the learner pursuing the same objective in the more conventional, teacher-involved learning situation. The principles of written test construction remain relatively constant, regardless of the situation in which the instrument is later used. The suggestions that follow in no way lessen the challenge of preparing a good test, but are made to assist the test writer in making decisions that will provide a good measure of the learner's knowledge, and be of benefit as he or she works toward attaining the particular learning objective.

Planning the Related Information Test

The related information test contains a variety of individual test items which constitute a sample of all possible questions that might be asked concerning the technical occupational information topics. The learner's ability to respond correctly to the various sample items reflects his or her knowledge of the total body of information from which the items are drawn. Before writing any of the test items, however, the writer must first know the learning objective, the technical occupational information topics associated with that objective, and the particular items of information that are crucial to the learner's successful performance of the objective. If the test is to be valid, i.e., test the material it is designed to test, it must contain a fair and representative number of items which are drawn from these informational resources.

Also, if the test is to be a good measure of a learner's understanding of a particular area of information, it must be well constructed — it has to be valid, reliable, objective, and comprehensive. A brief discussion of each characteristic follows.

Validity. A test is considered valid if it measures that which it is intended to measure. In the related information test, the individual test items are derived directly from the technical occupational information topics in the learning package. When prepared for a specific learning objective, the validity of the test and its individual items should be extremely high, since both reflect the specific informational topics found in the materials the learner has already read and studied.

Reliability. A test is said to be reliable if the score attained by a learner on the first attempt is approximately the same as the totals that would be earned if he or she were to repeat the same test a second or third time with no additional study or review.

Reliability is correlated to several criteria: the overall length of the test, its level of difficulty, the types of items included, objective or subjective, and the inherent clarity, consciousness, and quality of the individual items. Each must be considered by the test writer if a test of quality is to be achieved and maintained.

Objectivity. Objectivity of a test is achieved when scoring is free of scorer or rater bias and personal opinion. If several people evaluate the test and considerable variation in their results occurs, the test rates low in objectivity, and will not fairly and accurately represent the abilities of the learner.

In tests containing completion items, the scoring may be influenced by the learner's expression of terms, handwriting, personal characteristics or other extraneous qualities (Gronlund, 1968). When personal bias or opinion influences the scoring of the test, the instrument also loses its objectivity and becomes a less effective measure of learner achievement.

Comprehensiveness. A related information test is considered comprehensive if it contains test items which constituted a liberal sampling of all of the possible questions that could be asked about the body of information. While it is not necessary or practical to expect the learner to respond to each and every point covered in the learning materials, it is reasonable to expect the learner to have retained the information and to be able to respond to various questions pertaining to it in a test situation.

Preparing a comprehensive test is a matter of selecting those items which sample the learner's knowledge and understanding of an entire body of information.

Discrimination. A test which has the ability to distinguish the levels of achievement of good, average, and poor learners is said to be discriminating. However, while the need to differentiate between the attainment levels of learners is viewed as essential in some circumstances, this characteristic is not as crucial to the quality of the related information test found in the learning activities package. Because the test is used in an individualized learning situation, its role differs somewhat from that of the more conventional classroom achievement test. The major function of the related information test is to determine whether the learner has acquired the needed technical information to complete the learning objective, and, to signal his or her success and continuance in the learning activities sequence. In the individualized learning situation, the test is not used to discriminate between individual test scores, but rather to indicate successful assimilation or failure to assimilate specific points of information.

Writing Test Items

The various items found in the related information test are derived from the informational content cited in the various resources of the *knowledge-related* learning activities. The information contained in the various resources is reworded and presented to form the following types of test items:

- True–False
- Multiple Choice
- Completion
- Matching
- Essay

The first four types of test items are objective in nature, whereas the last item, the essay, is subjective because the opinions of the scorer enter into its final evaluation. A more detailed discussion of the characteristics of the various test items, their strengths and weaknesses, and suggestions for their development and evaluation appears in the following sections of the chapter.

True–False Items

The true–false test item is a statement which the learner must judge to be either right or wrong based on his or her knowledge of the material being tested. An example of a true–false item, together with directions for completion, appear below:

> If you think the statement is true, fill in the "0" under the "T" on the answer sheet. If you think the statement is false, fill in the "0" under the "F" on the answer sheet for that statement. You will receive one point for each correct response.
>
> 1. The term *green* applies to wood when its moisture content is over 30%.

The true–false item is a popular entry on classroom tests, but is also readily adaptable to individualized learning situations. Large numbers of true–false items with the same broad range of informational content can be included in a related information test. Because of their uncomplicated nature, these items can also be self-administered by the learner.

The true–false test item is basically designed to measure knowledge of specific points or facts. Hence, true–false items must have an absolute and uncompromising quality about them so as to permit the learner to distinguish them as either true or false.

The strengths of the true–false test item, used in a learning activities package, include its ease of application in the individualized situation, its potential for sampling a wide range of informational content within a relatively short period of time, its ease of scoring, and its objectivity. The major weakness of the true–false item is that all too often information being tested for is not of an either/or nature. Much learning revolves around generalizations, concepts, principles, or explanation, and while the true-false statement can be used in such situations, it is somewhat limited in measuring types of learning that appear higher on the cognitive taxonomy. Also, because of its absolute quality, a true-false statement must be precisely phrased and universally applicable if it is to permit no misconceptions on the part of the learner in responding to it. To write a statement in such a manner can be difficult.

Suggestions for Writing True-False Statements. Like any type of test item, true-false statements can be well or poorly written. Following are some suggestions that will serve as guides in writing good true-false items.

1. *Do not use statements that can be interpreted in different ways.* The best stated true-false test items are either totally true or totally false. They are absolute in that they permit only one clear response and do not give the learner any opportunity to cite other plausible alternatives. Any ambiguity that might be established in the way the statement is presented, or its authenticity as to either true or false, eliminates the item as a reliable and valid indicator of the learner's knowledge. See the example.

   Poor

   Fiber glass is an insulating material used in house construction.

   Improved

   Fiber glass is one type of insulating material used in house construction.

   The first statement, while it is true, is not all inclusive. Other materials such as wood, felt paper, and brick are also used for purposes of insulation. Also misleading is the phrase "house construction". Fiber glass is not used exclusively in houses, but in other types of buildings as well. The second statement is an improvement over the first because the inclusion of the phrase "one type of" qualifies the intention of the item with regard to function and situation.

2. *Include an approximately equal number of items that are true and false.* Approximately one-half of the items included in the true-false section of the related information test should have true responses and the other one-half, false responses. Also, the individual items should be ordered so as not to establish a pattern or series of like response items. The final result of the true-false test should reflect what the learner knows about certain technical information topics, and not that he or she was able to discover an inherent trend or pattern within the test.

3. *Avoid long, wordy, or complicated statements.* In each true-false statement, there is a point of information around which the test item is designed. If the meaning of the statement is obscured

by phrasing or by extraneous information, the test item is poorly constructed. In some instances, items might have to be discarded altogether or, as is more often the case, simplified by rephrasing to focus on the particular point of information.

Poor

Although banks, credit unions, and currency exchanges sell traveler's checks to their customers and, at the same time, accept and cash them, only one company, *American Express,* issues them to the various selling agencies for public sale.

Improved

The only U.S. company which issues traveler's checks to banks, and other agencies for public sale is *American Express.*

4. *Avoid using misleading or trick questions.* The purpose of each item in the related information test is to measure the learner's knowledge of a particular body of technical information as it relates to a learning objective. Therefore, rather than include items in the test which measure the learner's ability to recognize intentionally misleading questions, the individual items should be designed to evaluate the learner's knowledge of the requisite information and nothing else. An example of a misleading test item, together with an example of an improved statement appears below.

Poor

The chief component in a fuel-air mixture is nitrogen.

Improved

The chief component that supports combustion in a fuel-air mixture is nitrogen.

The first example misleads the learner because, while the statement is true, (nitrogen is the chief component in the fuel-air mixture), oxygen is the component of air that is used in combustion and is the element that should be stressed. The addition of the phrase "that supports combustion" in the improved item focuses the statement and makes it a better item than the first example.

5. *Avoid using words or phrases which give clues to the proper responses.* Certain words or phrases used in writing true–false statements connote, to the more experienced learner, a particular response. Some words or phrases are more associated with items that are intended by the test writer to be true, and other words

with those items designed to be false. Words and phrases such as "always", "never", "all", "will always be", have an absolute quality that indicates to the test-wise learner that the statement is false. In contrast, such words or phrases as "might be", "usually", "may" or "in some instances," are more closely associated with statements meant to be true. Again, the problem with such words and phrases is not the words or phrases themselves nor their intended meaning, but the fact that they alert and permit the learner to respond correctly to a test item on a basis other than his or her knowledge of the material.

Poor

Wood is the best insulating material used in house construction.

Improved

When compared to concrete, brick, or other masonry products, wood is a better insulator.

6. *Restrict the use of negatively stated test items.* In most instances, a positively stated test item is more desirable in a related information test than is a negatively stated item. By design, most informational tests seek to measure what the learner knows rather than what he doesn't know, and to overuse negative items in a test only emphasizes the latter condition. Statements which incorporate negative words complicate the meaning of the item, create confusion in the learner by drastically changing the direction from which he or she has approached preceding questions in the test, and induce careless errors by introducing a semantic twist to particular items.

   An example of a negatively stated item appears below with a complementing statement of the same item stated in more positive terms.

Poor

It is not the purpose of a test item to confuse the learner's thinking.

Improved

The purpose of the test item is to help in determining the learner's knowledge of a particular body of information.

Double negative statements, those that contain two negative words, should be avoided altogether because they maximize confusion and significantly affect the reliability of test items. A sample double negative item and a restatement of the same item, in a more positive form, appears below.

Poor

A high nitrogen fertilizer should not be used if, after its application, the amount of ground moisture will not be relatively high.

Improved

A high nitrogen fertilizer should be used only at times when the ground moisture will be relatively high during and following its application.

Scoring. To reduce the remaking of tests and facilitate the scoring process, it is suggested that learners respond to the various test items on a separate answer sheet. In scoring the true–false portion of tests, the usual practice is to award one point for each correct response made by the learner. The subtotal earned then for the true–false portion of the test can later be added with the other subtotals to determine the overall number of points earned.

Multiple-Choice Items

The multiple-choice item consists of two basic parts: an introductory statement or *stem*, and the alternatives or *responses* that complete the item. An example appears below.

Each of the items listed below is followed by four possible responses. Fill in the "0" under the letter on the answer sheet that *best* completes the statement. You receive one point for each correct response.

Which one of the following abrasives ranks hardest on the Moh's scale?

A. Corundum
B. Aluminum oxide
C. Silicon carbide
D. Boron carbide

Unlike the true–false item, which requires that the responses be of an absolute nature, the multiple-choice item provides the learner with a selection of alternative responses and requires him or her to select the one that *best* answers the question or completes the opening phrase. The multiple-choice item also reduces the effect of guessing on the part of the learner. A well-written mulitple-choice statement usually contains four or five responses, compared to two for a true–false question. The increased number of alternatives from which the learner must choose considerably reduces his or her chances of guessing the appropriate response. In turn, this characteristic of multiple-choice items increases the reliability of the test of which they are a part.

The multiple-choice test item, because of its list of alternative responses, is able to measure learning of concepts and principles, ability to reason, and other sophisticated and complex forms of cognitive learning. Like the true–false item, it can also be used to measure verbal relationships and ability to recall factual data, but because of its greater potential for detecting learning of a broader, more generalized nature, it should not be used solely for that purpose.

Like any type of test item, the multiple-choice design has its limitations. Its strengths rest in its ability to measure different types of cognitive learning, reduce the effects of guessing, and be objective in terms of scoring, but it also has limitations. Both the construction and the administration of a multiple-choice test require a considerable investment of time. The test writer is faced with the problem of not only identifying potential central ideas around which the test items will be constructed, but also with selecting alternative responses that are meaningful to the situation and yet have subtle enough differences that they test the learner's knowledge of the subject. In like fashion, the learner encounters the time factor as he or she reads each entry of each test item, makes a choice, and repeats the process until the test is complete. A peripheral drawback, but one that still should be mentioned, is the relatively large amount of space required by each multiple-choice item. Because of this, multiple-choice tests contain, in most cases, proportionately more pages per test than do tests comprised of other types of test items.

Suggestions for Writing Multiple-choice Items.

1. *Use either a direct question or incomplete statement.* The stem of a multiple-choice test item functions best when it is posed as either a direct question or a statement to be completed by the learner. In the first case, the statement is written in the form of a question and the responses that accompany it are all potential answers to the question. In the latter instance, the stem of the test item is an incomplete statement followed by individual responses which grammatically complete it. Regardless of format, the goal of the learner is to select the response that best answers the question or completes the test statement.

   Examples of the direct question and incomplete statement types of items appear below.

Direct Question

Which structural member is one of the components of a rough door opening?

A. Firestop

B. Trimmer stud

C. Joist

D. Threshold

Incomplete Statement

The term *gelding* is best associated with

A. Cattle

B. Sheep

C. Horses

D. Pigs

The style used in writing test items should be dictated by the central ideas taken from the related information. If it makes little or no difference for a particular item, use the style that is most comfortable. Neither approach is proven superior. However, for those who are not experienced in writing multiple-choice statements, the direct question approach generally produces a technically better item than does the incompleted statement item. The direct question approach encourages the test writer to select responses directly related to the stated question, whereas the incomplete-statement approach sometimes produces difficulties in identifying and ordering the various word and phrase responses to produce a well-designed test item. Again, however, added experience will allow the writer to use both styles effectively and with ease.

Another aspect of writing test items in either of the two formats is to make every effort to keep the items simple, direct, and focused on a central informational issue or problem. Like any other type of test item, difficult, unfamiliar, or irrelevant language should be avoided. Technical information and terms are acceptable, of course, but only if they pertain to the essential information.

2. *The central idea of the item should be included in the stem.* The central idea of the item, derived from the informational content, should be located in the stem of the test statement. Once the learner has read the opening statement, he or she should grasp the main thought being stressed and be able to proceed then in examining the alternative responses. The test item is poorly constructed if the learner has to rely on an individual response to gain the remainder of the central idea being emphasized.

An example follows.

Poor

The phrase *range of motion*

A. applies to the amount of movement an ambulatory patient can move without tiring.

B. defines the movement of an unborn baby in the womb.

C. applies to the extreme limits of movement that a person can make at a given joint.

    D. applies to the degrees that a joint can be hyper-extended beyond the "normal" range.

Improved

Range of motion applies to the limits of movement of the

    A. heart
    B. joints
    C. lower extremeties
    D. hyper-extended range of joints

3. *Make the stem and responses grammatically correct and compatible.* Grammatical correctness and compatibility between the stem and its responses are important in both the direct question and incomplete-statement types of multiple-choice items. However, difficulties in achieving these are more commonplace in the latter type. The direct question, by design, elicits a pointed response to a question, whereas the incomplete-statement item, to be successful, has to establish a continuity of thought between the stem of the item and each of its responses. It is in the establishment of this link that the difficulty sometimes arises, and precautions should be taken to prevent problems. In the following examples the first statement shows a lack of grammatical correctness and continuity of thought between the two components of the item. The second is an improvement on the first because the components are grammatically correct and compatible.

    Poor

Most automobile-pedestrian accidents occur

    A. where intersections are protected by stop signs
    B. traffic light
    C. no traffic signal
    D. jaywalking

    Improved

Most automobile-pedestrian accidents occur

    A. at intersections protected by stop signs.
    B. at intersections protected by traffic lights.
    C. at intersections where there are no traffic signals.
    D. between intersections where pedestrians are jaywalking.

The above examples also show another situation that can occur when writing multiple-choice test items, repetition of words or phrases in each of the responses of the test statement. Sometimes repetition is unavoidable, but the test writer should make every effort to limit repeating a word or phrase within a given test item. One way to prevent the problem is to rephrase the stem of the item to include that which would be repeated, and remove it from each of the responses.

4. *Avoid using negative statements.* The precautions noted for avoiding the use of negatively phrased true–false items apply equally to the writing of negative multiple-choice test items. The negative statement, while sometimes desirable, can be difficult for the learner to interpret and can confuse him or her about what exactly is being asked in the test statement. The following example points out the undesirable traits of a negatively stated test item.

> A check that is *stale-dated* does not refer to:
>
> A. a traveler's check that has exceeded the legal time limit in which it must be cashed.
>
> B. a personal check that has exceeded the legal time limit in which it must be cashed.
>
> C. a personal check.
>
> D. a counter check that has exceeded the legal time limit in which it must be cashed.

In the above example, the reader is immediately confronted with the problem of eliminating responses that "stale-dated" *does* refer to in order to determine the technically correct response. The association between the central term and what it does not mean contradicts the basic assumption that the related information test is designed to measure what the learner knows and not what he or she does not know. The confusion and uncertainty that is promoted and the reversal in the process of approaching the problem is contradictory to good testing logic and procedure.

5. *All of the responses should have potential as a possible right answer and have equal appeal to the learner who does not have the requisite knowledge.* The purpose of the related information test is to determine whether the learner has acquired the technical information needed to perform the learning objective. In a more limited sense, the role of each *item* on the test is to discern the individual's knowledge of the needed information. One technique used to determine whether the learner has acquired the essential information and to reduce the effect of guessing is selecting responses that all have the potential for being correct. Written in this manner, a test item will prove difficult to the learner who does not have the requisite information and must guess if he or she is to respond at all.

The following examples clearly demonstrate the effect of not having responses of approximately the same appeal.

Poor

What term is used to denote electrical *resistance*?

A. Transformer

B. Volt

C. Copper wire

D. Ohm

Improved

What term is used to denote electrical *resistance*?

A. Ampere

B. Volt

C. Watt

D. Ohm

6. *Avoid the tendency of making one response (A, B, C, etc.) the one that is predominately the correct answer.* When writing and ordering responses of the various multiple-choice items, make a conscious attempt to distribute the correct responses among the various choices. In this way no trends of correct responses will appear in the test and the knowledge of the learner, rather than his ability to detect patterns and other repetitious clues, will be assessed.

   Related to the above suggestion, is including only one best response within an individual multiple-choice item. While subtle discriminations can be made between various responses of a multiple-choice item, it is unfair to the learner to include responses that have an equal possibility of being correct. The test writer must use discretion when selecting responses to an item, always remembering that the learner has only one chance per item to make the best choice and that, while subtle differences among responses can be made, the writer must also be fair to the learner who must respond.

7. *For any given multiple-choice item, the central idea of each response should be independent and mutually exclusive of the others.* As stated earlier, a well written multiple-choice item includes one best response. Dangers that exist when two or more responses are interrelated, are that no one best response is listed, or that a combination of responses becomes the best choice. In either situation, the learner is still expected to make only one choice and any choice he or she makes will be incorrect. Interdependence also assists the learner by allowing him or her to eliminate wrong responses without essential knowledge and then choose from the remaining items. This significantly reduces the reliability of the test item.

An example appears below.

Poor

As a scuba diver rises from the bottom of a lake, the

A. water pressure increases

B. water pressure decreases

C. water pressure remains the same

D. water pressure is inversely proportional to his depth

Improved

The volume of air in the scuba diver's lungs increases as he rises from the bottom of the lake because the:

A. water pressure decreases

B. water pressure increases

C. density of the air in his lungs increases

D. volume of air in the scuba diver's lungs remains constant as he rises

In the first example, "D" is automatically excluded because "A", "B" and "C" cover the entire range, giving the learner now only three options from which to choose, rather than the original four. In the improved example all four responses are possible alternatives and the learner now can rely only on his or her knowledge of Boyle's Law to evaluate each response in light of the stated conditions and to select the one that best completes the stem of the item.

8. *Limit the use of* all of the above, none of the above *as responses.* When used sparingly, these two phrases can add to the overall value of the related information test. However, when the two responses are used extensively and without discretion, they tend to dilute the potency of the test. Too often they are used when the test writer cannot think of a fourth or fifth response to the stem. When used appropriately and with purpose, however, they can be used to collect information that pertains to the central idea of the item and evaluate the learner's knowledge of several areas at one time. An example of the use of the two phrases as responses to multiple-choice items appears below.

Which of the following are row crops?

A. swamp rice

B. alfalfa hay

C. sugar cane

D. none of the above

Which of the following makes of automobiles are manufactured in Germany?

A. Porsche

B. Volkswagen

C. Mercedes Benz

D. All of the above

Scoring. For purposes of economy and ease of grading it is suggested that the learner respond on a separate answer sheet. In most cases, one point is given per correct response. Like that of the true–false item, the quality of the multiple-choice item is quickly and easily determined in an item analysis. In an analysis the test writer can easily estimate the individual items as discriminators of the learner's knowledge of the information being tested.

Completion Items

Another type of test often included in a related information test is the completion, short-answer, recall, or supply-type item. In its most common form, the completion item is a statement in which one or two of the words are missing and are supplied by the learner. An example of a typical completion item and directions for its completion appear below.

> Complete the following items by writing in the appropriate response. Again, write your responses on the answer sheet that accompanies the test and NOT on this questionnaire. One point is earned for each correct response.
>
> 1. The glass portion of spark plug is called the _____ .

The completion item is similar to the essay item and to true–false and multiple-choice items. Like the essay, the completion item requires the learner to recall the information being sought and write it in the space provided. He or she is not given a single statement or series of responses to aid him or her in recognizing the answer, but, rather, must possess the knowledge to respond correctly. The completion item is like the true-false and multiple-choice item because, if it is carefully written, it will elicit a single, definite response which can be evaluated objectively from the learner. One of the problems with this type of item, discussed later, is the difficulty of stating items that have only a single correct response.

Because completion-type items can be constructed to test a wide range of material, are usually compact and space-saving, and can be evaluated quickly, they are appreciated by test writers. However, because of their intrinsic nature, they are less useful in measuring more abstract types of learning, — concept and principle learning, analyzing, synthesizing — and hence are used predominately to measure a learner's ability to recall certain points of information. As mentioned earlier, a major problem encountered in writing completion-type test items is to write them so that they elicit a single, specific response. It is always surprising to the person evaluating a series of completion items to find a number of responses which differ altogether from the intended one but yet might be correct. If this occurs occasionally, the individual items can be rewritten and improved. However, the reliability and quality of a test fraught with such items are considerably reduced. Great care should be taken to avoid writing items which can have more than one correct response.

Suggestions for Writing Completion Items. The following list of suggestions will assist and guide you in preparing completion-type test items for the related information test.

1. *Write the item in a concise manner and in a way that elicits the intended word(s) or phrase from the learner.* As in writing true–false and multiple-choice items, care should be taken to state the completion-type statement in such a way that it calls for a specific and concise response. The item should not be loosely worded nor ambiguous, but should clearly specify the word or phrase that completes the item in the desired manner. The reliability of the item is significantly reduced when the learner can misinterpret the meaning of the statement or evade the intended response with an alternative that works but is not the one being sought. An example appears below.

   A St. Bernard is a _____ dog.

   Because of the way in which the statement is phrased, a number of technically correct responses are possible. But, because the writer was looking for a more specific response, they would be considered incorrect. The intended answer has to do with the type of predominant activity for which the dog was bred, "work" or "rescue", but such responses as "large", "friendly", "long-haired", "outdoor", are also possible answers.

2. *Limit the number of responses for any one item to one or two.* At times, a potential completion-type test item contains a number of key words that are specific, concise terms and, therefore, potentially good recall responses. However, because there is a direct relationship between the number of blanks included in an item and the number of alternatives and combinations of responses that can be made, it is suggested that only one, and no more than two responses, be required for completion of any one test item. If a given item requires three, four, five, or more responses for completion, the difficulties faced increase. The result of deleting too many key words from the original statement is that its very essence and meaning are lost. Asking someone to reconstruct the statement goes beyond the scope and purpose of the information test.

   An example in which a number of the key words have been removed appears below. The difficulties in completing the item are more than apparent.

As the ___(voltage)___ in the ___(battery)___ is reduced, a signal is sent to the ___(voltage regulator)___ which, in turn, reacts and routes ___(current)___ being produced by the ___(generator)___ back to the ___(battery)___ to replenish it.

Another practice to be discouraged is placing the blanks to be completed throughout the test item. Preferably, the blanks should appear near the end of the statement. The statement, ideally, should be ordered so that the learner has as much of the essential information as possible before he or she is expected to recall the missing word or phrase.

3. *Avoid giving the learner clues to the desired response.* In any type of written test item, the rules of grammar can provide the learner with clues to the response. An immediate example involves the articles "a" and "an".

The elevated platform from which a painter works is called a

_____ .

In the example, the learner could, by elimination, exclude those alternatives that begin with a vowel. Admittedly, this does not provide the answer, but it does assist in arriving at it with knowledge other than that being tested. Solutions to the problem are to rewrite the statement or add the following insert:

The elevated platform from which a painter works is called a(an)

_____ .

Another type of clue involves the length of the blanks themselves. Subconsciously, test writers will sometimes adjust the length of the line to conform to the approximate physical length of the response being sought. A line only symbolically represents the portion of the statement that is excluded and does not, nor is it intended to, physically accommodate the omitted portion of the test statement.

On the other hand, the number of blanks included in a completion test item should equal the number of responses being sought. The blanks should also be arranged so that the correct response is grammatically correct. See the following example.

The major function of the carburetor is to mix ___(fuel)___ and ___(air)___ .

If the statement requires a compound response, then the ordering and appearance of the blanks should also reflect that condition.

The gas produced during photosynthesis is _____ _____ .

4. *In general, restrict the use of completion items to measuring recall knowledge.* The underlying premise of the completion item is that the learner must remember or recall the information being sought and respond in writing. No written clues or stimuli, other than the text of statement being responded to, are present to assist the learner in choosing a response.

5. *Avoid using as the completion statement statements taken verbatim from textbooks or other written sources.* A temptation that the test writer faces in preparing the completion portion of the related information test is to use sentences or phrases directly from a text. Occasionally this practice might be acceptable, but its widespread use encourages learners to search out and commit to memory those portions of the material that they think will appear on the test, rather than reading the material for content and interpretation.

6. *When used in situations where there are quantifiable answers, the degree to which the learner should respond should be specified.* Often, completion items are used in testing situations where the learner is expected to provide a quantitative response to a given statement. In such situations, the test writer should specify the degree of accuracy required. For instance, in the item presented below, the apprentice interior decorator is asked to compute the number of square feet, correct to two decimal places, of wall space in a room.

> A rectangular room is 8' high, 18.5' long and 12.8' wide. It has two door openings that each measure 3' $\times$ 6.5' and one picture window opening that measures 4' $\times$ 8'. The wall area of the room, correct to two decimal places, equals _____ square feet.

The degree to which the learner is expected to respond is made known, and any answer that does not carry the decimal to the requested two places would have to be counted as incorrect. A person who computed an answer beyond the two place figure, providing it was correct, would receive credit for the correct answer, but not for the unnecessary work.

It is easy for the instructor to overlook the process or procedure that the learner goes through to arrive at a particular answer. The final answer is important, but an incorrect final response might be the result of a mechanical error not of improper process. If the learner's worksheet is requested along with the examination answer sheet and reviewed as a part of the total evaluation then the difficulty is avoided. The practice of evaluating only the single, correct answer should be questioned.

Scoring. To score a completion type item, one point is awarded per correct response. If, for instance, a particular item requires a single word to complete it, one point is earned by the learner for the proper response.

Similarly, if two blanks appear in an item and both responses are correct, a total of two points is awarded.

Matching Items

Another style of test item that can be used in a related information test is the matching-type item. Comprised of two columns of words or phrases, the individual entries in the right-hand column, referred to as *responses*, are matched to the individual entries in the left-hand column, referred to as *premises*. See the following example.

> The two columns below contain the names of automobiles in the left-hand column and the nationalities of various automobile manufacturers in the right-hand column. To complete the item, read the name of the first automobile in the left column and select the nationality of its manufacturer from the right column. Enter the letter for the response you selected in the space provided at the left of the items in the left-hand column. Repeat the process until all of the blanks on the answer sheet are complete. One point is earned for each correct response.
>
> | *Column A* | | *Column B* | |
> |---|---|---|---|
> | (e) | 1. Mercedes Benz | a. | American |
> | ——— | 2. Saab | b. | Canadian |
> | ——— | 3. Toyota | c. | English |
> | ——— | 4. Renault | d. | French |
> | ——— | 5. BMW | e. | German |
> | ——— | 6. Ford | f. | Japanese |
> | ——— | 7. Bricklin | g. | Swedish |

To complete the item, the individual premises are read, the list of potential responses reviewed, the one that best matches the given premise selected, and its letter entered in the space provided to the left of the premise. The process is then repeated until each premise has a response.

The matching type of exercise provides the evaluator with a tried and true way of testing a learner's ability to associate various terms, statements, phrases, definitions, etc. that relate to one another. The item should include no more than ten premises and an equal or greater number of responses. If the list of premises increases much beyond ten, the number of associations the learner will be required to make reaches proportions that can overwhelm him or her and have a marked effect on the validity of the test item. An increased number of premises and responses also puts a burden on the test writer, because, for the matching exercise to be at its best, a certain degree of plausibility must exist between each premise and response. Increasing the numbers of each entry proportionately reduces chances of maintaining the needed relationships among the various entries in the item.

Other advantages associated with the matching exercise are that the learner can usually complete the matching item in a brief period of time, his or her responses can be scored quickly and objectively, and, because of its physical design and suggested limits on number of entries, it is a space-saving type of test item. Also, because all of the responses in a well-designed matching item are plausible alternatives to each of the premises, there is less motivation for the learner to guess and, in turn, reduce the reliability of the item.

Weaknesses associated with the matching item include its limited use in measuring the more complex forms of cognitive learning, a tendency for the test writer to include unimportant information in the item in order to maintain its validity, and, because of this inherent characteristic, encourage less than desirable learner study habits by promoting memorization and rote learning.

The first two weaknesses result from the need to maintain the validity of the item as a part of the related information test. By restricting the use of premise and response statements to those which have plausible relationships to one another, the higher levels of cognitive learning cannot be tested satisfactorily in most cases. The difficulties encountered when writing entries for a matching item that measure the higher levels of knowledge too often outweigh the advantages, and other types of testing items and procedures have to be used. Also, the need for a plausible relationship to exist among all entries can promote the use of unimportant or less-than-important material in the item.

The last characteristic of the matching item that detracts from its overall desirability is its effect on the individual's learning practices. If the matching type of test item is used extensively, it promotes memorization of a number of isolated facts, rather than encouraging the learner to grasp the entire or more generalizable meaning of the information being presented. To use the matching test item purposefully to elicit necessary memorized facts would be considered an appropriate application of the item, but to use it indiscriminately without knowledge of its effects on the study practices of the learner, would be to defeat a major tenet of occupational preparation, — the application and incorporation of knowledge to performance.

Suggestions for Writing Matching Items. The preparation of matching items, like that of each of the other types of test items, can be improved if certain considerations are made at the time of writing. Some of the suggestions listed below pertain only to preparing matching items, others also apply to each of the previously discussed items.

1. *Each of the responses in the matching item should be a plausible alternative to each of the premise statements.* In writing a matching test item, care should be taken to select only those responses that are logical and potential answers to *each* of the premise statements. If the responses do not have a plausible relationship to *each*

of the various premises, the validity and worth of the item will be diminished, because the learner will be able to respond correctly to the various premise stimuli from a basis other than the needed information. By design, the responses serve as distractors from the correct response and, in this way, help determine who has and does not have the required knowledge.

2. *Limit the list of premise and response statements.* The number of premise and response statements, as mentioned earlier in this section, should be restricted to approximately ten.

   A longer list of entries reduces the effectiveness and validity of the item. If the list is too long, the learner is required to make an unreasonable number of associations. For example, a learner confronted with a matching item containing twenty premise statements and twenty responses must make approximately 400 comparisons before completing the item.

   Another reason that has already been mentioned for restricting the matching test item to a workable length is that the chances of retaining the desired plausible relationship between the premises and responses are greater.

   The last point that has to do with the number of entries in a matching test item concerns the number of *responses* in the item compared to the number of premise statements. Teachers and test writers will, at times, include more responses than premises in an item. This restricts the effects of guessing on the part of the learner. As the learner nears the end of a paired list, his or her choices can be made more on elimination than on actual knowledge. To offset this, the test writer has only to introduce two, three, or four more alternative responses to the list and the learner is again back to relying more on knowledge of the material than other factors.

3. *Arrange the premise statements and responses in a logical and easily read order.* Matching test items can usually be completed in a relatively short period of time and without a lot of procedural difficulty, but they can be constructed in such a way that the learner will encounter unnecessary and time consuming obstacles. The longer, more complex statements should appear as premises and the shorter, briefer phrases posed as responses so that the learner does not have to waste time rereading long sentences for each response.

   Other potential problem areas are the listing of dates or numbers and names. Dates and other lists of numbers are best presented in either an ascending or descending order, and the names of people, places, or things that are inherently related might best be arranged alphabetically. Ordering in this manner also randomizes the responses and increases the reliability of the item and overall quality of the related information test.

4. *Avoid providing clues.* As was mentioned for each of the previously discussed test items, care should be taken in writing matching test items not to provide the learner with clues to the correct response. For example, if the premise reads "French scientist"

and the only French name listed in the series of responses is "Louis Pasteur," then regardless of whether the learner knows the answer, he or she can, with the clue, select the proper response. In instances where clues exist, the validity of the item as a good indicator of the learner's knowledge of the topic is significantly reduced.

Scoring. While individual teachers may have their own particular way of grading the matching test item or of assigning points, one point is typically awarded for each correct response selected by the learner. Hence, if a matching test item had ten entries and the learner responded to eight of the premises correctly, he or she would be awarded a total of eight points for the complete item.

Essay Items

The essay item is an integral and important part of the related information test. It is designed to elicit responses that directly reflect the learner's knowledge of a selected topic and require him or her to organize and present his or her thoughts on the matter in narrative style. Unlike the four previously discussed objective test items, the essay design requires the learner to respond to questions and problems directly without the benefit of other plausible alternatives to compare, examine, weigh, and select. The open-ended nature of the essay item allows types of learning appearing higher on the cognitive taxonomy can be better and more thoroughly tested and evaluated.

The single and most obvious problem associated with the essay item is reliability. The question or problematic situation should be presented so that the boundaries or limits within which the learner is to respond are established and the key points to be included in a correct response are listed. However, even if these conditions are met, the evaluator still must resort to subjective evaluation. The evaluator must decide whether the learner's response falls short of the established limits of the question and whether the key points have been fully discussed and the issue fully and completely dealt with. Too often with this type of item, such things as the evaluator's knowledge of the learner, and time of day (or night), etc. influence the evaluator's judgment and are reflected in the learner's final score.

Another problem inherent to the essay-type test, and one which affects its reliability, is that it provides only a limited sampling of the learner's knowledge. Because of the proportionately longer period of time required to complete an essay item, and the limited amount of time of the classroom testing period, only a portion of the information that the learner might be expected to know can be tested. The learner who does well in the essay test can only be assumed to have mastered the knowledge emphasized on the test. And, the learner who does poorly on the test, can only be assumed not to possess that information. Statements made about the learners' knowledge beyond the scope of the test, can, at best, be only generalizations. The learner who did well might have little or no knowledge of the other material. Likewise, the learner who, initially, did not fare well, might be very knowledgeable of other information.

From an educator's point of view, one of the major strengths of the essay test is that it encourages the learner to take more of an overall view of the material to be learned and to emphasize concepts, principles, and relationships of things and events. It definitely does not foster the memorization of isolated events and facts. Also, the essay item encourages the learner to express thoughts and ideas and to organize and incorporate them into a meaningful product.

The weaknesses of the essay item are its subjectivity in scoring, long periods of teacher time involved in evaluation and, as mentioned earlier, its limited ability to sample a wide range of information due to the time constraints inherent in the administration of the test.

Suggestions for Writing Essay Items. Following are several suggestions to assist in writing essay questions and situational problems.

1. *The question or situational problem to which the learner must respond should be stated in a specific and concise manner.* When preparing essay items, state the central question or situational problem to which you want the learner to respond clearly and precisely. If the learner is unsure what is expected of him or her, or is otherwise confused as to the nature, direction, scope, and intent of the item, his or her response will probably be marked by a lack of a central theme and stated in general and superficial terms. The essay item, by definition, does not seek one or two word responses, nor the repeating back of facts and isolated events. Rather, it is designed to elicit from the learner an in-depth response to a specific question or problem that shows substance and a knowledge of the key points and issues related to a specific topic.

   Consider the following example.

   Poor

   Discuss the four most commonly used computer program languages.

   Improved

   Discuss the purpose, intended applications, and limitations of the COBOL computer program language.

In the first example, the author has established no parameters or boundaries in which the learner can function and the learner may be confused as to exactly what should be included in his or her response. In contrast, the improved example specifies exactly what the learner should do and the parameters within which the response should fall. Providing he or she has the knowledge, the item causes no confusion on the part of the learner as to what is expected in response.

Test writers sometimes set the central idea of the item in a prefatory statement that describes a particular situation and influences the learner's response. See the example presented below.

> You are the first person to arrive at the scene of a two-car automobile accident. It is night and is raining; and the traffic, while light, is travelling at an average rate of 30–40 mph. List the things that you would do to aid those involved in the accident and discuss the reasons why you ordered the activities as you did.

While this is an excellent technique in writing essay-type items, care should be taken not to obscure the central activity expected of the learner.

Another point that relates to this suggestion is that the test item should be designed to elicit only one response from the learner. If the learner is confronted with having to choose between two, or three, or more right answers or, worse yet, to give all of them, he or she can quickly become confused and respond poorly to the item. Certainly, the learner can be expected to "discuss," "compare," "contrast," "differentiate," etc. topics. However, if he or she is required to perform one or more of these activities with several different concepts within the same item, the response will almost surely be of a lower quality than if only a single issue was dealt with.

2. *Use the essay item in situations where the objective-type items are not applicable.* The essay item is designed to measure knowledge as it applies to a comparison of events, conceptual learning, analysis, synthesis, etc. A common misuse of the item is in situations where objective-type items, true–false, multiple-choice, completion, and matching, are more applicable to the situation and perform in a more efficient and effective manner. The essay design should not be used to simply retrieve information that the learner possesses, but rather to apply the knowledge to a question or a specific problem.

In the following examples, the first does not call for any application of knowledge on the part of the learner, but simply has him or her recall the function of the compressor in a refrigeration system. A multiple-choice item would be more appropriate to the situation.

Poor

What is the function of the compressor in a cooling system?

Improved

Discuss the function of the compressor in a cooling system and its relationship to the other system components.

The improved statement requires the learner to use his or her knowledge of the cooling system as a whole and apply it in discussing the compressor, its function, and its relationship to the other components that comprise the total system.

3. *Allow a suitable amount of time for responding to the items.* Because the essay-type item requires the learner to develop and organize his or her thoughts about a particular question or problem and then record these thoughts in writing, significantly more time is required to complete an essay item than is required to complete objective items. While there is no specific formula for determining the exact amount of time required by the learner to complete a given item, an *approximate* time can be determined by multiplying the length of time it takes the text writer or teacher to write the answer by a factor of two or three. The multiplication selected depends a great deal on the nature and complexity of the particular item.

   This is only a suggested way of estimating the time requirement for a test item. Additional experience in writing and administering essay tests will be of the greatest benefit in determining the actual times required for completing individual essay items.

4. *It is preferable to use more short-response essay items than fewer long-response items.* As mentioned earlier, one of the disadvantages of an individual essay item is that it samples a narrow range of information. By design, it is most effective when it addresses a single topic and prompts the learner to respond to that topic. Therefore, to help offset its limited sampling characteristic, it is preferable to design the essay portion of the related information test so that it is made up of more short-response items rather than fewer long-response items. This will permit a wider sampling of information, reduce the complexity of the individual items, increase the reliability of the test and improve the process of reading and evaluating the individual items.

5. *The scope of the learner's response and the amount of detail to be included should be stated in the item.* Unless it is the intended purpose of the test item to determine a learner's ability to establish the parameters of a given topic and discuss in depth the details of the issue, the scope within which the learner should respond and the detail of the response should be specified in the essay statement. An example of an essay item in which the parameters and amount of detail are not specified, but should be, follows:

   Discuss the effects that the passage of a national health insurance act would have on health delivery agencies.

   In this example, the test writer could have specified the scope and amount of detail to be included in the response. Rather than requesting a discussion of all of the effects of the passage of such an act, the item could have directed the learner to discuss only two or three of them. Likewise, the item would have been further improved had it more specifically instructed the learner to discuss the results of such legislation on the "subsequent growth and quality of health manpower."

Another consideration in establishing the limits of the essay item is the selection of verbs used to introduce the statement and define the activity to be performed. Once the scope of the item is determined and the key points to be included are listed, the test writer should then select the verbs which best instruct the learner in answering the question or responding to the situational problem. Particular care must be taken to use verbs that will guide the learner in responding in the desired way. If the verb instructs the learner to list, then what should be expected is a listing of particular activities, events, items, etc. If the statement is such that the learner is instructed to "Identify and discuss two ways in which," then the response that can be rightly expected would include identification of two particular topics and a discussion of each.

Scoring.   The evaluation and scoring of essay questions or situational problems is subjective in nature and requires the evaluator to judge the quality of the learner's response. This subjectivity can and does cause problems, at times, in terms of reliability, but certain precautions can be taken at the time the test item is first written to dampen the effect of subjectivity and reduced reliability. As mentioned earlier, care should be taken initially to write specific and concise test statements and to establish the limits and amount of detail of the response. In conjunction with this, and affecting the scoring of the item, is the practice of establishing, for purposes of evaluation, a list of key points that should be included in the response. The listing of key points establishes a standard against which the essay item is evaluated and guides the evaluator in judging the learner's response.

Once the standard is established, the next step is to devise a system for assigning a numerical value to the test item as a whole and to its individual key points. However, because of the varying nature of each essay item, the person doing the evaluating will have to determine exactly the total number of points a given item is worth, and how the sum can be divided and assigned to the various key elements in the response. The more complete and thorough a response is, the greater the number of points it will earn. And, in those cases where only some of the key elements have been included in the response, proportionately fewer points will be earned on the item.

Answer Sheet.   For economy of time in reproduction and scoring and in the use of materials, it is suggested that an answer sheet be developed to be used by the learner during the administration of the related information test. An answer sheet is the sheet on which the learner responds to all of the questions and situational problems posed on the test. A sample answer sheet appears in Example 20.2.

The answer sheet is tailored to the related information test for which it is written. The organization and numbering of the various items on the sheet correspond exactly to those on the information test. The spaces in which the various responses are made are grouped and ordered as they appear in the test and labelled accordingly, e.g. true–false, multiple-choice, completion, etc. With the sheet arranged in this manner, the learner, as he or she progresses through the test, will also make orderly progress on the answer sheet.

Example 20.2

Name _____

Test Number _____

Answer Sheet

Learning Objective #11 — Selling Domestic Traveler's Checks

Objective Test Items

True–False	*Matching*
T F	_____ 10.
1. 0 0	_____ 11.
T F	_____ 12.
2. 0 0	_____ 13.
T F	_____ 14.
3. 0 0	

Multiple Choice

A B C D
4. 0 0 0 0
A B C D
5. 0 0 0 0
A B C D
6. 0 0 0 0

Completion

7. _____ _____
8. _____
9. _____ _____

Example 20.2   continued

Essay Items

15. Define the term *stale-dated* and explain why it is or is not important when dealing with traveler's checks.

16. What is the basic reason for having the customer initially sign each of the *loose-style* traveler's checks in the presence of the teller?

In the example, provisions are made for the name of the learner and the number of the test. The learning objective for which the related information test and answer sheet are written is also included. In the example, spaces for responses to true–false, multiple-choice, completion, matching, and essay-type items are included.

Another advantage of an answer sheet is that it can be easily made into an answer key for evaluating objective items. To make an answer key, the correct responses are first indicated for each item, and then punched out with a paper punch. The perforated key is then superimposed over the learner's answer sheet and his or her mistakes indicated. The key rapidly speeds up the scoring process of objective items and reduces the chances of making scoring errors to almost zero.

In Review

1. The related information test, as it is used in the learning activities package, is intended to measure what type of behavior?

2. Discuss how the related information test, as one of the learning activities in a given learning package, loses some of the negative connotations associated with the traditional pencil-paper test. (Clue: means rather than end.)

3. What is the rationale for locating the related information test in the position it occupies in the sequence of learning activities?

4. Define each of the following terms as they pertain to test writing: validity, reliability, objectivity, comprehensive, discriminating.

5. In most situations, discriminating between learners is a positive characteristic of a test. Discuss why this is not true when the test is used in an individualized learning situation.

CHAPTER 21

Preparing a Demonstration Outline

The demonstration is a technique used by the instructor to show and explain to the learner the procedure for performing a learning objective. Preceded by the various reading and written assignments, illustrated presentation, other knowledge-related learning activities considered relevant and appropriate, and the related information test, the demonstration is the first in the series of *performance-related* learning activities in the completed learning activities package.

The demonstration is the first opportunity for the learner to witness an actual performance of the learning objective and the application of the concepts and principles discussed in the preceding knowledge-related learning activities to the process. During the demonstration, the learner sees the information he or she has acquired directing, regulating, and influencing the performance of the objective and of its individual performance steps. From the demonstration, he or she gains a better knowledge of how each performance step is done, how the equipment, materials and supplies, if any, are incorporated into the procedure, and how information and values control and influence performance.

The demonstration of the learning objective and its subsequent steps is followed by the learner's practice of the activity and the final performance test. Other performance-related learning activities may or may not be included in the series, depending on the intentions of the instructor and the particular learning objective being sought.

Characteristics of the Demonstration

In some respects, the demonstration might be considered one of the most important activities that the learner completes as he or she works toward attaining the learning objective. Some characteristics of the demonstration that establish its value as a learning activity follow.

Focuses the Attention of the Learner. The demonstration immediately focuses the attention of the learner on the learning objective being performed. It points up the various performance steps that comprise the activity, the sequence in which they are performed, and the standards that are met as each step is completed. Another important contribution of a properly conducted demonstration is that it makes the learner very much aware of the need for technical information and judgment-making ability, and the relationships that exist between them and performance.

Efficient and Effective Way of Presenting Material. As stated earlier, the demonstration also deals with the procedural steps that the learner will later perform as he or she practises performing the objective and tests his or her mastery of them in a final performance situation. If done well, the demonstration shows the individual how to perform the various steps of the learning objective in an efficient and effective manner and in the prescribed sequence. It assists him or her in forming habits and developing skills that contribute to the successful completion of the objective. In addition, the demonstration reduces the time required for learning to perform the activity by showing exactly what has to be done. Time and effort spent in trial and error learning is reduced significantly if not altogether eliminated.

Encourages Safe Performance. Another desirable characteristic of the demonstration, is its effectiveness in promoting safe practices in performance of the objective. In those activities where a certain amount of danger exists, the demonstration alerts the learner to the potential problem and, in turn, reduces the possibility of its occurrence.

Complements the Other Learning Activities. The demonstration is an integral part of a systematic sequence of learning events. It is preceded by a number of knowledge-related learning activities that provide the individual with the information needed to perform the learning objective and is followed by those activities which guide him or her in its practice, and by a measure of final performance. Of singular importance, the demonstration is the first activity in the sequence in which the learner witnesses the synthesis of cognitive, affective, and psychomotor behavior. Here, he or she views for the first time the application of knowledge, regulatory affects of judgment and decisionmaking, and actual performance of the activity as a unified whole. It is because of this synthesizing characteristic that the demonstration, in one form or another, is considered absolutely essential to attainment of the learning objective.

The Demonstration in the Learning Activities Package

Most demonstrations in an occupational learning situation are readily adaptable to a form other than a live presentation. And, because one of the intended purposes of this Handbook is to guide the reader in developing individualized learning materials, the demonstration, like all of the heretofore discussed learning activities, is best suited to the learning activities package as a narrated filmstrip or slide series, videotape, or as an illustrated task procedure sheet.

By definition, the medium selected for recording the demonstration must be visual, but the exact form, videotape, pictures, etc., is dictated by the nature of the learning objective for which the demonstration is developed. If the actual movements of the demonstrator are important in themselves to the successful performance of the objective, a medium such as videotape or motion pictures should be used in recording the activity. In contrast, if the motions of the individual are universal in nature and do not have specific bearing on the outcome of the act, then filmstrips, slides, illustrations or other media where motion is not needed would be appropriate.

Planning the Demonstration

In most respects, planning a demonstration that is going to be presented as a written guide or recorded on film or videotape is almost the same as planning a demonstration that is going to be presented live. With exception of providing for the actual writing of a task procedure sheet or filming of the activity, making a recorded demonstration requires performing the same procedural steps to the same level of competence as does the production of its live counterpart.

The basic steps in planning the demonstration are listed, as they are for preparing all of the learning materials found in a learning activities package, on the *Learning Activities Development Sheet* discussed in Chapter 18. For purposes of review, however, the sequence of developmental steps is discussed here in greater detail.

Initially, the planner should review the *task detailing sheet* written for the task from which the learning objective was derived. The worksheet provides the individual preparing the demonstration with the sequence of performance steps of the objective, and the standards of performance statements for each step in the process.* With this basic data, the instructor planning the demonstration will know the procedural content and the criteria of performance.

With the task detailing sheet as reference, the instructor can now prepare the *Demonstration Outline and Practice Supervision Guide.* Dis-

---

*The *task detailing sheet* also contains technical occupational information topics from which the technical information questions that accompany each step are formulated. The development of the questions and their role will be discussed in the last section in the chapter.

cussed in detail in the last section of the chapter, the instrument, when used for purposes of demonstration, is an outline of the steps to be performed by the instructor as he or she demonstrates the learning objective. The outline serves as a guide as he or she walks through the demonstration and prepares for the actual recording of the activity.

With the outline now in hand, the site selected for giving the demonstration, the equipment, materials, and supplies arranged and accessible, and the necessary steps taken for filming or taping, the demonstration is ready for recording and eventual inclusion in the learning activities package.

The Demonstration Outline and Practice Supervision Guide

The *Demonstration Outline and Practice Supervision Guide*, is an instrument used by the instructor in each of two different learning activities. First, as mentioned earlier, it is used in its outline form as a guide in preparing the recorded demonstration for use in the learning activities package. Secondly, it is used by the instructor as a guide in supervising the practice session(s) of the learner and as a resource in testing his or her knowledge of the technical information as it applies to performance. An abbreviated example of the outline and guide appears in Example 21.1.

Example 21.1
Demonstration Outline
and Practice Supervision Guide

Learning Objective #11 — Selling Domestic Traveler's Checks

Equipment and Supplies

The following items are needed to complete the task:

- calculating machine
- money supply
- supply of assorted denominations of traveler's checks
- purchase application forms
- assortment of wallets

Procedure

Performance Steps	Standards of Performance
1. *Greet the customer*	The greeting is made in a friendly, courteous manner and includes the teller's offer of assistance. If the teller knows the customer's name, that should also be included in the greeting.

Example 21.1   continued

- What are some appropriate alternative greetings?
- Discuss a "business-like" and "personal" type greeting and why one or the other might be preferred.
-
-

2. *Take the customer's order*   The order is noted in writing and in terms of total dollar amount of checks desired and denomination(s).

- Why is an oral confirmation of the order necessary?
- What is the benefit of writing a note of the order?
-
-

Performance Steps   *Standards of Performance*

7. *Offer instruction on cashing the traveler's checks*   The customer is asked whether he or she has had previous experience in using traveler's checks and, if not, would he or she like some suggestions regarding their use. If instruction is requested, he or she is told the procedure of cashing the checks and keeping record of the transactions on the purchase application(s). The suggestion is also made as to the need to keep the application(s) and checks in different places. This practice is done to facilitate making a claim if the checks are lost or stolen.

- From a "customer service" point of view, why is this an important step?
- Why is it important that the traveler's checks and copies of the purchase applications be kept in separate places by the customer?
-
-

8. *Thank the customer*   The customer is thanked, wished a pleasant journey and invited back to the bank on his or her return.

- What is the psychology behind making the customer feel good as he or she leaves?
-
-

9. *Complete the sales transaction*   The cash or personal check received from the customer is attached to the original copy of the purchase application with a paper clip. It is then placed in the appropriate drawer to await final check out and settlement at the end of the business day.

- If, after the customer leaves, you find there is a difference between the total amount of money collected and the total indicated on the purchase application, what do you do?

·

References

1. "Training Manual for Tellers." Personnel Training Unit. The Fidelity Bank of Carbondale.

Taken primarily from the task detailing sheet developed during the analysis of the occupation, the contents of the outline/guide include the title of the sheet itself, the number and title of the learning objective for which it is written, a list of needed equipment and supplies, the procedural steps and standards of performance statements, and the list of references. A brief description of each entry follows.

The title of the sheet reflects both situations in which the sheet is used. In its first role it is an outline of the activity to be demonstrated, whereas, during the practice session, it is the instructor's guide to supervising the learner's performance and evaluating his or her technical knowledge. The number and title of the learning objective corresponds exactly to that of the learning activities package of which it is a part. The list of equipment and supplies itemizes those tools needed to perform the objective, and is a replication of the tools, materials, etc. found in the equipment, materials, and supplies portion of the "Performance Conditions" statement of the learning objective.

The performance steps and standards of performance, respectively, lead to attainment of the learning objective and establish the performance criteria of each step. The series of questions that accompany each performance step is used by the instructor to orally test the learner's knowledge of the technical information as it relates to the steps being performed. The questions are intended to be asked at the time the learner is practising the objective. As shown in the example, additional spaces are provided for other questions that the instructor might want to ask. This would make the form more flexible and adaptable to the individual learning situation.

Lastly, the references included in the outline/guide are the list of sources that are related to the objective being performed and provide additional information and insight to the person wanting to know more about the activity.

In Review

1. Discuss the rationale for having the knowledge-related learning activities appear before the performance-related learning activities in attaining a learning objective.

2. What role does the demonstration fulfill in attaining a particular learning objective?

3. The simplest ordering of performance-related learning activities is as follows: demonstration, practice session, and final performance test. What is the rationale for having the demonstration be the first activity?

4. Discuss the characteristics of a good demonstration and how they benefit the learner.

5. From which worksheet developed during the occupational data gathering process (Part Two, Section I) is most of the data for the demonstration obtained?

6. Discuss the purpose and benefits of the Demonstration Outline and Practice Supervision Guide.

CHAPTER 22

Preparing a Practice
Supervision Guide

The learning activity that follows the demonstration is practice of the demonstrated skill. The goal toward which the learner works is mastery of performance of the learning objective under the conditions specified in the objective statement and to the level of attainment stated in the evaluation criteria. Also, as the learner practises performing the objective, he or she integrates and applies the information gained from the knowledge-related learning activities to the activity. In sum, the practice is the first time in the sequence of learning activities that the learner has the opportunity to apply knowledge to performance and synthesize them into a total event.

Overtly, mastery of the objective appears to be the sole purpose of the three *performance-related* learning activities — the demonstration, practice, and performance test. However, while mastery of the steps and overall ability to perform the objective are important and contribute, in part, to successful performance in the occupation, they are only the observable portion of the total activity and should not be emphasized to a degree that diminishes or excludes development of other equally important, but less observable, abilities. During the demonstration and practice of an objective, the learner acquires skill in both the application of knowledge to performance and in forming judgments that regulate and influence performance direction and product. Both abilities are as crucial to the performance of the activity as is the completion of the steps that comprise it, and all three, occupational skill, applied knowledge, and judgment-forming ability, must be computed into the final outcome if total success is to be measured.

Instructor's Role in the Practice Session

Up until this time, the learner has been the only person directly involved in the series of learning activities in the learning activities package. Now, however, because of the nature of the activity and the need for outside supervision and comment, the instructor becomes involved in assisting the learner in attaining the learning objective. His or her major responsibility is to provide direction and perspective to the learner as the learner practises performing the objective and to assist him or her in preparing to successfully complete the performance test. The instructor also keeps records of the learner's progress in terms of his or her performance of the various steps and ability to answer impromptu questions pertinent to his or her performance.

As implied earlier, practice in performing an objective basically entails three events: developing skills required to perform the objective, applying the technical knowledge that has been acquired to performance, and learning to form judgments and make decisions that concern, direct, affect, and determine the outcome of the objective. The instructor is involved in each event as it relates to practice.

In an occupational education/training setting, the typical instructor is a recognized practitioner in the occupation he or she is teaching. Because of work experience in the occupation, mastery of the needed skills, and competence in teaching and supervision, he or she is well equipped to guide a learner in the practice and attainment of occupationally related learning objectives. He or she reviews technique and adds dimension to the previously viewed demonstration. Also, if new techniques or procedural steps are developed, he or she guides the learner in performing the new techniques and incorporating them into the procedure being performed.

The instructor also assists the learner in applying the technical information he or she has acquired to performance of the objective. By posing questions and other situational problems at the time of practice, he or she can quiz the learner orally on various matters of procedure, test his or her knowledge as it relates to particular situations and occurrences, and discuss alternative solutions to various other related problems. The list of possibilities varies depending on the learning objective, the number of performance steps, and the overall complexity of the activity.

Lastly, assisting the learner in making judgments about the outcome of his or her effort is another role that the instructor plays in supervising the practice session. An extension of the application of knowledge to performance, it is crucial that the learner becomes adept at making correct and accurate decisions about his or her performance at opportune times. The instructor, because of his or her experience in the occupation, is able to foresee difficulties that might arise and outcomes that would not be desirable. Once these are detected, the instructor is able to prompt the learner, make him or her aware of the situation, and assist him or her in deciding what to do or not to do to prevent or avoid the difficulty.

The Demonstration Outline and Practice Supervision Guide

The *Demonstration Outline and Practice Supervision Guide*, as it appears and is discussed in the preceding chapter, is also used by the instructor as a guide and key to supervising the learner's practice of an objective. A complete entry, taken from the example presented in the previous chapter, appears below.

Performance Steps	*Standards of Performance*
Have the customer complete his or her portion of the purchase application.	The customer's signature and printed name and address appear in the appropriate section of the purchase application.

- Why are both the customer's printed name and signature needed?
- Why is it important that the customer press firmly on the pen when he is filling out the application form?
-
-
-

The performance steps and standards of performance, respectively, are the sequence of steps that lead to completion of the learning objective, and the criteria statements which define when the individual steps have been properly performed. The series of technically related questions that are also a part of each entry on the outline/guide, but used only during the practice session, are questions that the instructor asks the learner as he or she practises the activity. Based on the portion of the "Evaluation Criteria" statement that refers to the learner being able to explain his or her performance at the request of the instructor, the questions are designed to assist the instructor in orally reviewing the learner's knowledge of the activity as it relates to performance.

Several blank spaces are provided within each entry on the outline/ guide to be used for the addition of other questions. These spaces provide the instructor with a place to write questions that are pertinent to the activity but are not already included.

Purpose and Scope of the Guide

In review, the three elements found in any one entry on the *Demonstration Outline and Practice Supervision Guide* are performance steps, standard of performance statements, and a list of technical questions. Derived from a *task detailing sheet* developed earlier in the occupational curriculum development process, the entries on the dual purpose form are used differently in the two situations for which they are designed. During the demonstration, the instructor uses the instrument as an outline for directing his or her performance in demonstrating the learning objective.

Major emphasis is placed on showing the learner how to perform the various steps of the objective in an occupationally acceptable manner. For purposes of practice, however, the instrument is used in another way. Its role changes from that of a *demonstration outline* to one of a *practice supervision guide* used in supervising a learner as he or she practises performing the objective.

In Review

1. What is the purpose of the practice session in the sequence of performance-related learning activities?

2. Discuss the logic of having the practice session appear where it does in the series of performance-related learning activities.

3. During the practice session and time of final performance, it is suggested that the instructor be directly involved in the learning process. Why is this important?

4. Discuss the instructor's role in supervising the practice of the learner.

5. How is the *Demonstration Outline and Practice Supervision Guide* used in supervising the practice of a learner?

6. What is the major difference between the ways the *Demonstration Outline and Practice Supervision Guide* is used in the two situations for which it is designed.

CHAPTER 23

Writing a Final
Performance Test

The performance test is the last in the series of learning activities that the learner must successfully complete to demonstrate his or her ability to perform the learning objectives. As one of the *performance-related* learning activities, it is designed to measure the learner's ability to synthesize knowledge, judgment-making skill, and psychomotor performance into a single act. It is a test designed to analyze and measure the learner's ability in performance of selected operations under *rigidly controlled conditions* (Micheels and Karnes, 1950). The test, as it is used within the context of an individualized learning activities package, serves several functions: it measures the learner's ability to perform the physical aspects of the objective, demonstrates his or her ability to apply the related technical information to performance, and determines the extent to which he or she can make decisions that direct performance and affect and gauge outcome.

Whereas the majority of learning activities can be successfully completed by the learner in an individualized setting, the performance test, like the preceding practice session, is most effective as a learning activity when it is administered and conducted in the presence of the instructor. The instructor's familiarity and experience with the objective being tested allows him or her to make critical decisions as to the learner's ability to perform it. He or she can orally quiz the learner as to process and product, alternative approaches, problem areas, etc. and gain insight into the learner's knowledge of the activity and how it is applied to performance. The instructor can also evaluate the learner's ability to sense and foresee problems that might arise and make decisions to avoid or reduce their effect.

As stated earlier, the performance test is the last in the series of activities that the learner must complete to attain the learning objective. See Example 23.1.

Example 23.1
Sample List of Learning Activities

1. Read Information Sheet "Grain Configuration, Color and Appearance." (30 mins)

2. Read Information-Assignment Sheet "Types and Styles of Casing and Trim" and complete the study questions. (60 mins)

3. Read Section #1, Chapter #7, "Finishing Rough Door Openings" in the text. (60 mins)

4. Read Task Procedure Sheet "Casing the Standard Rough Opening for an Interior Door." (10 mins)

5. View the taped illustrated presentation "Techniques and Materials for Casing Rough Openings." (60 mins)

6. Complete the Related Information Test "Casing Rough Door Openings." (60 mins)

7. Observe the demonstration of "Casing a Rough Opening for an Interior Door." (120 mins)

8. Practice the activity. (480 mins)

9. Take the final performance test of casing the rough opening for an interior door. (60 mins. $\times$ 6)

The test focuses on the knowledge and skill of the learner and his or her ability to integrate the two to perform the objective. The final performance test is preceded by a series of activities that direct the learner to various sources of information and eventually to a demonstration and practice of the activity. The test provides logical closure to the series of learning activities in the one learning activities package and psychologically prepares the learner for the next package in the occupational unit.

The final performance test can be likened, in some ways, to the previously discussed related information test. Like the information test, it provides the instructor with a means of determining the learner's progress toward the objective, his or her ability to perform the act, and a measure of the effectiveness of the preparatory activities in the total learning activities sequence. A common characteristic of the tests is that both instruments also indicate to the learner the level to which he or she has performed, and where his or her strengths and weaknesses lie in terms of performance. Unlike the related information test however, the performance test, when successfully completed, provides both the instructor and the learner with a composite measure of the latter's ability to physically perform the learning objective and apply his or her technical knowledge and decision-making ability to directing and controlling his or her effort.

Strengths and Limitations

The performance test, if well constructed, is an objective, valid, and reliable indicator of the learner's ability to perform the objective. It is a fair type of test in that it focuses on the psychomotor, cognitive, and affective abilities of the learner as they relate to performance of the objective. The test is also a valid instrument since it measures the composite behavioral skills that the learner has been developing from the time he or she began the sequence of learning activities. Lastly, the performance test is a reliable means of determining an individual's performance. If the instrument is written in a detailed and analytical way, it will consistently detect the more subtle aspects of the learner's performance as well as provide a good, overall view of his or her total effort.

Another aspect of the performance test which was mentioned earlier, but merits repeating, is the test's ability to evaluate not only the learner's physical performance of the objective, but also measure his or her technical knowledge and decision-making potential as it relates to application and performance. An information test is limited to determining the person's knowledge of a list of specific, informational topics, the scope of the performance test encompasses and measures the collective effect of his or her ability to perform the objective.

The performance test also has some inherent characteristics that cause problems in its development and application. First, because the activity being measured is of a complex, multi-behavioral nature, the test also has to be sufficiently detailed and analytical in its approach to detect acceptable performance. These conditions can, at times, cause difficulties in constructing the instrument and readying it for use in the learning activities package. However, the method for developing a final performance test that is suggested and discussed later in the chapter reduces some of the difficulties that might be encountered to a minimum.

The performance test also requires the presence of the instructor throughout the entire test period. While the test is not particularly difficult to administer with a properly constructed performance checksheet, it does require the constant attention of the evaluator. During the administration of the test he or she is expected to evaluate each step performed by the learner as well as the learner's overall ability in completing the objective.

Lastly, the final performance test can have a negative effect on the performance of the learner who has difficulty working in a highly organized and structured test environment. The detailed nature of the test, emphasis on performing at a given level of achievement, time constraints, and the general feeling of anxiety associated with taking tests are all variables which influence performance. However, measures can be taken to significantly reduce the problem. If, during the practice session, the learner is gradually brought to a point of performing the objective under the specified conditions and to the established standards, later, when performing the activity in the test situation, he or she will have already developed the needed degree of confidence. During the latter portion of the practice session, the instructor should intentionally have the learner practice as if he or she were taking the final test so when the time does arrive he or she will be prepared to demonstrate his or her mastery of the task unaffected by outside variables.

Writing a Final Performance Test

The *final performance test* is the instrument used by the instructor to evaluate the learner's performance of the objective and record the findings of the evaluation. The test is comprised of four major parts: the introduction, performance step evaluation section, task evaluation section, and the instructor's certification. The introduction includes the title of the sheet and the names of the program, course, unit, and learning objective for which it is written. It also includes an introductory paragraph which describes the purpose, direction, and scope of the instrument. A sample first page of the evaluation test appears in Example 23.2.

Example 23.2
Final Performance Test

Occupational Program — Teller Science

Course #1 — General Tellering

Unit #2 — Paying and Receiving

Learning Objective #11 — Selling Domestic Traveler's Checks

The performance test is made up of two sections: "Performance Step Evaluation" and "Task Evaluation". The first section focuses on the evaluation of the individual steps of the objective. The second section deals with the evaluation of the objective as a whole and completes the instrument.

Performance Step Evaluation

Directions: Below are the performance steps of the objective "Selling Domestic Traveler's Checks". Accompanying each performance step is a statement of its accepted standard of performance and a performance evaluation scale. As the learner completes a given step, read the performance standard for it and indicate on the evaluation scale how well you think he or she did in relation to the stated criteria. Evaluate each step in the procedure.

Performance Steps	*Standards of Performance*
1. *Greet the customer*	The greeting is made in a friendly, courteous manner and includes the teller's offer of assistance. If the teller knows the customer's name, that should also be included in the greeting.

Performed step very well	Performed step adequately	Performed step poorly	Did not perform step
5	4	3	2	1	0

Performance Step Evaluation. This portion of the performance test, as its name indicates, is used in evaluating the learner's performance of the various steps that comprise the learning objective. The section includes a set of directions, the individual performance steps with their respective standards of performance statements, and evaluation scale. The standards of performance statement of a given performance step specifies the criteria that must be attained by the learner before the step is considered complete. The scale provides a place for the instructor to record his or her evaluation of the learner's performance of the step. The scale ranges from "Performed the step well" which receives a total of five points to "Did not perform the step" which receives a rating of zero. Intermediate points which reflect evaluations between the two extremes are distributed along the scale. Provision for additional comments is also included at the end of the section.

The performance step evaluation section appears first in the checksheet since the individual steps are evaluated as the process evolves toward completion. Later, after the process is complete, the learning objective as a whole is evaluated and capability of the individual to perform it determined.

The performance steps and standards of performance statements were derived from the task detailing sheet prepared earlier in the occupational curriculum development process. Coupled with the evaluation scale, the three components formed the organizational basis of this section of the checksheet and established the approach for performance step evaluation.

Task Evaluation. The purpose of the task evaluation portion of the performance evaluation checksheet is to assist the evaluator in determining whether the learning objective has been completed in its entirety to the established set of criteria. This latter section of the checksheet is somewhat different in organization, content, and approach from the performance step evaluation section in that it deals with the evaluation of the objective as a whole. Together, the two parts of the instrument, when completed, will produce a comprehensive measure of the learner's ability to perform the learning objective.

A sample task evaluation section of the checksheet for *Selling Domestic Traveler's Checks* appears in Example 23.3. The task evaluation section includes as a part of the introduction the entire evaluation criteria statement of the learning objective for which the instrument is written. The criteria statement includes a description of the completed product or service as a whole, a summary evaluation of the process, a statement as to the learner's ability to orally respond to questions that test his or her knowledge of the process, time requirements for completing the objective, and lastly, the number of times the learner must repeat the activity over a given time frame to meet the standards.

Following the introduction are the various items used in evaluating the individual's overall performance of the learning objective. Preceded by a set of directions, the entries direct the focus of the evaluation to those aspects of performance specified in the evaluation criteria statement. Each entry is accompanied by a series of responses which include statements that describe different ways in which a learner might perform the objective. Typically, a series of responses includes two extreme alternatives and one, two, or three points between the extreme positions. In some of the entries, one of the extremes describes performance in terms of that of an experienced practitioner. In those entries, the satisfactory performance of the learner does not have to match that of the experienced worker to be acceptable (another alternative is available for that), but the option is included to recognize those pupils who demonstrate exceptional performance.

Example 23.3
Task Evaluation

This portion of the performance test will assist you in determining whether the learner has attained the objective of Selling Domestic Traveler's Checks. The evaluation criteria for the objective are as follows:

> The domestic traveler's checks are prepared according to the underwriter's sales directions and the transaction verified by the instructor. The sequence of performance steps listed on the task procedure sheet given at the time of demonstration of the objective was followed exactly. The learner was able to explain the procedure he or she performed at the instructor's request. He or she demonstrated the complete procedure within a 10 minute time period. The task was repeated a minimum of four times distributed equally over a two week time period.

As implied in the criteria statement, the learner will be evaluated in terms of his or her overall attainment of the learning objective, manipulative skill, knowledge and ability to apply it in performing the objective, professional attitudes and perceptive skills and ability to stay within the stated time constraints.

Directions: To complete this phase of the evaluation read the various criteria statements under each heading and indicate that statement which best describes the learner's total effort as you perceive it.

1. The learner completed the task of Selling Domestic Traveler's Checks as follows:

   ☐ Did not complete the task in accordance with the established criteria.

   ☐ Completed the task in accordance with the established criteria.

   ☐ Exceeded the established criteria. Demonstrated the task in the manner of an experienced teller.

2. During the completion of the task, the learner:

   ☐ Could not perform the performance steps of the task.

☐ Completed the performance steps of the sequence, but with hesitation and lack of confidence. Occasionally missed a performance step or performed it out of sequence.

☐ Technically performed the series of performance steps in an acceptable manner.

☐ Performed each performance step in the sequence with confidence and ability. Adapted to varying situations with little or no difficulty.

3. During the process, the learner:

☐ Could not respond correctly to questions/situational problems posed by the instructor.

☐ Responded to certain questions and/or contrived situational problems, but with hesitation and noticeable lack of confidence.

☐ Responded properly to questions/problems that were posed, but with no additional exploration or elaboration.

☐ Responded to all requests for information. Was able to anticipate various situations and problems and suggest possible solutions to them.

4. During the process, the learner:

☐ Displayed little or no professional behavior.

☐ Observed a simulation of acceptable professional behavior.

☐ Strived to emulate professional behavior.

☐ Consistently performed in a professional manner.

5. During the process, the learner:

☐ Was almost totally unaware of almost all non-verbal communiqués of the customer.

☐ Appeared to be aware of non-verbal communiqués and sometimes reacted to them.

☐ Was very aware of non-verbal communiqués, and once given, reacted in a positive, graceful manner.

6. In terms of time, the learner:

☐ Far exceeded the 10 minute time period for performing the objective.

☐ Did not perform the objective in the prescribed time, but exceeded it only slightly.

☐ Performed the objective within the prescribed time limit.

☐ Performed the objective in a time demonstrated by an experienced teller.

7. The learning objective was demonstrated by the learner "a minimum of *four* times distributed equally over a two-week period."

Test #1   Date: _____

Test #2   Date: _____

Example 23.3 continued

```
        Test #3              Date: _____

        Test #4              Date: _____

Additional Comments




Certification

In my professional judgment, _____
has attained the learning objective of Selling Domestic Traveler's Checks and is
capable of performing this task in a professionally acceptable manner.

                                      _____
                                              Signature

                                      _____
                                                 Date
```

The individual entries in the task evaluation section of the performance checksheet refer respectively to the learner's overall attainment of the learning objective, summary evaluation of the performance steps completed in the process, ability of the learner to respond to the questions posed by the instructor, professional behavior demonstrated by the learner during the activity, awareness of non-verbal communiqués, time constraints, and repetitions over a period of time. While the majority of entries, as mentioned earlier, are directly related to the various components of an evaluation criteria statement of a learning objective this is not always the case. For example, the two above items that concern professional behavior and non-verbal communiqués, while not integral parts of the established criteria, are important to this particular objective. In some cases, such items refer to intrinsic aspects of the performance process that the learner is expected to demonstrate and, while not specified in detail in the criteria statement, are emphasized at the time of final performance.

Certification

The last section of the performance evaluation checksheet contains a signed and dated statement by the instructor that verifies the learner's attainment of the performance objective. It confirms that the instructor has witnessed the learner's activities throughout the performance process, evaluated the objective in its completed state and found the learner's work acceptable in terms of the stated criteria. The signed statement is official recognition of the learner's mastery of the specified objective.

In Review

1. What is the purpose of the *final performance test* within the sequence of learning activities?

2. Discuss the position of the final performance test within the sequence of performance-related learning activities.

3. Discuss how the final performance test synthesizes all of the knowledge, attitudes, and ability acquired prior to this time in the sequence of learning activities.

4. Discuss the strengths and limitations of the performance test.

5. Why is the performance test divided into two distinct categories of evaluation, performance step evaluation and task evaluation?

6. Discuss how the entries included in the *task evaluation* section of the performance test parallel and reflect the purpose of the various entries in the evaluation criteria portion of the learning objective.

7. What is the purpose of the *certification* portion of the performance test?

CHAPTER 24

Preparing Individualized Learning Activities Packages

This last chapter of the Handbook deals with the packaging of learning materials once they have been developed. Up to this point in time, the emphasis in Section V has been on the preparation of learning materials needed to implement the learning activities of a particular learning objective. Now, however, the emphasis changes. The problem no longer is one of developing and preparing materials, but that of putting the readied materials into an organized and usable form. Hence, the learning activities package.

By definition, a learning activities package is a compilation or package of materials which guides and assists the learner in attaining a particular learning objective with little or no outside assistance from the instructor.

Containing all of the materials needed to implement the various learning activities of the objective, related information sheets, textbooks, audio and videotapes, slide series, written and performance tests, etc., the learning package becomes a package of "hands on" activities experienced by the learner as he or she makes his or her way to the desired objective. One learning activities package is prepared for each learning objective of the occupational unit. Therefore, if a particular unit has seven learning objectives, seven packages would comprise the unit.

The learning activities package is organized so that its contents are readily accessible to the learner and will assist him or her in attaining the learning objective in as efficient and effective manner as possible. The LAP is one response to the problem of organizing an array of different kinds of learning activities into an individualized, functioning learning experience. Bjorkquist (1971) discusses, with some semantic differences, a number of desirable features of individualized learning:

Based on what we know about the way in which individuals learn there are several features of individualized instruction which are necessary or highly desirable. Knowing these, the teacher may then better select or plan individualized instructional sequences which will effectively accomplish learner objectives. Several questions may be helpful to the teacher.

1. Does the instruction provide for knowledge of results to the learner? On the basis of this knowledge of results, the learner will make adjustments to perform a given task correctly. In addition, the reinforcement for correct performance becomes an incentive for the learner. Knowledge of results may be provided to the learner in several forms. A simple statement such as "that is correct" or "that is incorrect" is one such form. In other cases, the learner internalizes the feedback process (Gagné and Fleishman, 1959). He can learn to observe whether the results of his behavior produce correct outcomes. This can be facilitated by giving the learner a model for comparison. For example, a correctly made solder joint could serve as comparison for students learning to solder.

2. Does the instructional sequence allow the student to experience success? There is truth in the old adage, "success breeds success." Since individuals tend to repeat those experiences which they find enjoyable, they are inclined to do again the things at which they succeed. The implication for individualized instruction is that the units should be structured so the student is assured of success in learning. Instructional sequences should begin with small steps. These should be arranged in order, so the learner can proceed from those things that are basic to those which are more complex. As the learner finds success, this in itself will serve as reinforcement by relieving the tension of the learning situation (Sorenson, 1964). This, in turn, should help the student to develop confidence.

3. Are a variety of presentation modes used in instruction? The use of a variety of presentation modes seems to be justified, not because a variety in itself is beneficial to learning or because the use of two communication channels will produce more learning than the use of one. However, because of learner differences and content differences the use of a variety of presentation modes is recommended (Briggs, 1968).

Media appropriate to the content to be learned should be used with individualized instruction. If motion, as the flow of electrons, is important to learning the concept, the instruction should probably include motion pictures. Oversized or reduced photographs are helpful to the learner in developing accurate concepts. Amplified sounds can be used to good advantage in some cases. Most students will probably learn the correct sound of the pulse for measuring blood pressure best by listening to pulse sounds.

4. Does the instruction provide for some form of active response by the learner? This response may be spoken, written, or take some other form of action. The response may take the form of a simple "yes" or "no" answer or it may be considerably more complex. When learning manipulative skills it is especially important that early practice be correct. It may be as easy for the learner to practice and develop an incorrect skill as to develop a correct skill. Therefore, the instructional program should provide for the step-by-step advance of the student, and he should be required to actively participate in those learning steps (Flug, 1967). Without doing this the learner can easily assume that he is capable of performing or that he understands without trying the task at hand and eventually have difficulty when he does try to perform the correct behavior.

5. Does the instruction provide for different rates of presentation? If they are hurried, slow learners tend to make errors. Conversely, fast learners often need to have the pace set for them so they don't waste time (Gropper and Kress, 1965). An instructional system in which the speed of presentation can be adjusted will be adaptable to the needs of more learners.

6. Does the individualized instructional system provide for branching alternatives? This means that the instructional system would not force the learner to repeat those learnings he has already acquired. Branching alternatives make it possible to adjust for differences in background and capability of the student to learn. It allows the learner to skip those units of instruction which he gives evidence of knowing. Likewise it provides for the repeat of instructional units where mastery has not been achieved with one attempt (Briggs, 1968).

7. Does the instruction provide for periodic and spaced review? The effect of learning can probably be retained longer if such reviews are provided. This will probably be accomplished by an instructional system which provides for the review of learning materials within a single instructional session. Subsequent reviews may be spaced increasingly further apart, forcing the student to recall what he has previously learned.

Organization of a Learning Activities Package

The number and types of items contained in different learning packages vary somewhat, but the two general types of items found in most packages are printed materials and audio-visual resources. Printed materials, with the exception of books, are usually bound together in the form of a *resource guide* and include both written learning materials and materials of an administrative nature which guide the learner through the package. Books, where needed, are included as is. The audio-visual materials usually are audio and/or video tapes of teacher-made presentations and video tapes, slide sets, or film strips of demonstrations.

Printed Materials

The printed materials contained in a learning activities package either directly assist the learner in attaining the learning objective, or they are administrative and guide and direct him or her through the series of learning activities. The learning materials used directly by the learner in attaining the objective have been discussed in the previous seven chapters. A discussion of the latter types of printed materials, e.g. those that guide and direct the learner in performing the various learning activities, follows.

Title Page. The title page of the resource guide introduces the reader to the learning package. Also included on the title page is a statement which identifies the package part of a total curriculum development system and locates it within the occupational unit, course, and program. If the LAP is used in an academic situation and the person is expected to submit it for evaluation, such entries as those specifying to whom the work is presented, the parent educational department, college, university, etc. and the date of submission are also appropriate entries on the title page.

A sample title page appears in Example 24.1.

Example 24.1
a resource guide for the learning activities package . . .

. . . "ARRANGING THE MEDICAL RECORD"

by

Naomi Kuwada

The third in a series of thirteen learning activities
packages in the "Assembling Medical Records" unit in the
course "Analysis Technology" in the "Medical Records
Technology" Occupational Program

Acknowledgements. The acknowledgements are an optional entry in the completed learning activities package. They are the author's formal recognition of those people who contributed to the development of the learning package. The acknowledgement statement may be as brief as a sentence or two, or may continue for one, two, or more pages. Again, its inclusion and content is left entirely to the discretion of the author.

Table of Contents. The table of contents of the resource guide found in a learning activities package is a list of all of the written or duplicated entries. A sample table of contents appears in Example 24.2. The table informs the learner of the various entries in the guide and the order or sequence in which they occur.

The table of contents of a resource guide is not to be confused with the "Contents of the Learning Activities Package" entry. Whereas the table of contents is a listing of entries within the guide itself, the "Contents" section is a list of specific items found in a complete learning package. A discussion of the "Content" statement follows later in the chapter.

Introduction. The introduction included in the learner's guide, much like those found in a program description, course outline, and unit guide,

---

Example 24.2
Table of Contents

---

provides the reader with a general knowledge of the package and its nature and purpose. Supported by the content and activities, the introductory statement secures the total package within the curricular framework, and informs the reader of its direction, scope, and limitations.

While each author will have his or her own thoughts and ideas as to what to include in the opening statement, the purpose of the introduction will be served if the reader is made aware of the intent of the package, how it will benefit him or her in the learning situation, and what it will do to advance him or her toward the learning objective.

A sample introductory statement follows.

Introduction

"Arranging the Medical Record" is the last learning activities package in the series of three that comprise the "Medical Records Assembling" occupational unit. The dual purpose of the LAP is to guide the learner in completing the occupational unit and becoming employable as a medical records assembly clerk, or assist him or her in his or her work preparation and training toward other employment options in the medical records field.

The compilation of the learning activities packages is the last step performed by the curriculum designer in implementing the occupational curriculum development theory. Beginning with an analysis of the various occupational specialties and sub-specialties of a primary occupation into their respective lists of tasks, converting these tasks to learning objectives, and followed by the writing of the various occupational program, course, and unit descriptions, the end result is realized when the various LAPS are developed to implement the individual learning objectives of the various occupational units.

In this particular learning activities package, the student medical records assembly clerk will acquire the knowledge and skills necessary to successfully perform the task of arranging the medical record. En route to attaining the learning objective, he or she will gain information and become familiar with the procedure as it is commonly performed by assembly clerks in hospital and other health-care institutions.

Since this LAP is the last one in the occupational unit, its completion marks a point at which the learner has the choice of leaving school and seeking employment in the area of work for which he or she is trained or opting to continue work preparation education in the medical records field.

Prerequisites. The prerequisite statement identifies those skills and knowledge that the learner must possess and be able to demonstrate prior to undertaking the learning activities package. The results of a demonstration of his or her abilities indicates whether or not he or she should be allowed to begin work on the LAP or be given work that would prepare him or her to meet the prerequisites. Evaluation of the learner's capabilities with regard to the prerequisites can be considered a diagnosis and prescription for learning and thus, lends a high degree of individualization and personal tailoring of the LAP to the learner.

Following is a sample prerequisite statement.

The prerequisites for the learning activities package of "Arranging the Medical Record" are that the learner be able to spell and count, and be thorough, detailed, and orderly. The learner should already possess the skills to file materials both alphabetically and numerically.

Contents of the Learning Activities Package. The "Contents" statement specifies all of the items that are actually contained in a learning activities package. An example of a typical list would include a resource guide, video-taped presentation, slide series demonstration with taped narration, textbook, etc. The contents statement informs the user as to what and how many items there are in the package and alerts him or her if there are too few or too many items in the package, or if one or more items from another package inadvertently were placed in the package for which the statement was written. A sample list of contents for the learning activities package of *cutting hair* appears below.

The list of learning materials contained in this package is as follows:

1. A Resource Guide for the Learning Activities Package for "Cutting Hair."
2. *Standard Textbook of Cosmotology* by Malady. Revised Edition, 1972.

3. Videotaped presentation. Title: "Review of Informational Topics on Haircutting."
4. Videotaped demonstration. Title: "Cutting Hair."
5. Hair Cutting Equipment Kit.

Learning Objective.   The learning objective specifies what the learner will be able to do once he or she has completed the learning activities package. Accompanying the performance statement of the objective are two other components which have equal importance; the circumstances or conditions which will exist at the time the learner is seeking mastery of the specified skill, and the criteria which define and indicate the level of acceptable performance.

The learning objective that appears in the learning package is a direct transposition of the objective statement that appears on one of the unit learning modules in a given occupational unit guide. Taken verbatim from the module, the learning objective was originally derived from a task of an occupational sub-specialty and was written, via a task objective sheet, in performance terms. After appearing at several different stages of the curriculum development process, the learning objective finally assumes its intended role in the learning activities package; defining the particular occupational skill to be attained and serving as a guide to the learner working toward the specified end.

If you wish to review the writing of learning objectives, see Section II, Chapter 9.

Directions for Completing the Learning Activities Package.   This entry in the completed resource guide serves to guide the reader through the sequence of learning materials. It is comprised of two basic parts: the written directions or instructions for guiding the learner toward the objective, and the list of learning activities which specify what he or she will be doing en route. A sample "Direction" statement for the package "Washing Hands (Aseptic Technique)" follows.

The sequence of learning activities listed below will guide you in completing the learning activities package. The learning materials specified in each learning activities statement e.g., textbooks, related information and instruction sheets, tests, videotapes, slide series and audiotapes, comprise the LAP. To assist and guide you through the learning package, the various learning materials have been arranged and numbered to correspond with the list of learning activities. Hence, to begin the LAP, read the first learning activities statement, locate the appropriate learning activity in the package and complete it. Repeat the procedure with items 2, 3, 4, etc. until you have completed the remaining list of activities.

A word of caution. Be sure to follow the sequence of learning activities as they are listed. Their order is important in insuring your success in completing the LAP, and in attaining the learning objective.

Learning Activities.   The learning activities that appear in the resource guide identify various resources to be used in acquiring the knowledge and skill needed to perform the learning objective. The review of the learning activities listed that follows shows those activities that will guide the learner to the sources of essential information (learning activities 1–5), and those in which he or she will apply this knowledge in the observation, practice, and performance of the task (learning activities 6–8).

Learning Activities
The learning activities are as follows:

1. Read pages 1–67, "Introduction to Asepsis."
2. Read Information-Assignment Sheet "The Common Mode of Transmitting Pathogenic Bacteria."
3. Read Task Procedure Sheet "Washing Hands."
4. View film "Hospital Sepsis."
5. Take Related Information Test.
6. View flip chart demonstration of washing hands.
7. Practice washing your hands using aseptic technique.
8. Take the final performance test of washing hands.

Appendix.   In review, a completed learning activities package contains basically two types of learning materials: those that are printed and bound, and referred to as a learner's or resource guide, and those that appear as audio and/or visual aids, e.g. slide series, audio-tapes, video tapes, filmstrips. Appearing as the last major entry in the printed material guide is the appendix. While what is included is left to the discretion of the author, some of the entries that might be considered for inclusion are the *learning activities development sheet* which was used in the planning of the learning package, and the *task listing sheet*, *task detailing sheet*, *task objective sheet*, and *unit learning module* which were also instrumental in the development of the package. Other items which could be considered are the *presentation-discussion guide*, *answer key* to the related information test, *demonstration outline and practice supervision guide*, and *performance evaluation checksheet*.

The aforementioned entries may not be included if the learning activities package was prepared for immediate use by the learner. However, if the package was developed by a student enrolled in a curriculum development course, they might be included to help insure his or her understanding of the curriculum development process and aid in the evaluation of their work by the instructor.

Bibliography.   A bibliography is an optional item in the learner's guide. If included, it is a suggested source of materials that complement and add to other informational sources contained in the learning package. While valuable, because of its relationship to the learning materials already included in the package, the bibliography does not possess the same essential qualities as the other entries which are integral to the learning package. If included, the bibliography does, however, provide the learner with additional sources of pertinent information.

Identification Label. The identification label is the initial source of identification of the packaged learning materials. Affixed in a conspicuous place on the outside of the learning activities package, the label informs the reader of the occupational program, course, and unit of which the package is a part. It also includes the title of the learning objective, and the estimated time needed to complete all of the activities and attain the stated objective.

A sample identification label follows:

Occupational Program: Residential Carpentry

Course: Finish Carpentry

Unit: Hardwood Flooring Installation

Learning Objective: Installing Pre-Finished Tongue and Groove Flooring

Estimated Time: 12 hr. 30 mins.

Example 24.3   *Identification Label for a Learning Activities Package*

In Review

1. Define the *learning activities package.*

2. What are the two basic types of learning materials included in a learning activities package?

3. What is the purpose of the *learner's guide* found in the learning package?

4. How many learning activities packages would accompany a given *unit guide*? (See Chapter 15 for a review of unit guides.)

5. What is the purpose of the *Learning Activities Package Identification Label*?

Appendixes

APPENDIX A

Occupational Curriculum Development
Worksheet Series for Money
Distribution and Management-Related
Occupations

by
Beverly Faunce
and
Maria Varano Butz

Table of Contents

Employment-Curriculum Spiral

Occupational Curriculum Development Process

Learning Objective:

Developing a Long-Range *Employment Curriculum* Spiral

I. Gathering and Organizing Occupational Data

    A. Develop the component Long-Range *Employment* Spiral

        1. Determine the group title and list of primary occupations for the functionally related group of occupations.

        2. Determine the occupational specialties and sub-specialties of the primary occupational title.

        3. Write task listing sheets.

        4. Write task detailing sheets.

      *5. Write performance step detailing sheets.

      *6. Write related occupational information topics.

II. Converting Occupational Organization and Data to Work Preparation Curriculum

    A. Write task objective sheets.

III. Organizing the Occupational Curriculum

    A. Develop the component Long-Range *Curriculum* Spiral

        1. Determine the occupational program, course and unit titles.

        2. Write an outline of the program, course, unit and learning objective titles.

        3. Write unit learning modules.

IV. Writing Occupational Program, Course, and Unit Descriptions

    A. Write an Occupational Program Description.

    B. Write an Occupational Course Outline.

    C. Write an Occupational Unit Guide.

V. Preparing Occupational Learning Materials

    A. Prepare knowledge-related and performance-related learning materials.

    B. Prepare individualized learning activities packages (LAPS).

*These two activities are not steps in the proposed occupational development process. However, the data contained on each of the two worksheets are essential later in the development, preparation and writing of the occupational learning materials.

Figure A.1 *A Long-Range Employment-Curriculum Spiral for Money Distribution and Management-Related Occupations*

The Long-Range Occupational Employment-Curriculum
Spiral Description Sheet for Money Distribution and
Management-Related Occupations

The Long-Range Occupational Employment-Curriculum Spiral for the Money Distribution and Management-Related Occupations is an organizational plan for coordinating the educational and employment opportunities as they exist in that group of occupations. The purpose of the dual approach is to provide the person interested in preparing for work in a particular occupational group with a way in which he or she can attain his or her perceived occupational goal and, at the same time, realize a number of en route employment and educational alternatives should he or she need them prior to reaching that goal.

Long-Range Occupational Employment Spiral

The employment-curriculum spiral for the functionally related group of money distribution and management-related occupations is made up of two component spirals: a long-range occupational employment spiral and a long-range occupational curriculum spiral. The employment spiral is the conceptual model used in organizing and ranking the occupations, occupational specialties and occupational sub-specialties in the occupational group. The spiral assists the curriculum designer in establishing a hierarchy of occupational titles, and identifying the occupational entry and exit points distributed along it. The employment spiral serves as the organizational guide in developing the first phase of the occupational curriculum development process.

Components. Five primary occupations (PO) appear on the Long-Range Occupational Employment Spiral: General Office Clerk (entry-level occupation); Teller (technical occupation); Assistant Manager (professional occupation); Administrative Assistant (research occupation); Office Manager (administrative occupation). The five primary occupational titles define the primary "entry-exit" points on the spiral. Each point is defined by a triple-shafted arrow. The arcs of the spiral defined by the arrows, in turn, are made up of a series of dots that represent the respective lists of tasks of the five primary occupations in the spiral. The "highlighted" dots on the spiral symbolically represent the tasks of the occupation being analyzed, in this case, that of the "Teller". The title of the spiral is derived directly from the occupational *group* title for which the spiral is being constructed and is inclusive of all occupational titles that comprise that spiral.

While not depicted on the employment spiral, the occupational specialties and sub-specialties of each of the five primary occupations are implied. Later in the occupational curriculum development process, the employment spiral and its components will serve as the basis for developing the corresponding curriculum spiral and together, the two will form the dual Long-Range Occupational Employment-Curriculum Spiral for the particular occupational group.

Long-Range Occupational Curriculum Spiral

The long-range occupational curriculum spiral is the educational complement of the employment spiral. Whereas the employment spiral is an organizational concept allied to a group of functionally related occupations in the world of work, the curriculum spiral is a paralleling organizational concept that complements the employment spiral and adds educational dimension to it. The importance of such a relationship is that since occupational education would be organized in terms of and complement the world of work, horizontal movement from work to education and education to work could occur with little or no penalty to the "worker-learner." Vertical movement would also be enhanced in this work-education organizational system.

Once the tasks on the employment spiral are identified and listed for each of the primary occupational titles, the creation of the complementary curriculum spiral becomes a relatively simple matter: to write each task in performance terms. This single act serves as the change agent and catalyst. Whereas, on the employment spiral the activities are tasks, on the curriculum spiral they are learning objectives.

The conversion of tasks to learning objectives also affects a difference in the nature of the two spirals. Whereas the employment spiral is simply a hierarchical ordering of primary occupational titles, together with a series of spirally arranged dots representing the tasks of the related occupations, the curriculum spiral is a spirally configured *timeline* made up of individual learning objectives of a total occupational curriculum.

Components. The Long-Range Occupational Curriculum Spiral for Money Distribution and Management-Related Occupations is comprised of five occupational programs. The programs and their respective objectives are derived from and coincide with the five primary occupational titles listed on the employment spiral. The titles of the programs are: General Office Procedures (entry-level program); Teller Science (technical program); Management Trainee Program (professional program); Administrative Assistant Program (research program); and Office Management (administrative program).

The course and unit titles that comprise each of the above occupational programs are implied on the curriculum spiral. Like the title of the "Teller Science" program the title on the curriculum spiral is derived from and corresponds to the primary occupational title of "Teller", the course and unit titles of the program are derived from and correspond to the occupational specialty and sub-specialty titles of the occupation of teller. This same logic is extended to naming the other programs, courses and units that make up the total curriculum spiral.

Employment Spiral

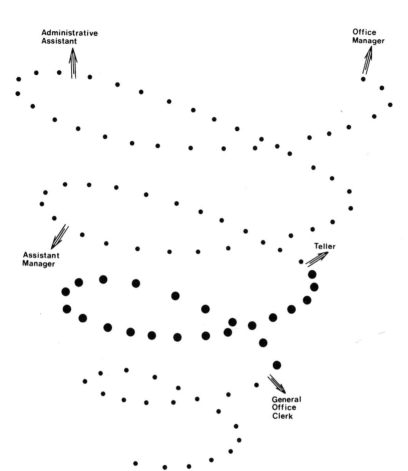

Figure A.2 *A Long-Range Employment Spiral for Money Distribution and Management-Related Occupations*

**Determining the Group Title and List of Primary
Occupations for Developing a Long-Range Occupational
Employment Spiral for Money Distribution and
Management-Related Occupations**

I. *Occupational Area of Interest:*　Banking-Related Occupations

II. *Occupational Category:*　Clerical and Sales-Related Occupations

III. *Functional Divisions:*

    A.　Stenography, Typing and Filing-Related Occupations

   *B.　Computing and Account Recording-Related Occupations

    C.　Material and Production Recording-Related Occupations

    D.　Information and Message Distribution-Related Occupations

    E.　Miscellaneous Clerical Occupations

    F.　Service Sales-Related Occupations

    G.　Commodities Sales-Related Occupations

    H.　Merchandising-Related Occupations (other than sales)

IV. *Functional Groups:*

    A.　*Functional Division:*　Computing and Account Recording-Related
                 Occupations

     *1.　Money Distribution and Management-Related Occupations

      2.　Cashier-Related Occupations

      3.　Bookkeeper-Related Occupations

      4.　Automatic Data Processing Equipment Operator-Related
         Occupations

      5.　Billing-Machine Operator-Related Occupations

      6.　Bookkeeper-Machine Operator-Related Occupations

      7.　Computing-Machine Operator-Related Occupations

      8.　Account-Recording-Machine Operator-Related Occupations

      9.　Computing and Account-Recording-Related Occupations

V. *Occupational Titles:*

    A.　*Functional Division:*　Computing and Account Recording-Related
                 Occupations

    B.　*Functional Group:*　Money Distribution and Management-Related
                 Occupations

    C.　*Random List of Primary, Occupational Specialty and Occupational
       Sub-Specialty Titles:*

    **1.　Teller

      2.　General Teller

      3.　Mail Credit Teller

      4.　Paying and Receiving Teller

5. Payroll Teller
6. Return Items Teller
7. Savings Teller
8. Special Deposits Teller
9. Collection and Exchange Teller
10. Bond Teller
11. Contract Collections Teller
12. Domestic Exchange Teller
13. Foreign Exchange Teller
14. Note Teller
15. Collateral Teller
16. Commercial Note Teller
17. Discount Teller
18. Real Estate Loan Teller
19. Utility Teller
20. Head Teller
*21. Assistant Manager
*22. Administrative Assistant
23. Business Office Machine Operator
*24. Office Manager
*25. General Office Clerk

Determining the Occupational Specialties and
Sub-Specialties of the Primary Occupational Title

I. *Primary Occupation (PO):*   Teller

II. *Occupational Specialties (OS):*
  A.   General Teller
  B.   Collection and Exchange Teller
  C.   Note Teller
  D.   Utility Teller

III. *Occupational Sub-Specialties (OSS):*

  A.   *Occupational Specialty:*   A — General Teller
    1.   Mail Credit Teller
    2.   Paying and Receiving Teller
    3.   Payroll Teller
    4.   Return Items Teller
    5.   Savings Teller
    6.   Special Deposits Teller

  B.   *Occupational Specialty:*   B — Collection and Exchange Teller
    1.   Bond Teller
    2.   Domestic Exchange Teller
    3.   Foreign Exchange Teller

  C.   *Occupational Specialty:*   C — Note Teller
    1.   Collateral Teller
    2.   Commercial Note Teller
    3.   Discount Teller

  D.   *Occupational Specialty:*   D — Utility Teller
        (None)

Task Listing Sheets

Task Listing Sheet

Primary Occupation (PO): Teller

Occupational Specialty (OS): General Teller

Occupational Sub-Specialty (OSS): Mail Credit Teller
  Tasks:
- Opening Envelopes
- Receiving Checks for Deposit
- Examining Checks for Endorsements
- Verifying Deposits
- Entering Deposit in Depositors Passbook or Checking Account
- Issuing Receipts

Occupational Sub-Specialty: Paying and Receiving Teller
  Tasks:
- Counting Currency
- Cashing Checks
- Handling Check Deposits
- Handling Cash Deposits
- Receiving Personal Loan Payments
- Receiving Christmas Club Payments
- Issuing Treasurer's Checks
- Selling Money Orders
- Withdrawing Funds From No Passbook Savings Accounts
- Ordering the Daily Cash Supply
- Selling Domestic Traveler's Checks
- Balancing the Cash Drawer and Settlement
- Accepting Night Depository Deposits

Occupational Sub-Specialty: Payroll Teller
  Tasks:
- Receiving Payroll Requests from Depositors
- Preparing Cash in Requested Denominations
- Verifying Totals
- Accepting Debit to Offset Payroll
- Assuring Funds are Available
- Computing Service Charges

Occupational Sub-Specialty: Return Items Teller

   Tasks:

- Returning Item to Cashing Tellers for Collection
- Debiting Checking Accounts for Deposited Items
- Returning Deposited Saving Account Items to Originating Office Head Tellers for Collection
- Assessing Service Charges
- Charging-Off Uncollectable Return Items

Occupational Sub-Specialty: Savings Teller

   Tasks:

- Verifying Cash Deposits
- Securing Endorsements on Deposited Items
- Verifying Total on Deposit Tickets
- Posting Customer's Passbooks
- Withdrawing Funds Upon Signature Verification
- Posting Annual Interest
- Placing Holds on Withdrawals
- Issuing Treasurer's Checks
- Microfilming Transactions
- Balancing Cash Drawer

Occupational Sub-Specialty: Special Deposits Teller

   Tasks:

- Reporting Unusual Deposits of $10,000.00 or More to Satisfy Bank Secrecy Act
- Accepting Certified Checks for Deposit
- Accepting Sight Drafts for Collection
- Accepting Government Bond Interest Coupons for Deposit
- Receiving Withholding Tax Deposits

Task Listing Sheet

Primary Occupation (PO):   Teller

Occupational Specialty (OS):   Collection and Exchange Teller

Occupational Sub-Specialty (OSS):   Bond Teller

 Tasks:
- Issuing Series "E" Bonds
- Preparing Transmittal Letters
- Ordering Bond Inventory
- Maintaining Activity Records
- Exchanging Series "E" Bonds for Series "H" Bonds
- Computing Interest on Bonds Presented for Redemption
- Issuing Treasurer's Checks
- Counting Money

Occupational Sub-Specialty: Domestic Exchange Teller

 Tasks:
- Presenting for Collection Items Bearing Guaranteed Endorsements
- Redeeming Treasury Bills
- Collecting Bearer Bonds When Due
- Issuing Letters of Credit

Occupational Sub-Specialty: Foreign Exchange Teller

 Tasks:
- Counting Currency
- Selling Foreign Currency
- Identifying and Classifying Foreign Currency
- Computing Exchange Rates and Exchanging Foreign Currency
- Preparing Foreign Drafts
- Preparing Cable Transfers
- Preparing Air Mail Transfers
- Selling Tip Packs
- Selling Foreign Travelers Cheques
- Maintaining Controls

Task Listing Sheet

Primary Occupation (PO):   Teller

Occupational Specialty (OS):   Note Teller

Occupational Sub-Specialty (OSS):   Collateral Teller
  Tasks:
- Typing Documents
- Examining Collateral for Negotiability
- Securing Necessary Documentation
- Monitoring Stock Margins
- Maintaining Securities Vault
- Releasing Securities
- Computing Current Value of Loan Collateral Held

Occupational Sub-Specialty: Commercial Note Teller
  Tasks:
- Recording Judgements and Second Mortgages
- Accepting Payments on Loans
- Issuing Receipts
- Examining Collateral for Negotiability
- Typing Documents
- Satisfying Judgements and Second Mortgages

Occupational Sub-Specialty: Discount Teller
  Tasks:
- Computing Interest
- Posting Payments
- Maintaining Ledgers
- Issuing Receipts
- Verifying Ledger Balances

Task Listing Sheet

Primary Occupation (PO):   Teller

Occupational Specialty (OS):   Utility Teller

Occupational Sub-Specialty (OSS):   None

   Tasks:

- Collecting Payments from Customers
- Totaling Items on Bill Using Adding Machine
- Recording Transactions
- Issuing Receipts
- Adjusting Bill Complaints
- Handling Partial Payments of Bill
- Crediting Utility Company Accounts

Task Detailing Sheets

Task Detailing Sheet

Primary Occupation (PO): Teller

Occupational Specialty (OS): General Teller

Occupational Sub-Specialty (OSS): Paying and Receiving Teller

Task: Counting Currency

Performance Steps	Standards of Performance
1. Identify currency	Student has discriminated between various denominations of currency to the instructor's satisfaction.
2. Sort money	Money is individually stacked, face up, by denomination.
3. Count money	Total equals instructor's.
4. Store money	Money is placed in appropriate bin in cash drawer.

Technical Occupational Information Topics

1. Handling Money
2. Unit Count Method
3. Basic Arithmetic

Task Detailing Sheet

Primary Occupation (PO): Teller

Occupational Specialty (OS): General Teller

Occupational Sub-Specialty (OSS): Paying and Receiving Teller

Task: Cashing Checks

Performance Steps	*Standards of Performance*
1. Examine the check	Check is completed properly and endorsed.
2. Verify the maker's signature	Maker's signature is verified.
3. Identify the payee	Payee is identified.
4. Place "hold" on the maker's account	Computer has accepted "hold" for specified amount.
5. Process the check	Check is "cashed out" for the designated amount and placed in appropriate bin for transit pickup.
6. Give funds to payee	Payee has received currency equal to amount of check.

Technical Occupational Information Topics

1. Cashing Checks
2. Circle Scan Method
3. Demand Inquiry System
4. Clearing House Recommendations
5. Identification With and Without Credentials
6. Burrough's Teller Machine
7. Microfiche/Signature Verification
8. Definition of Terms

Task Detailing Sheet

Primary Occupation (PO):   Teller

Occupational Specialty (OS):   General Teller

Occupational Sub-Specialty (OSS):   Paying and Receiving Teller

Task: Handling Check Deposits

Performance Steps	*Standards of Performance*
1. Examine the deposit ticket	Deposit ticket is legible and completed properly.
2. Verify checks are endorsed	Checks are properly endorsed by the depositor.
3. Receipt the deposit ticket	Deposit ticket is receipted for the exact amount of the deposit.
4. Issue the customer a receipt	A receipt is given to the customer for the exact amount of the deposit.
5. Process the deposit	Deposit ticket and check(s) are placed in appropriate bin for transit pickup.

Technical Occupational Information Topics

    1.   Handling Deposits

    2.   Burrough's Teller Machine

Task Detailing Sheet

Primary Occupation (PO):   Teller

Occupational Specialty (OS):   General Teller

Occupational Sub-Specialty (OSS):   Paying and Receiving Teller

Task: Handling Cash Deposits

Performance Steps	*Standards of Performance*
1. Examine the deposit ticket	Deposit ticket is legible and completed properly.
2. Count the cash	Cash is counted and equals the amount listed on the deposit ticket.
3. Identify the cash total	A red check-mark appears next to the cash total.
4. Place money in the cash drawer	Money is placed by denominations, in the appropriate bins in the cash drawer.

5. Receipt the deposit ticket	Deposit ticket is receipted for the exact amount of the deposit and the deposit is "cashed in" on the teller's tape only.
6. Issue customer receipt	Receipt is given to the customer for the exact amount of the deposit.
7. Process the deposit	Deposit ticket is placed in the appropriate bin for transit pickup.

Technical Occupational Information Topics

1. Handling Deposits
2. Basic Arithmetic
3. Burrough's Teller Machine
4. Definition of Terms

Task Detailing Sheet

Primary Occupation (PO): Teller

Occupational Specialty (OS): General Teller

Occupational Sub-Specialty (OSS): Paying and Receiving Teller

Task: Receiving Personal Loan Payments

Performance Steps	*Standards of Performance*
1. Accept payment	Payment is accepted from the customer and equals the amount of the loan payment.
2. Receipt the coupon book	The teller's stamp appears on the coupon and stub.
3. Process the coupon	The coupon is "cashed in", on the reverse side, and placed in the appropriate bin for transit pickup.

Technical Occupational Information Topics

1. Other Services
2. Burrough's Teller Machine
3. Definition of Terms

Task Detailing Sheet

Primary Occupation (PO): Teller

Occupational Specialty (OS): General Teller

Occupational Sub-Specialty (OSS): Paying and Receiving Teller

   Task: Receiving Christmas Club Payments

Performance Steps	*Standards of Performance*
1. Accept payment	Payment is accepted from the customer and equals the amount of the coupon(s) paid.
2. Receipt the coupon book	The teller's stamp appears on the succeeding coupon.
3. Process the coupon	The coupon(s) is "cashed in", on the reverse side, and placed in the appropriate bin for transit pickup.

Technical Occupational Information Topics

   1. Other Services
   2. Burrough's Teller Machine

Task Detailing Sheet

Primary Occupation (PO): Teller

Occupational Specialty (OS): General Teller

Occupational Sub-Specialty (OSS): Paying and Receiving Teller

   Task: Issuing Treasurer's Checks

Performance Steps	*Standards of Performance*
1. Ascertain amount of check to be issued and accept payment	The accepted payment is equal to the amount of the check to be issued.
2. Prepare the Treasurer's check	The Treasurer's check is "cut" for the exact predetermined amount. The current date, numeric amount, and the payee's name appear in the appropriate places on the check.
3. Have the Treasurer's check signed	The check is signed by an authorized bank signer.
4. Process the Treasurer's check	The original is given to the customer. The credit copy is "cashed in" on the reverse side for the exact amount of the check and placed in the appropriate bin for transit pickup.

The office copy is filed numerically, chronologically and by date in the appropriate file drawer.

Technical Occupational Information Topics

1. Other Services
2. Protectograph Machine
3. Definition of Terms
4. Burrough's Teller Machine
5. Alphabetic, Numeric Filing Procedures

Task Detailing Sheet

Primary Occupation (PO): Teller

Occupational Specialty (OS): General Teller

Occupational Sub-Specialty (OSS): Paying and Receiving Teller

   Task: Selling Money Orders

Performance Steps	*Standards of Performance*
1. Ascertain amount of check to be issued and accept payment	The accepted payment is equal to the amount of the check to be issued.
2. Prepare the money order	The money order is "cut" for the exact predetermined amount, and the current date appears on the check portion.
3. Process the money order	The original is given to the customer. The credit copy is "cashed in" on the reverse side for the exact amount of the check and placed in the appropriate bin for transit pickup. The office copy is filed numerically, chronologically and by date in the appropriate file drawer.
4. Collect commission	Fifty cent commission is collected from customer.

Technical Occupational Information Topics

1. Other Services
2. Protectograph Machine
3. Burrough's Teller Machine
4. Definition of Terms
5. Alphabetic, Numeric Filing Procedures

Task Detailing Sheet

Primary Occupation (PO): Teller

Occupational Specialty (OS): General Teller

Occupational Sub-Specialty (OSS): Paying and Receiving Teller

    Task: Withdrawing Funds From No Passbook Savings Accounts

Performance Steps	*Standards of Performance*
1. Examine the withdrawal ticket	The withdrawal ticket is legible and completed properly.
2. Verify signature	Signature is verified.
3. Place "hold" on the savings account	Computer has accepted "hold" for specified amount.
4. Process the withdrawal ticket	The withdrawal ticket is "cashed out" for the designated amount and placed in the appropriate bin for transit pickup.
5. Issue a receipt to the customer	A receipt is given to the customer for the exact amount of the withdrawal and the teller's stamp is affixed to it.
6. Give funds to customer	Customer has received currency equal to amount withdrawn.

Technical Occupational Information Topics

    1. Microfiche/Signature Verification
    2. Savings Inquiry System
    3. Burrough's Teller Machine
    4. No Passbook Withdrawal Procedures

Task Detailing Sheet

Primary Occupation (PO): Teller

Occupational Specialty (OS): General Teller

Occupational Sub-Specialty (OSS): Paying and Receiving Teller

    Task: Ordering the Daily Cash Supply

Performance Steps	*Standards of Performance*
1. Complete cash order form #1586	The amount of each denomination needed is listed in the appropriate column. Columns are totaled. Head teller and teller have signed both copies of cash order form #1586.

2. Process cash order form #1586   The head teller received the original.
The teller kept the duplicate copy.

Technical Occupational Information Topics

    1. Handling Money

Task Detailing Sheet

Primary Occupation (PO): Teller

Occupational Specialty (OS): General Teller

Occupational Sub-Specialty (OSS): Paying and Receiving Teller

    Task: Selling Domestic Traveler's Checks

Performance Steps	Standards of Performance
1. Greet the customer	The greeting is made in a friendly, courteous manner and includes the teller's offer of assistance. If the teller knows the customer's name, that should also be included in the greeting.
2. Take the customer's order	The order is noted in writing and in terms of total dollar amount of checks desired and denomination(s).
3. Count out the number of traveler's checks requested by the customer	The total dollar amount and denomination(s) of the checks are counted and totaled to equal the customer's request. If the denominations of the checks requested are the same, and the total dollar amount equals that of a booklet of checks as received from the issuing company, then the booklet of bound checks is selected for sale. However, if the request is made for two or more denominations of checks and/or is not for an amount equal to a booklet of checks as packaged by the issuing agency, individual checks are then selected, counted and totaled. In a series of like denomination checks, the serial numbers are consecutively arranged in ascending order, and the *number* of checks sold verified by subtracting the serial number of the first check

Performance Steps	Standards of Performance
	from the serial number of the last check and adding one. The *number* of like denomination checks, when multiplied by that denomination, should equal the total dollar amount requested.
4. Have the customer complete his portion of the purchase application	The customer's signature and printed name and address appear in the appropriate section of the purchase application.
5. Complete filling out the purchase application	The serial numbers of the series of traveler's checks appear in the appropriate section of the purchase application.
6. Collect the money from the customer	The total amount of money collected or personal check accepted equals the total amount of the checks sold plus one percent (1%) of the total amount purchased.
7. Secure purchaser's signature on each traveler's check	The purchaser signs each check in the designated place.
8. Verify the signing of each traveler's check	The signature of the purchaser appears on each check in the designated place.
9. Count out the traveler's checks to the customer	Total amount of traveler's checks equals total amount of money collected. Checks arranged in ascending order by serial number.
10. Request the customer's choice of wallet	Customer's choice of wallet is selected and the series of traveler's checks enclosed.
11. Give the traveler's checks and copies of the purchase application to the customer	Customer acknowledges receipt of checks and purchase application.
12. Offer instruction on cashing the traveler's checks	The customer is asked if he has had previous experience in using traveler's checks and, if not, would he like some suggestions regarding their use. If instruction is requested, he is told the procedure of cashing the checks and keeping record of the transactions on the purchase application(s). The suggestion is also made as to the need to keep the application and checks in different places. The prac-

Performance Steps	*Standards of Performance*
	tice is done to facilitate making a claim if the checks are lost or stolen.
13. Thank the customer	The customer is thanked, wished a pleasant journey and invited back to the bank on his return.
14. Complete the sales transaction	The cash or personal check received from the customer is attached to the original copy of the purchase application with a paper clip. It is then placed in the appropriate drawer to await final check out and settlement at the end of the business day.

Technical Occupational Information Topics

1. Terms
2. Traveler's Checks — Function and Purpose
3. Types of Traveler's Checks
4. Nomenclature
5. Purpose of the Purchase Application

Task Detailing Sheet

Primary Occupation (PO): Teller

Occupational Specialty (OS): General Teller

Occupational Sub-Specialty (OSS): Paying and Receiving Teller

    Task: Balancing the Cash Drawer and Settlement

Performance Steps	*Standards of Performance*
1. Clear Burrough's teller machine	Machine is cleared and totals retrieved.
2. Total "cash in" tickets	"Cash in" tickets are totaled.
3. Total "cash out" tickets	"Cash out" tickets are totaled.
4. Count the currency and coin and record on cash on hand form	All currency and coin is counted and recorded in appropriate place. Form is totaled.
5. Prepare settlement sheet	Starting cash plus "cash ins" for the day are entered on the credit side and are subtotaled. "Cash outs" for the day are listed on the debit side and subtracted. The total equals the total on the cash on hand form.

Technical Occupational Information Topics

    1. Settlement

    2. Settlement — Cash on Hand

    3. Settlement — Settlement Sheet

    4. Unit Count Method

    5. Burrough's Teller Machine

Task Detailing Sheet

Primary Occupation (PO):   Teller

Occupational Specialty (OS):   General Teller

Occupational Sub-Specialty (OSS):   Paying and Receiving Teller

   Task: Accepting Night Depository Deposits

Performance Steps	*Standards of Performance*
1. Accept night depository bag(s)	Night bag form #1361–1 is signed by the teller for bag(s) received.
2. Unlock night depository bag	Lock is opened by master key.
3. Process the deposit	The deposit is processed in the usual manner and the receipt is placed inside the bag.
4. Place the bag in designated drawer	The bag is placed in the designated drawer for customer pickup.

Technical Occupational Information Topics

   1. Other Services
   2. Burrough's Teller Machine
   3. Unit Count Method

Task Objective Sheets

Task Objective Sheet

  I. *Primary Occupation (PO):*　Teller

 II. *Occupational Specialty (OS):*　General Teller

III. *Occupational Sub-Specialty (OSS):*　Paying and Receiving Teller

IV. *Learning Objective:*　Counting Currency

 V. *Performance Conditions:*　In the simulated bank teller station area of the classroom, given a cash drawer and currency, given no instructional aids, and in the presence of the instructor,

VI. *Desired Behavior:*　The learner will count currency.

VII. *Evaluation Criteria:*　The money is prepared for counting according to established procedures outlined and demonstrated in class. The money is then counted and the total equals that of the instructor's. The student was able to explain the procedure he or she performed at the instructor's request. He or she demonstrated the complete procedure within a fifteen minute time period. The task was repeated a minimum of three times over a two week period.

Task Objective Sheet

  I. *Primary Occupation (PO):*　Teller

 II. *Occupational Specialty (OS):*　General Teller

III. *Occupational Sub-Specialty (OSS):*　Paying and Receiving Teller

IV. *Learning Objective:*　Cashing Checks

 V. *Performance Conditions:*　In the simulated bank teller station area of the classroom, given a Burrough's teller machine, microfiche equipment, a push button telephone, a demand deposit inquiry manual, cash drawer, and checks, given no instructional aids, and in the presence of the instructor,

VI. *Desired Behavior:*　The learner will cash checks.

VII. *Evaluation Criteria:*　The check is properly examined, processed and paid out according to established procedures outlined and demonstrated in class. The student was able to explain the procedure he or she performed at the instructor's request. He or she demonstrated the complete procedure within a five minute time period. The task was repeated a minimum of three times over a two week period.

Task Objective Sheet

   I. *Primary Occupation (PO):*   Teller

  II. *Occupational Specialty (OS):*   General Teller

 III. *Occupational Sub-Specialty (OSS):*   Paying and Receiving Teller

 IV. *Learning Objective:*   Handling Check Deposits

  V. *Performance Conditions:*   In the simulated bank teller station area of the classroom, given a Burrough's teller machine, receipts, deposit tickets, checks, given no instructional aids, and in the presence of the instructor,

 VI. *Desired Behavior:*   The learner will handle check deposits.

VII. *Evaluation Criteria:*   The deposit transaction is accurately completed according to established procedures outlined and demonstrated in class. The student was able to explain the procedure he or she performed at the instructor's request. He or she demonstrated the complete procedure within a five minute time period. The task was repeated a minimum of three times over a two week period.

Task Objective Sheet

   I. *Primary Occupation (PO):*   Teller

  II. *Occupational Specialty (OS):*   General Teller

 III. *Occupational Sub-Specialty (OSS):*   Paying and Receiving Teller

 IV. *Learning Objective:*   Handling Cash Deposits

  V. *Performance Conditions:*   In the simulated bank teller station area of the classroom, given a Burrough's teller machine, receipts, deposit tickets, and cash drawer, given no instructional aids, and in the presence of the instructor,

 VI. *Desired Behavior:*   The learner will handle cash deposits.

VII. *Evaluation Criteria:*   The deposit transaction is accurately completed according to established procedures outlined and demonstrated in class. The student was able to explain the procedure he or she performed at the instructor's request. He or she demonstrated the complete procedure within a five minute time period. The task was repeated a minimum of three times over a two week period.

Task Objective Sheet

I. *Primary Occupation (PO):*   Teller

II. *Occupational Specialty (OS):*   General Teller

III. *Occupational Sub-Specialty (OSS):*   Paying and Receiving Teller

IV. *Learning Objective:*   Receiving Personal Loan Payments

V. *Performance Conditions:*   In the simulated bank teller station area of the classroom, given a Burrough's teller machine, teller stamp, loan payment book and cash drawer, given no instructional aids, and in the presence of the instructor,

VI. *Desired Behavior:*   The learner will receive personal loan payments.

VII. *Evaluation Criteria:*   The payment accepted is equal to the loan payment amount, and the payment book is receipted and processed according to the established procedures outlined and demonstrated in class. The student was able to explain the procedure he or she performed at the instructor's request. He or she demonstrated the complete procedure within a five minute time period. The task was repeated a minimum of three times over a two week period.

Task Objective Sheet

I. *Primary Occupation (PO):*   Teller

II. *Occupational Specialty (OS):*   General Teller

III. *Occupational Sub-Specialty (OSS):*   Paying and Receiving Teller

IV. *Learning Objective:*   Receiving Christmas Club Payments

V. *Performance Conditions:*   In the simulated bank teller station area of the classroom, given a Burrough's teller machine, teller stamp, cash drawer, and Christmas Club payment book, given no instructional aids, and in the presence of the instructor,

VI. *Desired Behavior:*   The learner will receive Christmas Club payments.

VII. *Evaluation Criteria:*   The payment accepted equals the Christmas Club payment, and the Christmas Club payment book is receipted and processed according to established procedures outlined and demonstrated in class. The student was able to explain the procedure he or she performed at the instructor's request. He demonstrated the complete procedure within a five minute time period. The task was repeated a minimum of three times over a two week period.

Task Objective Sheet

I. *Primary Occupation (PO):* Teller

II. *Occupational Specialty (OS):* General Teller

III. *Occupational Sub-Specialty (OSS):* Paying and Receiving Teller

IV. *Learning Objective:* Issuing Treasurer's Checks

V. *Performance Conditions:* In the simulated bank teller station area of the classroom, given a Burrough's teller machine, Protectograph machine, cash drawer and blank treasurer's checks, given no instructional aids, and in the presence of the instructor,

VI. *Desired Behavior:* The learner will issue treasurer's checks.

VII. *Evaluation Criteria:* The Treasurer's check is accurately prepared and processed according to established sequential procedures outlined and demonstrated in class, and the office copy is filed according to standard filing procedures. The student was able to explain the procedure he or she performed at the instructor's request. He or she demonstrated the complete procedure within a fifteen minute time period. The task was repeated a minimum of three times over a two week period.

Task Objective Sheet

I. *Primary Occupation (PO):* Teller

II. *Occupational Specialty (OS):* General Teller

III. *Occupational Sub-Specialty (OSS):* Paying and Receiving Teller

IV. *Learning Objective:* Selling Money Orders

V. *Performance Conditions:* In the simulated bank teller station area of the classroom, given a Burrough's teller machine, Protectograph machine, a cash drawer, and blank money orders, given no instructional aids, and in the presence of the instructor,

VI. *Desired Behavior:* The learner will sell money orders.

VII. *Evaluation Criteria:* The money order is accurately prepared and processed according to established sequential procedures outlined and demonstrated in class. The student was able to explain the procedure he or she performed at the instructor's request. He or she demonstrated the complete procedure within a ten minute time period. The task was repeated a minimum of three times over a two week period.

Task Objective Sheet

  I. *Primary Occupation (PO):*   Teller

 II. *Occupational Specialty (OS):*   General Teller

III. *Occupational Sub-Specialty (OSS):*   Paying and Receiving Teller

IV. *Learning Objective:*   Withdrawing Funds From No Passbook Savings Accounts

 V. *Performance Conditions:*   In the simulated bank teller station area of the classroom, given a Burrough's teller machine, Burrough's savings machine, microfiche equipment, push button telephone, savings inquiry manual, receipts and a cash drawer, given no instructional aids, and in the presence of the instructor,

VI. *Desired Behavior:*   The learner will withdraw funds from no passbook savings accounts.

VII. *Evaluation Criteria:*   The funds are withdrawn and paid to the customer after standard established procedures outlined and demonstrated in class have been accurately performed. The student was able to explain the procedure he or she performed at the instructor's request. He or she demonstrated the complete procedure within a five minute time period. The test was repeated a minimum of four times over a two week period.

Task Objective Sheet

  I. *Primary Occupation (PO):*   Teller

 II. *Occupational Specialty (OS):*   General Teller

III. *Occupational Sub-Specialty (OSS):*   Paying and Receiving Teller

IV. *Learning Objective:*   Ordering the Daily Cash Supply

 V. *Performance Conditions:*   In the simulated bank teller station area of the classroom, given a cash order form, given no instructional aids, and in the presence of the instructor,

VI. *Desired Behavior:*   The learner will order the daily cash supply.

VII. *Evaluation Criteria:*   The cash order form is prepared, totaled, and processed accurately according to procedures outlined and demonstrated in class. The student was able to explain the procedure he or she performed at the instructor's request. He or she demonstrated the complete procedure within a five minute time period. The task was repeated a minimum of three times over a two week period.

Task Objective Sheet

I. *Primary Occupation (PO):* Teller

II. *Occupational Specialty (OS):* General Teller

III. *Occupational Sub-Specialty (OSS):* Paying and Receiving Teller

IV. *Learning Objective:* Selling Domestic Traveler's Checks

V. *Performance Conditions:* At a simulated bank teller's station in the classroom, given a cash drawer, supply of traveler's checks and purchase applications, desk calculator, inter-office general ledger tickets, and an assortment of wallets, and with no learning aids, but in the presence of the instructor,

VI. *Desired Behavior:* The learner will sell domestic traveler's checks.

VII. *Evaluation Criteria:* The domestic traveler's checks are prepared according to the underwriter's sales directions and the transaction verified by the instructor. The sequence of performance steps listed on the task procedure sheet given at the time of demonstration of the objective was followed exactly. The learner was able to explain the procedure he or she performed at the instructor's request. He or she demonstrated the complete procedure within a ten minute time period. The task was repeated a minimum of four times distributed equally over a two week time period.

Task Objective Sheet

I. *Primary Occupation (PO):* Teller

II. *Occupational Specialty (OS):* General Teller

III. *Occupational Sub-Specialty (OSS):* Paying and Receiving Teller

IV. *Learning Objective:* Balancing the Cash Drawer and Settlement

V. *Performance Conditions:* In the simulated bank teller station area of the classroom, given a Burrough's teller machine, "cash in" forms, "cash out" forms, "cash on hand" forms, "settlement sheet" and cash drawer, given no instructional aids, and in the presence of the instructor,

VI. *Desired Behavior:* The learner will balance his cash drawer and settle.

VII. *Evaluation Criteria:* The Burrough's teller machine is cleared, coin and currency is accurately counted and amounts are listed in the appropriate columns on the cash on hand form. The settlement sheet is prepared according to established procedures outlined and demonstrated in class and the debit and credit totals equal. The student was able to explain the procedure he or she performed at the instructor's request. He or she completed the procedure within a twenty-five minute time period. The task was repeated a minimum of four times over a two week period.

Task Objective Sheet

  I. *Primary Occupation (PO):*   Teller

 II. *Occupational Specialty (OS):*   General Teller

III. *Occupational Sub-Specialty (OSS):*   Paying and Receiving Teller

IV. *Learning Objective:*   Accepting Night Depository Deposits

 V. *Performance Conditions:*   In the simulated bank teller station area of the classroom, given a Burrough's teller machine, receipts, a cash drawer, a master key and night depository bag(s), given no instructional aids, and in the presence of the instructor,

VI. *Desired Behavior:*   The learner will accept night depository deposits.

VII. *Evaluation Criteria:*   The night depository bag(s) is accepted, unlocked, counted, and receipted accurately. Procedures outlined and demonstrated in class were followed exactly. The student was able to explain the procedure he or she demonstrated at the instructor's request. He or she demonstrated the complete procedure within a twenty minute time period. The task was repeated a minimum of three times over a two week period.

Curriculum Spiral

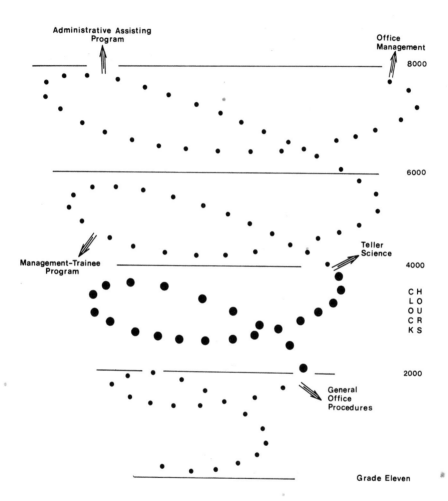

Figure A.3 *A Long-Range Curriculum Spiral for Money Distribution and Management-Related Occupations*

**Determining the Occupational Program, Course and
Unit Titles from the List of Occupational Specialties
and Sub-Specialties of the Primary Occupation**

Occupation, Occupational Specialty and Sub-Specialty Titles	*Program, Course and Unit Titles*
I. *Primary Occupation (PO):* Teller	I. *Occupational Program:* Teller Science
II. *Occupational Specialties (OS):*	II. *Occupational Courses:*
A. General Teller	A. General Tellering
B. Collection and Exchange Teller	B. Collection and Exchange Tellering
C. Note Teller	C. Note Tellering
D. Utility Teller	D. Utility Teller Procedures
III. *Occupational Sub-Specialties (OSS):*	III. *Occupational Units:*
A. Occupational Specialty: General Teller	A. Course: General Tellering
1. Mail Credit Teller	1. Mail Deposits
2. Paying and Receiving Teller	2. Paying and Receiving
3. Payroll Teller	3. Payroll
4. Return Items Teller	4. Return Items
5. Savings Teller	5. Savings
6. Special Deposits Teller	6. Special Deposits
B. Occupational Specialty: Collection and Exchange Teller	B. Course: Collection and Exchange Tellering
1. Bond Teller	1. Bonds
2. Domestic Exchange Teller	2. Domestic Exchange
3. Foreign Exchange Teller	3. Foreign Exchange
C. Occupational Specialty: Note Teller	C. Course: Note Tellering
1. Collateral Teller	1. Collateral
2. Commercial Note Teller	2. Commercial Notes
3. Discount Teller	3. Discount
*D. Occupational Specialty: Utility Teller	D. Course: Utility Teller Procedures

*In the analysis, there were no occupational sub-specialties for the specialty of "Utility Teller". Hence, there are no unit titles for the course in "Utility Teller Procedures".

**An Outline of the Teller Science Occupational Program
with Course, Unit and Learning Objective Titles**

Occupational Program: Teller Science

Course #1:   General Tellering

Unit #1:   Mail Deposits

Learning Objectives:
- Opening Envelopes
- Receiving Checks for Deposit
- Examining Checks for Endorsements
- Verifying Deposits
- Entering Deposits in Depositor's Passbook or Checking Account
- Issuing Receipts

Unit #2:   Paying and Receiving
Learning Objectives:
- Counting Currency
- Cashing Checks
- Handling Check Deposits
- Handling Cash Deposits
- Receiving Personal Loan Payments
- Receiving Christmas Club Payments
- Issuing Treasurer's Checks
- Selling Money Orders
- Withdrawing Funds from No Passbook Savings Accounts
- Ordering the Daily Cash Supply
- Selling Domestic Traveler's Checks
- Balancing the Cash Drawer and Settlement
- Accepting Night Depository Deposits

Unit #3:   Payroll
Learning Objectives:
- Receiving Payroll Requests from Depositors
- Preparing Cash in Requested Denominations
- Verifying Totals
- Accepting Debit to Offset Payroll
- Assuring Funds are Available
- Computing Service Charge

Unit #4:   Return Items

  Learning Objectives:

- Returning Item to Cashing Tellers for Collection
- Debiting Checking Accounts for Deposited Items
- Returning Deposited Savings Account Items to Originating Office Head Tellers for Collection
- Assessing Service Charges
- Charging-Off Uncollectable Return Items

Unit #5:   Savings

  Learning Objectives:

- Verifying Cash Deposits
- Securing Endorsements on Deposited Items
- Verifying Total on Deposit Tickets
- Posting Customer's Passbooks
- Withdrawing Funds Upon Signature Verification
- Posting Annual Interest
- Placing Holds on Withdrawals
- Issuing Treasurer's Checks
- Microfilming Transactions
- Balancing Cash Drawer

Unit #6:   Special Deposits

  Learning Objectives:

- Reporting Unusual Deposits of $10,000.00 or More to Satisfy Bank Secrecy Act
- Accepting Certified Checks for Deposit
- Accepting Sight Drafts for Collection
- Accepting Government Bond Interest Coupons for Deposit
- Receiving Withholding Tax Deposits

Occupational Program: Teller Science

Course #2:   Collection and Exchange Tellering

Unit #1:   Bonds

   Learning Objectives:

- Issuing Series "E" Bonds
- Preparing Transmittal Letters
- Ordering Bond Inventory
- Maintaining Activity Records
- Exchanging Series "E" Bonds for Series "H" Bonds
- Computing Interest on Bonds Presented for Redemption
- Issuing Treasurer's Checks
- Counting Money

Unit #2:   Domestic Exchange

   Learning Objectives:

- Presenting for Collection Items Bearing Guaranteed Endorsements
- Redeeming Treasury Bills
- Collecting Bearer Bonds When Due
- Issuing Letters of Credit

Unit #3:   Foreign Exchange

   Learning Objectives:

- Counting Currency
- Selling Foreign Currency
- Identifying and Classifying Foreign Currency
- Computing Exchange Rates and Exchanging Foreign Currency
- Preparing Foreign Drafts
- Preparing Cable Transfers
- Preparing Air Mail Transfers
- Selling Tip Packs
- Selling Foreign Travelers Cheques
- Redeeming Foreign Travelers Cheques
- Maintaining Controls

Occupational Program: Teller Science

Course #3:   Note Tellering

Unit #1:   Collateral

   Learning Objectives:

- Typing Documents
- Examining Collateral for Negotiability
- Securing Necessary Documentation
- Monitoring Stock Margins
- Maintaining Securities Vault
- Releasing Securities
- Computing Current Value of Loan Collateral Held

Unit #2:   Commercial Note

   Learning Objectives:

- Recording Judgements and Second Mortgages
- Accepting Payments on Loans
- Issuing Receipts
- Examining Collateral for Negotiability
- Typing Documents
- Satisfying Judgements and Second Mortgages

Unit #3:   Discount

   Learning Objectives:

- Computing Interest
- Posting Payments
- Maintaining Ledgers
- Issuing Receipts
- Verifying Ledger Balances

Occupational Program: Teller Science

Course #4:   Utility Teller Procedures

   Learning Objectives:

- Collecting Payments from Customers
- Totaling Items on Bill Using Adding Machine
- Recording Transactions
- Issuing Receipts
- Adjusting Bill Complaints
- Handling Partial Payments of Bill
- Crediting Utility Company Accounts

Unit Learning Modules

Unit Learning Module

Occupational Program:　Tellering Science

Course #1:　General Tellering

Unit #2:　Paying and Receiving

Learning Objective #1:　Counting Currency

Performance Conditions:　In the simulated bank teller station area of the classroom, given a cash drawer and currency, given no instructional aids, and in the presence of the instructor.

Desired Behavior:　The student will count money.

Evaluation Criteria:　The money is prepared for counting according to established procedures outlined and demonstrated in class. The money is then counted and the total equals the instructor's. The student was able to explain the procedure he or she performed at the instructor's request. He or she demonstrated the complete procedure within a fifteen minute time period. The task was repeated a minimum of three times over a two week period.

Learning Activities:

1. Read the section on "Handling Money" in Teller's manual (85 minutes)
2. Answer questions on "Handling Money" (30 minutes)
3. Take the Related Readings Test on "Counting Currency" (45 minutes)
4. Observe the demonstration of counting currency (60 minutes)
5. View film "Money Handling for Tellers" (20 minutes)
6. Critique the film (15 minutes)
7. Practice counting currency (240 minutes)
8. Take the final performance test (15 minutes/each of three tests: 45 minutes)

Estimated Time: 9 hours

Complementary Learning Activities:

1. Tour Money Reserve so students will understand the operations of a large currency counting facility (90 minutes)
2. Research methods of counting currency and discuss the pros and cons of each (120 minutes)
3. Prepare a report on various ways to detect counterfeit currency (90 minutes)

Equipment and Materials:

Equipment:　Projector, screen, cash drawer

Materials:　Currency, film, Teller's manual, handouts

Unit Learning Module

Occupational Program: Teller Science

Course #1: General Tellering

Unit #2: Paying and Receiving

Learning Objective #2: Cashing Checks

Performance Conditions: In the simulated bank teller station area of the classroom, given a Burrough's teller machine, Micro-Fiche equipment, a push button telephone, a demand deposit inquiry manual, cash drawer, and checks, given no instructional aids, and in the presence of the instructor,

Desired Behavior: The student will cash checks.

Evaluation Criteria: The check is properly examined, processed and paid out according to established procedures outlined and demonstrated in class. The student was able to explain the procedure he or she performed at the instructor's request. He or she demonstrated the complete procedure within a five minute time period. The task was repeated a minimum of three times over a two week period.

Learning Activities:

1. Read section on "Cashing Checks" in Teller's manual (90 minutes)
2. Read American Banker's Association booklet "Identification With and Without Credentials" (90 minutes)
3. Read Chapter on "Signature Verification" in text (60 minutes)
4. Read "Clearing House Recommendations" (20 minutes)
5. Read "Demand Deposit Inquiry System" (60 minutes)
6. Take the Related Readings Test on "Examining and Cashing Checks" (60 minutes)
7. Participate in a discussion/review of test (45 minutes)
8. Read Handout on "Equipment and Forms" (15 minutes)
9. Observe the demonstration of examining and cashing checks (120 minutes)
10. Practice examining and cashing checks (240 minutes)
11. Take the final performance test (5 minutes/each of three tests: 15 minutes)

Estimated Time: 13 hrs. 35 mins.

Complementary Learning Activities:

1. View audio/videotape "Journey of a Check" to see "in house" routing of item after teller cashes it for a customer (25 minutes)
2. Tour Bookkeeping department to learn the function of the various units and how their operations relate to tellering (90 minutes)

3. Listen to a representative from Computer and Systems discuss the importance of proper demand deposit formating (60 minutes)

4. Tour the Information Center where on-line terminals are housed for a lecture and demonstration (60 minutes)

Equipment and Materials:

Equipment: Burrough's teller machine, Micro-Fiche/Signature Verification viewer and card index, push button telephone, cash drawer, coin machine

Materials: Teller's manual, handouts, checks, currency, coin

Unit Learning Module

Occupational Program: Teller Science

Course #1: General Tellering

Unit #2: Paying and Receiving

Learning Objective #3: Handling Check Deposits

Performance Conditions: In the simulated bank teller station area of the classroom, given a Burrough's teller machine, receipts, deposit tickets, and checks, given no instructional aids, and in the presence of the instructor,

Desired Behavior: The student will handle check deposits.

Evaluation Criteria: The deposit transaction is accurately completed according to established procedures outlined and demonstrated in class. The student was able to explain the procedure he or she performed at the instructor's request. He or she demonstrated the complete procedure within a five minute time period. The task was repeated a minimum of three times over a two week period.

Learning Activities:

1. Read section on "Handling Deposits with Checks" in Teller's manual (90 minutes)

2. Take Related Readings Test on "Handling Check Deposits" (30 minutes)

3. Participate in a presentation/discussion on Handling Check Deposits (60 minutes)

4. View film "Handling Deposits" (20 minutes)

5. Observe the demonstration on handling check deposits (30 minutes)

6. Practice the activity (120 minutes)

7. Take the final performance test (5 minutes/each of three tests: 15 minutes)

Estimated Time: 5 hrs. 5 mins.

Complementary Learning Activities:

1. Tour Transit Proof Operations to see a demonstration of how the teller's work is verified and further processed (90 minutes)
2. Observe experienced tellers at a major financial institution and prepare a report on their method of handling deposits (120 minutes)
3. View and critique film "Uncollected Funds" (45 minutes)

Equipment and Materials:

Equipment: Burrough's teller machine, projector, screen

Materials: Teller's manual, film, handouts, deposit tickets, receipts

---

Unit Learning Module

Occupational Program: Teller Science

Course #1:   General Tellering

Unit #2:   Paying and Receiving

Learning Objective #4:   Handling Cash Deposits

Performance Conditions: In the simulated bank teller station area of the classroom, given a Burrough's teller machine, receipts, deposit tickets, and cash drawer, given no instructional aids, and in the presence of the instructor,

Desired Behavior: The student will handle cash deposits.

Evaluation Criteria: The deposit transaction is accurately completed according to established procedures outlined and demonstrated in class. The student was able to explain the procedure he or she performed at the instructor's request. He or she demonstrated the complete procedure within a five minute time period. The task was repeated a minimum of three times over a two week period.

Learning Activities:

1. Read section on "Handling Deposits with Cash" in Teller's manual (90 minutes)
2. Take the Related Readings Test on "Handling Cash Deposits" (45 minutes)
3. Participate in a presentation/discussion on handling cash deposits (60 minutes)
4. View film "Handling Deposits" (20 minutes)
5. Observe the demonstration on handling cash deposits (30 minutes)
6. Practice the activity (120 minutes)
7. Take the final performance test (5 minutes/each of three tests: 15 minutes)

Estimated Time: 6 hrs. 20 mins.

Complementary Learning Activities:

1. Tour Transit Proof Operations to see a demonstration of how the teller's work is verified and further processed (90 minutes)
2. View and critique film on "Kiting" (60 minutes)
3. Prepare a report on the "Bank Secrecy Act" (90 minutes)

Equipment and Materials:

Equipment: Burrough's teller machine, projector, screen, cash drawer

Materials: Teller's manual, film, handouts, currency, deposit tickets, receipts

---

Unit Learning Module

Occupational Program: Teller Science

Course #1:   General Tellering

Unit #2:   Paying and Receiving

Learning Objective #5:   Receiving Personal Loan Payments

Performance Conditions: In the simulated bank teller station area of the classroom, given a Burrough's teller machine, teller stamp, loan payment book and cash drawer, given no instructional aids, and in the presence of the instructor,

Desired Behavior: The student will receive personal loan payments.

Evaluation Criteria: The payment accepted is equal to the loan payment amount, and the payment book is receipted and processed according to the established procedures outlined and demonstrated in class. The student was able to explain the procedure he or she performed at the instructor's request. He or she demonstrated the complete procedure with a five minute time period. The task was repeated a minimum of three times over a two week period.

Learning Activities:

1. Read section on "Personal Credit Accounts" in Teller's manual (30 minutes)
2. Read handout "Definition of Terms" (10 minutes)
3. Take the Related Readings Test on "Receiving Personal Loan Payments" (40 minutes)
4. Participate in a presentation/discussion on receiving personal loan payments (45 minutes)
5. Observe the demonstration on receiving personal loan payments (30 minutes)
6. Practice the activity (90 minutes)
7. Take the final performance test (5 minutes/each of three tests: 15 minutes)

Estimated Time: 4 hrs. 20 mins.

Complementary Learning Activities:

1. Have a representative from Personal Credit direct a tour of his facilities so that the student will have a comprehensive view of the operations, and understand the importance of processing personal loan payments accurately (120 minutes)

2. View film "Money and Banking" and prepare a written report on the Federal Reserve Bank's control over the flow of currency (120 minutes)

Equipment and Materials:

Equipment: Burrough's teller machine, teller stamp, cash drawer, coin machine

Materials: Teller's manual, handouts, loan payment books, currency, coin

---

Unit Learning Module

Occupational Program: Teller Science

Course #1: General Tellering

Unit #2: Paying and Receiving

Learning Objective #6: Receiving Christmas Club Payments

Performance Conditions: In the simulated bank teller station area of the classroom, given a Burrough's teller machine, teller stamp, cash drawer, and Christmas Club payment book, given no instructional aids, and in the presence of the instructor,

Desired Behavior: The student will receive Christmas Club payments.

Evaluation Criteria: The payment accepted equals the Christmas Club payment, and the Christmas Club payment book is receipted and processed according to established procedures outlined and demonstrated in class. The student was able to explain the procedure he or she performed at the instructor's request. He or she demonstrated the complete procedure within a five minute time period. The task was repeated a minimum of three times over a two week period.

Learning Activities:

1. Read section on "Christmas Club Accounts" in Teller's manual (40 minutes)

2. Take the Related Readings test on "Receiving Christmas Club Payments" (30 minutes)

3. Participate in a presentation/discussion on receiving Christmas Club payments (45 minutes)

4. Observe the demonstration on receiving Christmas Club payments (30 minutes)

5. Practice the activity (90 minutes)

6. Take the final performance test (5 minutes/each of three tests: 15 minutes)

Estimated Time: 4 hrs. 10 mins.

Complementary Learning Activities:
1. Prepare an exhibit of Christmas Club coupons for display in the class-room (45 minutes)

Equipment and Materials:

Equipment: Burrough's teller machine, teller stamp, cash drawer, coin machine

Materials: Teller's manual, handouts, Christmas Club Books, currency, coin

---

Unit Learning Module

Occupational Program: Teller Science

Course #1: General Tellering

Unit #2: Paying and Receiving

Learning Objective #7: Issuing Treasurer's Checks

Performance Conditions: In the simulated bank teller station area of the class-room, given a Burrough's teller machine, Protectograph machine, cash drawer and blank treasurer's checks, given no instructional aids, and in the presence of the instructor,

Desired Behavior: The student will issue treasurer's checks.

Evaluation Criteria: The treasurer's check is accurately prepared and processed according to established sequential procedures outlined and demonstrated in class, and the office copy is filed according to standard filing procedures. The student was able to explain the procedure he or she performed at the instructor's request. He or she demonstrated the complete procedure within a fifteen minute time period. The task was repeated a minimum of three times over a two week period.

Learning Activities:
1. Read section on "Treasurer's Checks" in Teller's manual (20 minutes)
2. Read handout on "Related Banking Teminology" (10 minutes)
3. Take the Related Readings Test on "Issuing Treasurer's Checks" (30 minutes)
4. Review the test and answer questions (30 minutes)
5. Participate in a presentation/discussion on issuing treasurer's checks (50 minutes)
6. View transparencies on proper completion and distribution of treasurer's checks (45 minutes)
7. Observe the demonstration on issuing treasurer's checks (30 minutes)
8. Practice the activity (120 minutes)
9. Take the final performance test (15 minutes/each of three tests: 45 minutes)

Estimated Time: 6 hrs. 20 mins.

Complementary Learning Activities:

1. Prepare a chart on the proper completion and routing of Treasurer's Checks for the classroom (60 minutes)

2. Prepare a written report on "What is a Treasurer's Check"? (60 minutes)

Equipment and Materials:

Equipment: Burrough's teller machine, Protectograph machine, file drawer, overhead projector, screen, typewriter, cash drawer, coin machine

Materials: Teller's manual, handouts, Treasurer's Checks, transparencies currency, coin

---

Unit Learning Module

Occupational Program: Teller Science

Course #1:   General Tellering

Unit #2:   Paying and Receiving

Learning Objective #8:   Selling Money Orders

Performance Conditions: In the simulated bank teller station area of the classroom, given a Burrough's teller machine, Protectograph machine, a cash drawer, and blank money orders, given no instructional aids, and in the presence of the instructor,

Desired Behavior: The student will sell money orders.

Evaluation Criteria: The money order is accurately prepared and processed according to established sequential procedures outlined and demonstrated in class. The student was able to explain the procedure he or she performed at the instructor's request. He or she demonstrated the complete procedure within a ten minute time period. The task was repeated a minimum of three times over a two week period.

Learning Activities:

1. Read section on "Money Orders" in Teller's manual (15 minutes)

2. Read handout on "Related Bank Terminology" (15 minutes)

3. Answer questions on selling money orders (30 minutes)

4. Take the Related Readings Test on "Selling Money Orders" (30 minutes)

5. Review the test (30 minutes)

6. Observe the demonstration on selling money orders (45 minutes)

7. Practice the activity (120 minutes)

8. Take the final performance test (10 minutes/each of three tests: 30 minutes)

Estimated Time: 5 hrs. 15 mins.

Complementary Learning Activities:

1. Prepare a written report on the advantages and disadvantages of money orders versus checking account (60 minutes)

Equipment and Materials:

Equipment: Burrough's teller machine, Protectograph machine, file drawer, cash drawer, coin machine

Materials: Teller's manual, money orders, handouts, currency, coin

---

Unit Learning Module

Occupational Program: Teller Science

Course #1:   General Tellering

Unit #2:   Paying and Receiving

Learning Objective #9:   Withdrawing Funds from No Passbook Savings Accounts

Performance Conditions: In the simulated bank teller station area of the classroom, given a Burrough's teller machine, Burrough's savings machine, Micro-Fiche equipment, push button telephone, savings inquiry manual, receipts and a cash drawer, given no instructional aids, and in the presence of the instructor,

Desired Behavior: The student will withdraw funds from no passbook savings accounts.

Evaluation Criteria: The funds are withdrawn and paid to the customer after standard established procedures, outlined and demonstrated in class, have been accurately performed. The student was able to explain the procedure he or she performed at the instructor's request. He or she demonstrated the complete procedure within a five minute time period. The task was repeated a minimum of four times over a two week period.

Learning Activities:

1. Read section on "No Passbook Savings Accounts" in the Savings Fund Manual (60 minutes)
2. Read chapter on "Signature Verification" in text (60 minutes)
3. Read "Time Deposit Accounts Inquiry System" (60 minutes)
4. Answer questions on reading assignments (60 minutes)
5. Take the Related Readings Test on "Withdrawing Funds from No Passbook Savings Accounts" (60 minutes)
6. Participate in presentation/discussion on withdrawing funds from no passbook savings accounts (120 minutes)
7. Observe the demonstration of established procedures for withdrawing funds from no passbook savings accounts (90 minutes)
8. Practice the activity (180 minutes)

9. Take the final performance test (5 minutes each/each of four tests: 20 minutes)

Estimated Time: 11 hrs. 50 mins.

Complementary Learning Activities:
1. Tour Savings Fund Bookkeeping for lecture and discussion (60 minutes)
2. Tour Information Center for a lecture and demonstration on information available from the computer (60 minutes)

Equipment and Materials:

Equipment: Burrough's Teller machine, Burrough's savings machine, cash drawer, coin machine

Materials: Teller's manual, Savings manual, handouts, currency, receipts, coin

---

Unit Learning Module

Occupational Program: Teller Science

Course #1:   General Tellering

Unit #2:   Paying and Receiving

Learning Objective #10:   Ordering the Daily Cash Supply

Performance Conditions: In the simulated bank station area of the classroom, given a cash order form, given no instructional aids, and in the presence of the instructor,

Desired Behavior: The student will order a supply of cash to meet his daily needs.

Evaluation Criteria: The cash order form is prepared, totalled and processed accurately according to procedures outlined and demonstrated in class. The student was able to explain the procedure he or she performed at the instructor's request. He or she demonstrated the complete procedure within a five minute time period. The task was repeated a minimum of three times over a two week period.

Learning Activities:
1. Read section on "Ordering Coin and Currency" in Teller's manual (30 minutes)
2. Take the Related Readings Test on "Ordering Supply of Cash to Meet Daily Needs" (30 minutes)
3. Participate in a presentation/demonstration on ordering coin and currency (45 minutes)

4. Observe the demonstration on form completion and procedures for ordering coin and currency (45 minutes)
5. Practice the activity (60 minutes)
6. Take the final performance test (5 minutes/each of three tests: 15 minutes)

Estimated Time: 3 hrs. 45 mins.

Complementary Learning Activities:

1. Prepare a report on office and teller limitations for a particular branch (60 minutes)
2. Prepare a report on security measures each teller must adhere to in regard to storing excess coin and currency (60 minutes)

Equipment and Materials:

Equipment: None

Materials: Teller's manual, cash order forms, handouts

Unit Learning Module

Occupational Program: Teller Science

Course #1: General Tellering

Unit #2: Paying and Receiving

Learning Objective #11: Selling Domestic Traveler's Checks

Performance Conditions: At a simulated bank teller's station in the classroom, given a cash drawer, supply of traveler's checks and purchase applications, desk calculator, inter-office general ledger tickets, and an assortment of wallets, and with no learning aids, but in the presence of the instructor,

Desired Behavior: The learner will sell domestic traveler's checks.

Evaluation Criteria: The domestic traveler's checks are prepared according to the underwriter's sales directions and the transaction verified by the instructor. The sequence of performance steps listed on the task procedure sheet given at the time of demonstration of the objective was followed exactly. The learner was able to explain the procedure he or she performed at the instructor's request. He or she demonstrated the complete procedure within a ten minute time period. The task was repeated a minimum of four times distributed equally over a two week time period.

Learning Activities:

1. Read the Information Sheet "Terms" (10 minutes)
2. Read the Information-Assignment Sheet "Traveler's Checks" (30 minutes)

3. Complete the assignment portion of the above Information-Assignment Sheet (30 minutes)

4. Read pages 44–48 in the "Training Manual for Tellers", Fidelity Bank of Carbondale (30 minutes)

5. Read the Task Procedure Sheet "Selling Domestic Traveler's Checks" (20 minutes)

6. View the video-taped illustrated presentation "Traveler's Checks — an Informational Review" (60 minutes)

7. Complete the related information test on traveler's checks (60 minutes)

8. Observe the narrated slide tape demonstration of "Selling Domestic Traveler's Checks" (15 minutes)

9. Practice the activity (8 hours)

10. Take the final performance test of selling domestic traveler's checks (10 minutes/each of four tests: 40 minutes)

Estimated Time: 12 hrs. 55 mins.

Complementary Learning Activities:

1. Purchase traveler's checks as a customer in preparation for a trip (30 minutes)

2. Write a paper on stolen traveler's checks

Equipment and Materials:

Equipment: 2 X 2 slide projector, speaker, and screen

Materials: None

Unit Learning Module

Occupational Program: Teller Science

Course #1:   General Tellering

Unit #2:   Paying and Receiving

Learning Objective #12:   Balancing the Cash Drawer and Settlement

Performance Conditions: In the simulated bank teller station area of the classroom, given a Burrough's teller machine, "cash-in" forms, "cash-out" forms, "cash-on-hand" forms, "settlement sheet" and cash drawer, given no instructional aids, and in the presence of the instructor,

Desired Behavior: The student will balance his cash drawer and settle.

Evaluation Criteria: The Burrough's teller machine is properly cleared, coin and currency is accurately counted and amounts are listed in appropriate columns on the cash on hand form. The settlement sheet is prepared according to established procedures outlined and demonstrated in class and the debit and credit totals equal. The student was able to explain the procedure he or she performed at the instructor's request. He or she completed the procedure within a twenty-five minute time period. The task was repeated a minimum of four times over a two week period.

Learning Activities:
1. Read section on "Settlement" in Teller's manual (60 minutes)
2. Read handout on "Banking Terminology" (15 minutes)
3. Answer questions on "Balancing the Cash Drawer and Settlement", and terminology (45 minutes)
4. Take Related Readings Test on Balancing the Cash Drawer and Settlement (50 minutes)
5. Participate in a presentation/discussion on balancing the cash drawer and settlement (60 minutes)
6. View transparencies on "Form Completion and Procedures for Balancing the Cash Drawer and Settlement" (45 minutes)
7. Observe the demonstration on balancing the cash drawer and settlement (30 minutes)
8. Practice the activity (180 minutes)
9. Take the final performance test (25 minutes/each of 4 tests: 100 minutes)

Estimated Time: 9 hrs. 45 mins.

Complementary Learning Activities:
1. Prepare a procedures manual on each step of "Balancing the Cash Drawer and Settlement" (240 minutes)
2. Observe experienced tellers "Balancing the Cash Drawer and Settling" (60 minutes)

Equipment and Materials:

Equipment: Overhead projector, screen, adding machine, Burrough's teller machine, cash drawer, coin machine

Materials: Teller's manual, handouts, transparencies, cash in forms, cash out forms, cash on hand forms, settlement forms, currency, coin

Unit Learning Module

Occupational Program: Teller Science

Course #1:   General Tellering

Unit #2:   Paying and Receiving

Learning Objective #13:   Accepting Night Depository Deposits

Performance Conditions: In the simulated bank teller station area of the classroom, given a Burrough's teller machine, receipts, a cash drawer, master key and night depository bag(s), given no instructional aids, and in the presence of the instructor,

Desired Behavior: The student will accept night depository deposits.

Evaluating Criteria: The night depository bag(s) is accepted, unlocked, counted, and receipted accurately. Procedures outlined and demonstrated in class were followed exactly. The student was able to explain the procedure he or she demonstrated at the instructor's request. He or she demonstrated the complete procedure within a twenty minute time period. The task was repeated a minimum of three times in a two week period.

Learning Activities:

1. Read "Night Depository Deposits" in Teller's manual (30 minutes)
2. Answer questions on "Accepting Night Deposits" (30 minutes)
3. Take Related Readings Test on "Accepting Night Depository Deposits" (45 minutes)
4. Participate in a presentation/discussion on accepting night depository deposits (60 minutes)
5. Observe the demonstration on accepting night depository deposits (60 minutes)
6. Practice accepting, opening, counting, and processing night depository deposits (120 minutes)
7. Take the final performance test (20 minutes/each of three tests: 60 minutes)

Estimated Time: 6 hrs. 45 mins.

Complementary Learning Activities:

1. Prepare a report on security measures taken to safeguard night bags (90 minutes)
2. Observe experienced tellers "Accepting Night Depository Deposits" (60 minutes)

Equipment and Materials:

Equipment: Burrough's teller machine, cash drawer, coin machine, night bags, master key

Materials: Currency, coin, handouts

Record Forms and Achievement Awards

Record Forms

BLACK DIAMOND COMMUNITY COLLEGE

Teller Science Occupational

Program Transcript

I. *Performance Record of:*

Name: _____

Address: _____
 Street

_____
City   State   Zip

Telephone Number: ( ) _____

II. *Biographical Data:*

Date of Birth: _____

Place of Birth: _____

Social Security No.: _____

Date of Admission: _____

III. *Program:* Teller Science:

A. Applied Courses:

Course#1: General Tellering

Unit #1: Mail Deposits

Learning Objectives: Date   Initial

- Opening Envelopes   ____   ____
- Receiving Checks for Deposit   ____   ____
- Examining Checks for
  Endorsements   ____   ____
- Verifying Deposits   ____   ____
- Entering Deposit in Depositor's
  Passbook or Checking Account   ____   ____
- Issuing Receipts   ____   ____

Unit #4: Return Items

Learning Objectives: Date   Initial

- Returning Item to Cashing
  Tellers for Collection   ____   ____
- Debiting Checking Accounts
  for Deposited Items   ____   ____
- Returning Deposited Savings
  Account Items to Origi-
  nating Office Head Tellers
  for Collection   ____   ____

290

Unit #2: Paying and Receiving

Learning Objectives:

	Date	Initial
· Counting Currency		
· Cashing Checks		
· Handling Check Deposits		
· Handling Cash Deposits		
· Receiving Personal Loan Payments		
· Receiving Christmas Club Payments		
· Issuing Treasurer's Checks		
· Selling Money Orders		
· Withdrawing Funds From No Passbook Savings Accounts		
· Ordering the Daily Cash Supply		
· Selling Domestic Traveler's Checks		
· Balancing the Cash Drawer and Settlement		
· Accepting Night Depository Deposits		
· Assessing Service Charges		
· Charging-Off Uncollectable Return Items		

Unit #5: Savings

Learning Objectives:

	Date	Initial
· Verifying Cash Deposits		
· Securing Endorsements on Deposited Items		
· Verifying Total on Deposit Tickets		
· Posting Customer's Passbooks		
· Withdrawing Funds Upon Signature Verification		
· Posting Annual Interest		
· Placing Holds on Withdrawals		
· Issuing Treasurer's Checks		
· Microfilming Transactions		
· Balancing Cash Drawer		

Unit #6: Special Deposits:

Learning Objectives:

	Date	Initial
· Reporting Unusual Deposits of $10,000 or More to Satisfy Bank Secrecy Act		
· Accepting Certified Checks for Deposit		
· Accepting Sight Drafts for Collection		
· Accepting Government Bond Interest Coupons for Deposit		
· Receiving Withholding Tax Deposits		

Unit #3: Payroll

Learning Objectives:

	Date	Initial
· Receiving Payroll Requests From Depositors		
· Preparing Cash in Requested Denominations		
· Verifying Totals		
· Accepting Debit to Offset Payroll		
· Assuring Funds Are Available		
· Computing Service Charge		

Course #2: Collection and Exchange Tellering

Unit #1: Bonds

Learning Objectives: Date   Initial
- Issuing Series "E" Bonds
- Preparing Transmittal Letters
- Ordering Bond Inventory
- Maintaining Activity Records
- Exchanging Series "E" Bonds for Series "H" Bonds
- Computing Interest on Bonds Presented for Redemption
- Issuing Treasurer's Checks
- Counting Money

Unit #2: Domestic Exchange

Learning Objectives: Date   Initial
- Presenting for Collection Items Bearing Guaranteed Endorsements
- Redeeming Treasury Bills
- Collecting Bearer Bonds When Due
- Issuing Letters of Credit

Unit #3: Foreign Exchange

Learning Objectives: Date   Initial
- Counting Currency
- Selling Foreign Currency
- Identifying and Classifying Foreign Currency

Unit #2: Commercial Note

Learning Objectives: Date   Initial
- Recording Judgments and Second Mortgages
- Accepting Payments on Loans
- Issuing Receipts
- Examining Collateral for Negotiability
- Typing Documents
- Satisfying Judgments and Second Mortgages

Unit #3: Discount:

Learning Objectives: Date   Initial
- Computing Interest
- Posting Payments
- Maintaining Ledgers
- Issuing Receipts
- Verifying Ledger Balances

Course #4: Utility Teller Procedures

Unit #1:

Learning Objectives: Date   Initial
- Collecting Payments for Customers
- Totaling Items on Bill Using Adding Machine
- Recording Transactions
- Issuing Receipts

- Computing Exchange Rates and Exchanging Foreign Currency
- Preparing Foreign Drafts
- Preparing Cable Transfers
- Preparing Air Mail Transfers
- Selling Tip Packs
- Selling Foreign Traveler's Cheques
- Redeeming Foreign Traveler's Cheques
- Maintaining Controls

Course #3: Note Tellering

Unit #1: Collateral

Learning Objectives: Date   Initial

- Typing Documents
- Examining Collateral for Negotiability
- Securing Necessary Documentation
- Monitoring Stock Margins
- Maintaining Securities Vault
- Releasing Securities
- Computing Current Value of Loan Collateral Held

- Adjusting Bill Complaints
- Handling Partial Payments of Bill
- Crediting Utility Company Accounts

B. *Related Subjects*

1. *Grading*

   S – Satisfactory
   U – Unsatisfactory

2. *Courses*   Grade   Initial

- Basic Mathematics
- Business English
- Principles of Loss Prevention
- Principles of Bank Operations
- Principles of Economics
- Savings and Time Deposit Banking
- English Composition
- Basic Accounting
- Interpersonal Communication
- Principles of Data Processing
- Money and Banking
- Federal Reserve System

Course Achievement Record
General Tellering

I. *Performance Record of:*   II. *Student Data:*

Name: _____   Date of Entry: _____

Address: _____   Date of Completion: _____

_____

Telephone: ( )_____

III. *Units with Learning Objectives:*

Unit #1: Mail Deposits

Learning Objectives: *Date*   *Initial*

- Opening Envelopes   ____   ____
- Receiving Checks for Deposit   ____   ____
- Examining Checks for Endorsement   ____   ____
- Verifying Deposits   ____   ____
- Entering Deposit in Depositor's Passbook or
  Checking Account   ____   ____
- Issuing Receipts   ____   ____

Unit #2: Paying and Receiving

Learning Objectives:

- Counting Currency   ____   ____
- Cashing Checks   ____   ____
- Handling Check Deposits   ____   ____
- Handling Cash Deposits   ____   ____
- Receiving Personal Loan Payments   ____   ____
- Receiving Christmas Club Payments   ____   ____
- Issuing Treasurer's Checks   ____   ____
- Selling Money Orders   ____   ____
- Withdrawing Funds From No Passbook Savings
  Accounts   ____   ____
- Ordering the Daily Cash Supply   ____   ____
- Selling Domestic Traveler's Checks   ____   ____
- Balancing the Cash Drawer and Settlement ____   ____
- Accepting Night Depository Deposits   ____   ____

Unit #3: Payroll

Learning Objectives: *Date*   *Initial*

- Receiving Payroll Requests from Depositors ____   ____
- Preparing Cash in Requested Denominations ____   ____
- Verifying Totals   ____   ____
- Accepting Debit to Offset Payroll   ____   ____
- Assuring Funds Are Available   ____   ____
- Computing Service Charge   ____   ____

Unit #4: Return Items

Learning Objectives:	*Date*	*Initial*
• Returning Item to Cashing Tellers for Collection	____	____
• Debiting Checking Accounts for Deposited Items	____	____
• Returning Deposited Savings Account Items to Originating Office Head Tellers for Collection	____	____
• Assessing Service Charges	____	____
• Charging-Off Uncollectable Return Items	____	____

Unit #5: Savings

Learning Objectives:	*Date*	*Initial*
• Verifying Cash Deposits	____	____
• Securing Endorsements on Deposited Items	____	____
• Verifying Total on Deposit Tickets	____	____
• Posting Customer's Passbooks	____	____
• Placing Holds on Withdrawals	____	____
• Issuing Treasurer's Checks	____	____
• Microfilming Transactions	____	____
• Balancing Cash Drawer	____	____

Unit #6: Special Deposits

Learning Objectives:	*Date*	*Initial*
• Reporting Unusual Deposits of $10,000 or More to Satisfy Bank Secrecy Act	____	____
• Accepting Certified Checks for Deposit	____	____
• Accepting Sight Drafts for Collection	____	____
• Accepting Government Bond Interest Coupons for Deposit	____	____
• Receiving Withholding Tax Deposits	____	____

IV. *Remarks:*

V. *Attainment:*

The learner has attained all of the above learning objectives and is prepared to work as a teller or continue his preparation for employment in the Teller Science Occupational Program.

_____   _____
Instructor's Signature   Date

Black Diamond Community College

Business Occupations

B

Certificate

This certifies that _____ has successfully

completed the course _____

given this _____ day of _____ 19 ___

_____   _____
INSTRUCTOR   CHAIRMAN

Black Diamond Community College

B

On recommendation of the President and Faculty,
the Board of Trustees, by virtue of the authority vested in it, has
conferred on

the degree of

and has granted this Diploma as evidence thereof

....
President

....
Dean

....
Chairman of Board

APPENDIX B

A Curriculum Guide of Selected Program, Course
and Unit Descriptions for the Money Distribution and
Management-Related Occupational Curriculum

by
Beverly Faunce
and
Maria Varano Butz

Table of Contents

Foreword

The "Curriculum Guide of Selected Program, Course, and Unit Descriptions in the Money Distribution and Management-Related Occupational Curriculum" is a product of the occupational curriculum development process proposed by Bortz.[1] The process includes developing a theory of organization, gathering and organizing occupational data, converting occupational activities and information to occupational curriculum, developing occupational programs, courses and units of study, and, lastly, preparing learning materials.

The following manuscript is a product of the first two major steps of the occupational curriculum development process. The sequential completion of the procedural steps established the organizational basis and direction of the entire occupational curriculum development process, and guided the learner in writing the occupational program, course, and unit descriptions found herein. The products of the last step of the development process, while not contained in the manuscript, contain the learning materials needed to attain the learning objectives of the occupational unit, and evaluation instruments for measuring their effectiveness in the learning process.

Organization

The organizational theory provided the theoretical basis for the development of the Long-Range Employment-Curriculum Spiral for Money Distribution and Management-Related Occupations. The employment spiral component of the dual employment-curriculum spiral served as the organizational concept for ranking and ordering occupations in the money distribution field. It provided a means of establishing a hierarchy of related occupational titles and their respective tasks, which, when accompanied by the component curriculum spiral, defined points of passage between work and education and education and work.

The analysis of the occupation of teller provided the necessary occupational data. The analysis contained a listing of the occupational specialties and sub-specialties of the teller occupation and the tasks performed in each. This list of functionally related occupational titles and tasks would eventually provide the organization and content of the Teller Science Occupational Program.

With the analysis complete, the conversion of employment-related activities to curricular activities was then made. Basically, this entailed writing each of the tasks mentioned above as learning objectives, and extending the organizational plan developed in the analysis to the occupational program, courses and units.

Once completed, the organization and content of the Teller Science Occupational Program was established and ready for further development. For a detailed study of the proposed occupational curriculum development process the reader can refer to the Appendix in this guide.

---

[1] Bortz, Richard F. "Developing Occupational Curriculum." (Unpublished manuscript, Southern Illinois University at Carbondale, 1978.)

Source of Occupational Data

As mentioned above, the occupational curriculum materials contained in this manuscript were derived from an analysis of the occupation of teller. In this particular study, the teller worked in the main office of a bank whose assets total three billion dollars.

The teller worked with ten other tellers. The office staff comprised only a small percentage of the bank's total number of employees. The teller was familiar with a few of the various departments within the company and dealt either directly or indirectly with those departments.

The teller was supervised by the Head Teller of the branch and at times, by the Branch Manager. The teller had no supervisory responsibility.

A Description of the
Teller Science
Occupational Program

by
Beverly Faunce
and
Maria Varano Butz

The second program in a series of five occupational
programs in the Money Distribution and Management-Related
Occupational Curriculum

Although the rate of technological change is hard to measure, no one seems to argue that the useful life of technical training is growing ever shorter. The assumption that ten percent of all technical knowledge becomes obsolete each year is generally accepted. Such obsolescence is likely to take one of two forms: inability to keep up to date with job requirements, and inability to maintain professional versatility.

Programs to combat manpower obsolescence should be based on comprehensive manpower planning and curriculum design.

The program content has to be related to the individual's desire to acquire the new knowledge and techniques. The program may increase the effectiveness of the individual's performance or may serve to extend or enlarge his or her capabilities for a position in a higher level. No matter what the purpose, the program material must be relevant to the real world.

The Teller Science Program is the second in a series of five occupational programs that comprise the Long-Range Occupational Curriculum Spiral for Money Distribution and Management-Related Occupations. The two-fold purpose of the program is to prepare the student for work in any one of the occupational specialties or sub-specialties of the occupation of teller, or to prepare him or her for entry into the Management Trainee Occupational Program. Completion of each of the applied courses in the program prepares the person for employment in one of the occupational specialties of the occupation of teller. Collectively, they prepare the individual for work as a teller. Individually, they prepare him or her for work as a general teller, collection and exchange teller, note teller and/or utility teller.

Goals

The goals of the program are to:

- Create for the student an understanding of the design, character, and service of the teller position in the banking system, and to provide the knowledge to master all responsibilities in the occupation.
- Supply a basic understanding of the banking system and foster attitudes in the student that will allow him or her to grow in the banking industry.
- Develop the skills and knowledge necessary to obtain employment as a teller or any one of the occupational specialties that comprise it.

Admission and Retention Requirements

Any person 18 years of age or older, interested in the banking field will be admitted to the program. The learner must maintain a reasonable rate of attaining the learning objectives to continue in the program. He or she must have command of basic arithmetic and communications skills.

Costs and Financial Assistance

Costs of training will vary according to the school attended and may range from $1,000 to $2,000 for the program. Most large financial institutions have either a tuition advance or tuition reimbursement policy to assist the employee in his or her educational growth and development. There are also various state and federally funded programs which offer the student financial assistance.

Courses

The Teller Science Program requires approximately 2,500 clock hours for completion. Subtotals and times for the individual courses appear in the listing of courses below. The time factors are computed on the assumption that the student has no prior tellering education background and will be taking each course in its entirety. A listing of the applied and related subject matter courses with their respective clock hour requirements appears below.

	Clock Hours		Clock Hours
Basic Mathematics	100	English Composition	90
*General Tellering	720	*Collection and Exchange Tellering	500
Business English	90	Basic Accounting	80
Principles of Loss Prevention	80	Interpersonal Communication	90
Subtotal	990	Subtotal	760

	Clock Hours		Clock Hours
*Utility Teller Procedures	80	*Note Tellering	120
Principles of Bank Operations	90	Principles of Data Processing	90
Principles of Economics	90	Money and Banking	100
Savings and Time Deposit Banking	90	Federal Reserve System	90
Subtotal	350	Subtotal	400
		Grand Total	2,500

The clock hours listed may vary somewhat with each student in relation to his or her learning ability.

Career and Employment Opportunities

On successful completion of the program, the student may obtain employment in any size financial institution throughout the continental United States.

Salaries for tellers average $560 per month. Senior tellers and head tellers average $700 per month. Salaries may vary in different parts of the country and are affected by length of service and experience.

The teller position is a non-supervisory responsibility level.

For those people who do not complete the Teller Science occupational program, employment opportunities in one or more of the occupational specialties or sub-specialties are available. However, these openings are typically limited to the larger financial institutions.

Educational Opportunities

Upon completion of the Teller Science Program, the student may continue his or her educational work in the Money Distribution and Management-Related Occupational Curriculum. The programs which serially follow the teller program are the "Management Trainee Program", "Administrative Assistant Program" and "Office Management". The occupations for which a person would be prepared upon completion of these programs would respectively be assistant manager, administrative assistant, and office manager. An individual obtaining any one of these positions must have acquired work experience as a teller.

Additional Information

For additional information about the Teller Science Program contact:

Ms. Beverly Faunce, Program Coordinator
Business Occupations
Black Diamond Community College
Carbondale, IL   62901
Telephone: (215) 715–6002

An Outline of the General Tellering Occupational Course

by
Beverly Faunce
and
Maria Varano Butz

The first in a series of four applied occupational
courses in the Teller Science Program in the
Money Distribution and Management-Related Occupational Curriculum

"General Tellering" is the first in a series of four applied courses in the Teller Science Occupational Program. Its purpose and scope is derived from the analysis of the occupational specialty of general teller. On completion of the course, the student will be qualified to work as a general teller or as any one of its occupational sub-specialties, or continue his or her training in the occupational curriculum.

With the growing acceptance of specialization in banking, it becomes apparent that necessary skills and knowledge are defined. This course is designed to provide individuals with the necessary skills for immediate employment as a general teller or in the related occupational sub-specialties of mail credit teller, paying and receiving teller, payroll teller, return items teller, savings teller or special deposits teller. In any case, the result is employability.

On completion of the course, the student will enjoy the option of being prepared for work, or if he or she chooses, he or she can elect to continue his or her occupational education in one or more of the other courses in the next program.

Goals

The goals of the course are to:

- Create for the student an understanding of the design, character, and service of the teller position in the banking system, and to provide the knowledge to master all responsibilities in the occupation.
- Supply a basic understanding of the banking system and foster attitudes in the student that will allow him or her to grow in the banking industry.
- Develop the skills and knowledge necessary to obtain employment as a teller or any one of the occupational specialties that comprise it.

Admission and Retention Requirements

Any person 18 years of age or older, interested in the banking field will be admitted to the program. The student must be able to accurately perform the learning objectives of the course within the time period allotted. He or she must also be able to do basic arithmetic functions and demonstrate common communications skills.

Costs and Financial Assistance

The total cost of the course is $150. This figure includes the costs incurred for materials and supplies, needed equipment, text, booklets, and duplicating, collating, and binding the materials developed in the course.

The cost of the course is covered by tuition aid and tuition reimbursement programs, and recognized scholarship programs.

Units

The General Tellering course is comprised of six units and requires approximately 735 clock hours for completion. The units are as follows:

Unit One: Mail Credit Tellering (127 hrs)

Unit Two: Paying and Receiving Tellering (100 hrs)

Unit Three: Payroll Tellering (127 hrs)

Unit Four: Return Items Tellering (100 hrs)

Unit Five: Savings Tellering (180 hrs)

Unit Six: Special Deposits Tellering (100 hrs)

Text

Vergari, James V. *Negotiable Instruments and the Payment Mechanism.* 1st ed. New York: American Institute of Banking, The American Bankers Association, 1975.

Additional References

Waldren, Harold. *Principles of Bank Operations.* New York: American Institute of Banking, The American Bankers Association, 1966.

Career and Employment Opportunities

Upon successful completion of the above course, the student will be qualified to work as a general teller or in any of the occupational sub-specialties prepared for during the completion of this course. Due to the degree of specialization, most employment opportunities will be limited to larger institutions. With additional study, or through experience gained while employed, the teller can acquire the necessary additional skills to qualify for other teller-related occupations.

For the beginning teller, salaries are lower than those of other office workers. However, pay increases do come with experience.

With the expansion of branch banking and the possibility of state-wide banking, tellers are in demand and will be even more so in the near future.

Educational Opportunities

Once the course is completed, the student may continue his or her educational work in the Teller Science Program or he or she may begin employment and continue his or her education at a later date. However, with additional study, the student can eventually become qualified as a teller or any of the other occupations in the teller field.

Course Products

On completion of the course the student will have the following course products:

- A Mini-Reference Manual
- Sample Transactions Manual

Additional Information

For additional information or assistance, contact

Ms. Ina Derrick, Teller Trainer
Business Occupations
Black Diamond Community College
Carbondale, IL 62901

Telephone: (215) 715-6002

A Guide to the
Paying and Receiving
Occupational Unit

by

Beverly Faunce

and

Maria Varano Butz

The second in a series of six occupational
units in the General Tellering Course
in the Teller Science Occupational Program

Table of Contents

Introduction

"Paying and Receiving" is the second of six units in the "General Tellering" Course. The two-fold purpose of the unit is to prepare students for employment as a paying and receiving teller, and/or to further their occupational education toward employment in other teller-related occupations. The unit title and the learning objectives are directly derived from the analysis of the occupational sub-specialty of the paying and receiving teller. While attaining the objectives of the unit, the student paying and receiving teller will acquire the skills and knowledge needed to perform such tasks as: examination and encashment of checks, acceptance of cash and check deposits, issuance of Treasurer's checks, balancing the debits and credits, etc. Indeed, every task that comprises the sub-specialty of paying and receiving teller will be acquired so that he or she can function effectively in the banking system.

Much like the program and course descriptions, the unit description provides the learner with various employment and educational options. On completion of the unit objectives, he or she will enjoy the options of being prepared for work as a paying and receiving teller, or if he or she chooses, continuing his or her occupational education in one or more of the other teller-related occupational curriculum offerings.

Goals

The goals of the unit are to:

- Create for the learner an understanding of the design, character, and services of the teller position in the banking system, and to provide the knowledge to master all responsibilities in the occupation.
- Foster attitudes that will allow the learner to grow in the banking industry.
- Develop skills in the learner that will prepare him or her for employment as a teller or serve as a basis for continuing his or her occupational education.

Learning Objectives

The learning objectives are derived from the list of tasks of the occupational sub-specialty of paying and receiving teller. The thirteen learning objectives for the unit are:

- Counting Currency
- Cashing Checks
- Handling Check Deposits
- Handling Cash Deposits
- Receiving Personal Loan Payments
- Receiving Christmas Club Payments
- Issuing Treasurer's Checks
- Selling Money Orders
- Withdrawing Funds From No Passbook Savings Accounts
- Ordering the Daily Cash Supply
- Selling Domestic Traveler's Checks

- Balancing the Cash Drawer and Settlement
- Accepting Night Depository Deposits

The occupational unit requires approximately one hundred clock hours for completion. This total is based on the estimated amounts of time required to attain all of the above learning objectives. The total time figure is increased or reduced proportionately depending on the individual learner's need for more or less time to attain a particular objective.

The estimated times for each of the above learning objectives appear on the individual unit learning modules that follow in the last section of this unit.

Admission and Retention Requirements

Previous tellering experience is not required for entry into the occupational unit. Retention in the unit is dependent on the learner's continuing attainment of the learning objectives.

Text

Vergari, James V. *Negotiable Instruments and the Payment Mechanism,* 1st edition. New York: American Institute of Banking and the American Bankers Association, 1975.

Additional References

Waldren, Harold. *Principles of Bank Operations*. New York: American Institute of Banking and the American Bankers Association, 1966.

Costs and Financial Assistance

The costs incurred in the unit total fifty dollars. No financial assistance is available at this time through any funding or scholarship agencies.

Unit Learning Modules

The thirteen unit learning modules that comprise this unit appear on pages 28 through 40. Together with the learning objectives, the modules contain lists of learning activities that will guide the learner to the defined end.

Career and Employment Opportunities

At the end of the occupational unit, the student will be qualified for work as a paying and receiving teller. Due to the degree of specialization, most employment opportunities will be limited to larger institutions where specialized teller help is employed. Only such large institutions can accommodate people whose skills are so specialized.

For the beginning paying and receiving teller, salaries are usually at the minimum. Opportunities for advancement within the occupational sub-specialty are few. However, pay increases come with experience and other opportunities are available with additional training in other teller-related occupations.

NOTE: Whereas the entire set of unit learning modules is included in a complete unit guide, only one has been included here for purposes of example.

Educational Opportunities

Additional occupational education opportunities lie within the teller occupations field. By completing the remaining units of the "General Tellering" course, the student will be qualified to work as a general teller or in any one of the six occupational sub-specialties that comprise it.

Additional Information

For additional information or assistance contact

> Ms. Ina Derrick, Teller Trainer
> Business Occupations
> Black Diamond Community College
> Carbondale, IL   62901
> Telephone: (215) 715-6002

Unit Learning Module

Occupational Program: Teller Science

Course #1:   General Tellering

Unit #2:   Paying and Receiving

Learning Objective #11:   Selling Domestic Traveler's Checks

Performance Conditions: At a simulated bank teller's station in the classroom, given a cash drawer, supply of traveler's checks and purchase applications, desk calculator, inter-office general ledger tickets, and an assortment of wallets, and with no learning aids, but in the presence of the instructor,

Desired Behavior: The learner will sell domestic traveler's checks.

Evaluation Criteria: The domestic traveler's checks are prepared according to the underwriter's sales directions and the transaction verified by the instructor. The sequence of performance steps listed on the task procedure sheet given at the time of demonstration of the objective was followed exactly. The learner was able to explain the procedure he or she performed at the instructor's request. He or she demonstrated the complete procedure within a ten minute time period. The task was repeated a minimum of four times distributed equally over a two week time period.

Learning Activities:

1. Read the Information Sheet "Terms" (10 minutes)
2. Read the Information-Assignment Sheet "Traveler's Checks" (30 minutes)
3. Complete the assignment portion of the above Information-Assignment Sheet (30 minutes)
4. Read pages 44–48 in the "Training Manual for Tellers", Fidelity Bank of Carbondale (30 minutes)
5. Read the Task Procedure Sheet "Selling Domestic Traveler's Checks" (20 minutes)

6. View the video-taped illustrated presentation "Traveler's Checks — an Informational Review" (60 minutes)

7. Complete the related information test on traveler's checks (60 minutes)

8. Observe the narrated slide tape demonstration of "Selling Domestic Traveler's Checks" (15 minutes)

9. Practice the activity (8 hours)

10. Take the final performance test of selling domestic traveler's checks (10 minutes/each of four tests: 40 minutes)

Estimated Time: 12 hrs. 55 mins.

Complementary Learning Activities

1. Purchase traveler's checks as a customer in preparation for a trip (30 minutes)

2. Write a paper on stolen traveler's checks

Equipment and Materials

Equipment: 2 X 2 slide projector, speaker and screen

Materials: None

APPENDIX C

A Resource Guide for the
Learning Activities Package of . . .
. . . Selling Domestic Traveler's Checks

by
Beverly Faunce
and
Maria Varano Butz

The eleventh in a series of thirteen learning
activities packages in the Paying and Receiving Unit of
the General Tellering Course in the
Teller Science Occupational Program

Table of Contents

Introduction

"Selling Domestic Traveler's Checks" is the eleventh in a series of thirteen learning activities packages that comprise the occupational unit in "Paying and Receiving". The purpose of the learning activities package is to assist the learner in acquiring the requisite knowledge and skill so as to be able to perform the task of selling domestic traveler's checks. Once the learning objective is attained, the learner is one step nearer to completing the unit of instruction and being qualified for employment as a paying and receiving teller.

The LAP is the resultant product of a culminating series of events that preceded it. Beginning with an analysis of the various occupational specialties and sub-specialties of the occupation of teller into their respective lists of tasks, converting of tasks to learning objectives, and writing of the various occupational program, course, and unit descriptions, the result is realized when the various LAPs are developed and used in attaining the individual learning objectives of the particular unit of which they are a part. In those situations which demand it, the LAPs can be used alone by a person to attain the given objective, or if need be, put with other selected learning packages to give an individual a tailor-made grouping of occupational skills.

In this particular learning activities package, the student paying and receiving teller will acquire the knowledge and skills necessary to successfully perform the task of selling domestic traveler's checks. Enroute to attaining the learning objective, he or she will gain essential information as it pertains to performing the task and become familiar with the procedure as it is commonly performed by tellers in banks and other money handling institutions.

Since this LAP is only one in a series of thirteen learning activities packages, its completion does not mark a point at which the learner is fully prepared for employment. Rather, completion of this LAP recognizes the learner's attainment of the skill of selling domestic traveler's checks, and at the same time, mentally prepares him or her to begin attainment of the next learning objective in the series.

Prerequisites

The prerequisites for the learning activities package for selling domestic traveler's checks are that the learner be able to read, write, and count. He or she should also possess the quality of being friendly and courteous and, at the same time, thorough, organized and businesslike. The learner should also already possess a working knowledge of ten-key and full-keyboard adding machines.

Contents of the Learning Activities Package

The list of learning materials contained in this learning package is as follows:

1. "A Guide to the Informational and Activities Resources for the Learning Activities Package of Selling Domestic Traveler's Checks."
2. "Training Manual for Tellers." Personnel Training Unit. The Fidelity Bank of Carbondale.
3. "Review of Necessary Information for Selling Domestic Traveler's Checks." Video-taped presentation.
4. "Selling Domestic Traveler's Checks" slide series and audiotape.

Learning Objective

Title: Selling Domestic Traveler's Checks

Performance Conditions: At a simulated bank teller's station in the classroom, given a cash drawer, supply of traveler's checks and purchase applications, desk calculator, inter-office general ledger tickets, and an assortment of wallets, and with no learning aids, but in the presence of the instructor,

Desired Behavior: The learner will sell domestic traveler's checks.

Evaluation Criteria: The domestic traveler's checks are prepared according to the underwriter's sales directions and the transaction verified by the instructor. The sequence of performance steps listed on the task procedure sheet given at the time of demonstration of the objective was followed exactly. The learner was able to explain the procedure he or she performed at the instructor's request. He or she demonstrated the complete procedure within a ten minute time period. The task was repeated a minimum of four times distributed equally over a two-week time period.

Directions for Completing the Learning Activities Package

The sequence of learning activities listed below will guide you in completing this learning activities package. The learning materials specified in each learning activities statement, e.g., textbook, related information and instruction sheets, tests, videotapes, slide series, and audiotapes, etc., comprise the LAP.

    To assist and guide you through the learning package, the various learning materials have been arranged and numbered to correspond with the list of learning activities. Hence, to begin the LAP, read the first learning activities statement, locate the specified learning materials in the package and complete the activity. Repeat the procedure with items 2, 3, 4, and so on until you have completed the entire list of activities.

    A word of caution. Be sure to follow the sequence of learning activities as they are listed. Their order is important in insuring your success in completing the LAP and attaining the learning objective.

    The LAP will take approximately thirteen hours to complete. This total is based on estimated time it will take to complete each learning activity. The times are not absolute and if it takes you a little more or a little less time to complete either the individual learning activities or the package itself, do not be overly concerned. The package is designed to accommodate you and your rate and style of learning.

Learning Activities

The learning activities are as follows:

1. Read the Information Sheet "Terms" (10 minutes)
2. Read the Information-Assignment Sheet "Traveler's Checks" (30 minutes)
3. Complete the assignment portion of the above Information-Assignment Sheet (30 minutes)
4. Read pages 44–48 in the "Training Manual for Tellers", Fidelity Bank of Carbondale (30 minutes)

5. Read the Task Procedure Sheet "Selling Domestic Traveler's Checks" (20 minutes)

6. View the videotaped illustrated presentation "Traveler's Checks — An Informational Review" (60 minutes)

7. Complete the related information test on traveler's checks (60 minutes)

8. Observe the narrated slide tape demonstration of "Selling Domestic Traveler's Checks" (15 minutes)

9. Practice the activity (8 hours)

10. Take the final performance test of selling domestic traveler's checks (10 minutes/each of four tests: 40 minutes)

Terms

The terms associated with the task of selling domestic traveler's checks and their definitions appear below.

- Countersign — The act of signing a traveler's check a second time. Done by the holder of the check in the presence of the party who is going to cash the check at the time of cashing.

- Countersignature — The signature made by the holder of the check at the time of cashing. For the check to be valid, the *countersignature* must correspond in name and handwriting to the signature made at the time of purchase.

- Denomination — The dollar value of the traveler's check. Appears as a number ($10, $20, $50, etc.) at several different places on the check. Denominations of traveler's checks are $10, $20, $50, $100, $500 and $1,000.

- Initial Signature — The handwritten name of the purchaser that appears in a designated place on the traveler's check and is made in the presence of the teller at the time of purchase.

- Loose Checks — Traveler's checks which may be sold individually or in any combination of denominations. Those traveler's checks which are not pre-packaged.

- Pre-Packaged Checks — Checks which are packaged and sold in predetermined check denomination and total value amounts. Example: a package of ten $20 checks totalling $200.00.

- Private Brand — The term used to describe traveler's checks which are issued and guaranteed by companies other than American Express, Bank of America, or First National City Bank of New York. In many cases, the "private brands" are still financially backed by one of the major issuing companies.

- Purchase Application — The multiple copy form completed by the teller at the time of purchase. Used as proof and record of sale by the issuing agency, the seller, and the purchaser.

- Serial Number — The number that appears on each individual traveler's check and is used to identify that particular check. No two serial numbers are the same on any checks issued by a given agency.

- Stale-Dated — The term used to describe a check that has exceeded the legal time limit in which it must be cashed. After that time, the check is said to be "stale-dated" or non-negotiable.
- Transit Routing Number — One of several numbers that appears on a traveler's check. It defines the particular bank or issuing agency in the Federal Reserve Banking System on which the check is drawn. It facilitates high speed processing of the check through the banking system.
- Traveler's Check — A prepaid, negotiable note. A check drawn against an issuing company or agency which guarantees that funds are on deposit equal to the face value of the check and available to reimburse the party who cashes it.
- Wallet — A billfold or checkbook-like holder in which the traveler's checks are placed and presented to the customer at the time of sale. Usually made of a thin, waterproof, plastic material.

References

Wallgren, Harold. *Principles of Bank Operations.* New York: American Institute of Banking and American Bankers Association, 1975.

Traveler's Checks

A traveler's check is a legal, negotiable check whose recognized value is guaranteed by the issuing bank, express office, or other funding agency. Most often the checks are used, as their name implies, by travelers to purchase various goods and services both in this country and abroad. Like cash, traveler's checks are a recognized and readily spendable form of currency. However, unlike cash, their value to the original purchaser is not lost if they are inadvertently misplaced, lost, stolen, damaged, or destroyed. It is because of their nationwide and international recognition and acceptance, and the guaranteed return on investment, that traveler's checks are so widely used. They are a great convenience to those who travel and do business in places and situations where they are not known and where cashing a personal check might be very difficult if not impossible.

Also, traveler's checks, unlike personal checks, do not become "stale-dated," e.g., there is no expiration date fixed to their time of purchase. Once a traveler's check is purchased it is valuable to the customer until it is cashed.

Brands of Traveler's Checks

The three most commonly used traveler's checks are those issued by American Express, Bank of America, and First National City Bank of New York. While all three agencies issue traveler's checks that are somewhat different in appearance, closer study reveals marked similarities. A sample traveler's check appears in Figure 1.

In each case, the physical size of the check approximates the size of U.S. currency. The properties, e.g., type of paper, watermarking, and impregnations in the checks themselves, differ somewhat depending on the dictates of the issuing company. However, even in these cases, these differences share the same purpose, e.g., to reduce alterations to the rightful owner's signature or counterfeiting of the note itself.

The entries on the various checks are also about the same. (See Figure 2.) Each has the name of the issuing company, the denomination of the check appearing in

Figure 1.　*Sample Traveler's Check*

several different places, a serial number, a transit routing number, provision for the signature of the buyer as witnessed by the seller at the time of purchase, a space for entering the name of the individual or business to whom the check is being paid, space for the countersignature of the person cashing the check, and lastly, the date of the transaction.

Denominations and Packaging

Traveler's checks are usually issued in $10, $20, $50, $100, $500 and $1,000 denominations. Traveler's checks which bear "private brand" insignias are typically only available in $10, $20, $50, and $100 denominations. In either case, however, the denomination specifies the dollar value of the check, and is recognized as such in a business transaction.

Traveler's checks are sold in one of two ways: as *loose* checks or in a *pre-packaged* form. As loose checks, the buyer specifies the total amount of checks he or she wishes to purchase and the denomination(s) of the checks to be included. The total figure has

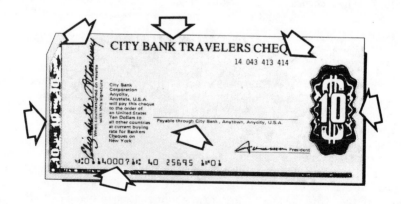

Figure 2.　*Various Entries on a Traveler's Check*

to be compatible with the sum total of the individual checks purchased. The loose checks, once verified and signed, are then assembled and packaged by the teller and given to the customer.

Pre-packaged traveler's checks, in contrast, are issued by the parent company to the seller in pre-packaged, self-contained units. The packages contain varying numbers of checks of a given denomination and are sold in that form for the defined amount.

There are advantages and disadvantages to selling the checks in each of the two ways. For the customer, "loose" checks are more appealing in that he or she can purchase a greater variety of denominations of checks if his or her needs are such. The disadvantage to the customer of purchasing "loose" checks is that the entire process of signing all of the checks has to occur at the teller's window and be witnessed by him or her before the transaction can be made. If time is of the essence at the time of purchase, then the "loose check" method becomes a disadvantage.

The advantages realized by the selling institution in selling loose-style checks is the flexibility of the service afforded its customers. On the other hand, the difficulties encountered in keeping accurate records of check sales, maintaining the sequence of checks to be sold, and other problems that arise when selling checks in "loose" form, have prompted some institutions to abandon that approach and begin selling pre-packaged checks.

For the customer, pre-packaged traveler's checks reduce the amount of time spent in purchasing the checks and the possibility of receiving an incorrect number of checks at the time of purchase. For the selling agency, pre-packaged checks permit a better and more efficient means of inventorying and auditing the supply of checks, reduce the number of minutes spent by the tellers in making the transaction with the customer, and reduce the number of errors made at the time of sale.

Purchase Applications

A *purchase application* is a multiple copy form that is completed both by the teller and customer at the time of sale of the traveler's checks. Its purpose is to formalize and make record of the sale of checks between the two parties. Two types of forms are available. One type is used for the sale of *loose* checks and another for the sale of *pre-packaged* checks. Figure 3 shows a sample purchase application.

Both forms are similar in that they include the name, address, and code number of

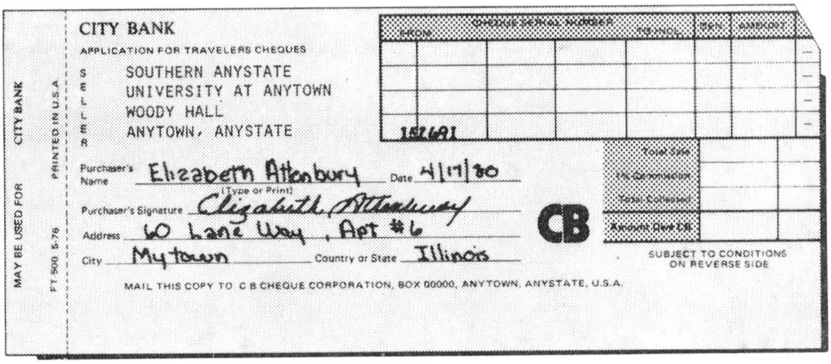

MAY BE USED FOR CITY BANK
PRINTED IN U.S.A.
FT 500 5-76

CITY BANK
APPLICATION FOR TRAVELERS CHEQUES

SELLER
SOUTHERN ANYSTATE
UNIVERSITY AT ANYTOWN
WOODY HALL
ANYTOWN, ANYSTATE

CHEQUE SERIAL NUMBER FROM | TO (INCL.) | DEN | AMOUNT
152691

Purchaser's Name Elizabeth Attenbury (Type or Print) Date 4/17/80
Purchaser's Signature Elizabeth Attenbury
Address 60 Lane Way, Apt #6
City Mytown Country or State Illinois

CB

Total Sale
1% Commission
Total Collected
Amount Due CB

SUBJECT TO CONDITIONS ON REVERSE SIDE

MAIL THIS COPY TO C B CHEQUE CORPORATION, BOX 00000, ANYTOWN, ANYSTATE, U.S.A.

Figure 3. *Purchase Application Form*

the selling agent, space for the signature and printed or typed name of the buyer, date of sale and provision for entering the data regarding the checks themselves. The application form for the sale of loose checks, however, is more detailed in this latter provision than it is for pre-packaged checks. Quantities, denominations, check numbers, subtotals, charge rate, and totals comprise the list of entries on the purchase application form, whereas the only entries required on the pre-packaged form are the date of sale, control number of the selling agency, and amount of money due the issuing company resulting from the sale.

As mentioned above, the purchase application is a multi-copy form. A purchase application form contains one original (the front sheet) and various copies. The copies typically are color coded. The original, when completed, is returned to the issuing company. Included with the original is a check equal to the amount of the service charge rate on the sale. Two copies of the same color are kept by the seller for his or her record. One copy is given to the customer for a record of the transaction.

Purchase application forms of the different companies differ somewhat in their physical appearance and make-up. However, their purpose is the same, to make record of the sale of the traveler's checks between the selling agent and the customer.

Wallets

A plastic cover or *wallet* is used to protect the unused checks until they are cashed. Pre-packaged checks, when received by the seller and sold to the customer, are already enclosed in their own protective cover. However, loose checks do not come packaged in this way and must be put in a protective cover at the time of sale.

Two types of wallets are available: the *flat* or *pocket* style, and the *in-stub* wallet. (See Figure 4.) The customer can choose the style of wallet he or she wishes. The flat wallet is much like a checkbook and can be carried conveniently in a coat, pants pocket, or purse. The in-stub type of wallet is somewhat more compact and is convenient for carrying in a hip or shirt pocket or smaller handbag.

Usually the wallets are made of a thin, flexible plastic. They come in assorted colors with the most common colors being black and dark blue. Being plastic, they help protect the checks from moisture damage, as well as any type of physical abuse or damage to which they might be subjected.

Figure 4. *Types of Wallets for Traveler's Checks*

For Study and Discussion

1. What is a "traveler's check?"
2. What guarantee accompanies a traveler's check but that is not associated with a personal check?
3. Who legally guarantees a given traveler's check?
4. What advantages do traveler's checks have over cash? Disadvantages?
5. Define the term "stale-dated." Does this term apply to traveler's checks?
6. What are the names of the three major U.S. agencies that issue traveler's checks?
7. What is the difference between a traveler's check issued by one of the major issuing companies and one issued by a "private brand" company?
8. What are the two ways in which traveler's checks are packaged?
9. What is a "purchase application?"
10. Who is responsible for filling out the purchase application?
11. Two types of covers or "wallets" are used to package and protect *loose* traveler's checks once they have been sold to the customer. What are the two types of wallets?

References

Chapin, Albert F. and George E. Hassetts, Jr. *Credit and Collection Principles and Practices,* 7th edition. New York: McGraw-Hill, 1960.

Vergari, James V. *Negotiable Instruments and the Payment Mechanism,* 1st edition. New York: American Institute of Banking and the American Bankers Association, 1975.

Waldren, Harold, *Principles of Bank Operations.* New York: American Institute of Banking and the American Bankers Association, 1966.

Procedure for Selling Domestic Traveler's Checks

The performance steps of the task of *Selling Domestic Traveler's Checks* appear below. The task is one of thirteen performed by a Paying and Receiving Teller in the course of a business day. The performance steps are for the task of selling traveler's checks in their loose form. Illustrations are included, as needed, to assist the learner in better understanding and performing the various steps of the task.

Equipment and Supplies

The following items are needed to complete the task:

- calculating machine
- money supply
- supply of assorted denominations of traveler's checks

- purchase application forms
- assortment of wallets

Performance Steps

The procedure for selling traveler's checks is as follows:

1. *Greet the customer.* The greeting is made in a friendly, courteous manner and includes the teller's offer of assistance. If the teller knows the customer's name, that should also be included in the greeting. For example, an appropriate greeting might be, "Good morning, Mr. Smith. Nice day, isn't it? May I help you?" (See Figure 1.)

Figure 1. *Greeting the Customer*

2. *Take the customer's order.* When the customer specifies that he or she wants to buy traveler's checks, the question is asked by the teller as to the total dollar amount and the denomination(s) desired. The order is noted in writing by the teller in abbreviated form as shown in Figure 2.

3. *Count out the number of traveler's checks requested by the customer.* Referring to the handwritten note, the total dollar amount and denomination(s) of checks are counted and totalled to equal the customer's request. If the denominations of the checks requested are the same, and the total dollar amount equals that of a booklet of checks as received from the

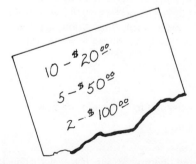

Figure 2. *Teller's Notes of Number of Checks by Denomination*

issuing company, then the booklet of bound checks is selected for sale. However, if the request is made for two or more denominations of checks and/or is not for an amount equal to a booklet of checks as packaged by the issuing agency, individual checks are then selected, counted, and totalled.

In each of the above cases, a precautionary step is taken to verify the number of checks of the same denomination being sold. Assured that the serial numbers of the like denomination checks are consecutive, the *number* of checks being sold is verified by subtracting the serial number of the first check from the serial number of the last check and adding one. Multiply the number of checks then by their denomination (they must be all the same) and the product should equal the subtotal or total (depending on the situation) dollar amount requested.

4. *Have the customer complete his portion of the purchase application.* Once the number and denomination(s) of traveler's checks are counted, the customer is then requested to complete one portion of the purchase application. This entails having the customer *sign* his or her name, *print* his or her name and write in his or her address in the spaces provided on the form. The customer should also be reminded to press firmly as he or she writes, since all of the copies of the application must bear the requested information. (See Figure 3.)

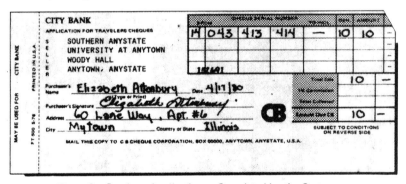

Figure 3. *Purchase Application as Completed by the Customer*

5. *Complete filling out the purchase application.* Once the customer has completed his portion of the purchase application, the teller must then finish completing the form. (See Figure 4.) The name, address and code number of the selling agency, together with the signature and other information provided by the customer, must be checked and verified. Also, entries are made as to the quantity and denomination of checks sold, their numerical sequence, the line and total dollar value of the checks sold in the transaction, the service charge (1% of the total), the total dollar amount collected from the customer, and the amount due the issuing company. The date of the sale is also recorded on the application form.

6. *Collect the money from the customer.* Once the purchase application form is complete, the money owed on the checks is collected from the customer. The sum collected equals the total amount due for the traveler's checks plus the 1% service charge.

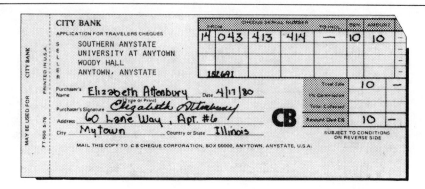

Figure 4. *Completed Purchase Application*

7. *Secure the customer's signature on each check.* The customer is instructed to sign *each* traveler's check in the space marked "Signature" on the front side of each check, and should be advised to sign the checks in his or her normal handwriting style. The teller should witness the signing of each check and verify the signatures on the checks with that on the purchase application. (See Figure 5.)

8. *Verify the signing of each traveler's check.* When the customer has returned the signed checks, confirm his or her signatures by looking at each check. As stated above, the customer's signature should appear in the designated place on the front side of each check.

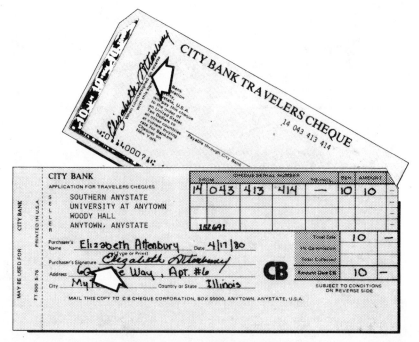

Figure 5. *Signed Traveler's Check*

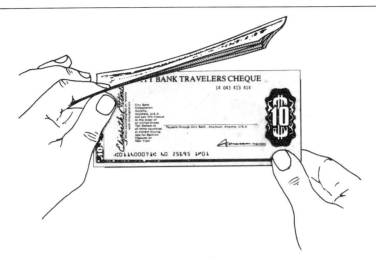

Figure 6. *Recounting the Traveler's Checks*

9. *Count out the traveler's checks to the customer.* With the money collected and the customer's signatures verified, the traveler's checks are counted out again to the customer. The sum total of the traveler's checks should equal the amount of money collected. A check is made by the teller at this time to see that the checks are arranged, by serial number, in ascending order. (See Figure 6.)

10. *Request the customer's choice of wallet.* Before the checks are given to the customer, he or she is shown the types of wallets available and asked his or her preference. Basically, the two styles of wallets are the *pocket* type and the *in-stub* type. (See Figure 7.) If the pocket style wallet is selected,

Figure 7. *Types of Wallets*

Figure 8. *Placing the Checks in the Pocket Style Wallet*

the checks are inserted, as is, into the pocket of the wallet and the wallet folded over or closed to protect them from dirt and moisture damage. (See Figure 8.)

If the in-stub wallet is chosen, the holes in the left end of the packet of checks are fitted over a metal fastener and secured in place. The wallet is then folded in half and secured by a snap. (See Figure 9.)

11. *Give the traveler's checks and copies of the purchase application to the customer.*   The sale of the traveler's checks is considered complete once the customer is presented with the checks and two copies of the purchase application. (See Figure 10.) Remind the customer, at this time, to keep each of the two copies of the application form separate from the checks and to maintain a record of all of the checks that he or she cashes. Later, these records would assist him or her, if he or she should have to claim lost, stolen, or otherwise missing checks.

12. *Thank the customer.*   At the conclusion of the transaction the customer is thanked for his or her business and wished a safe journey. A typical parting

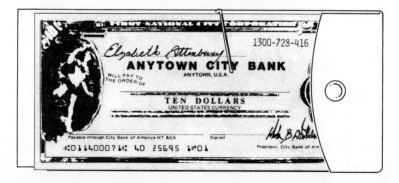

Figure 9. *In-Stub Type Wallet*

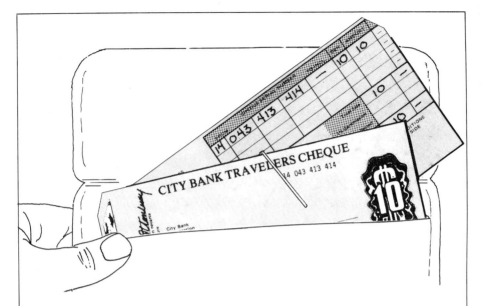

Figure 10. *Giving the Traveler's Checks and Purchase Applications*

comment might be, ". . . Thanks for stopping by. Hope you have a good trip and do stop back and tell us about it when you get back."

13. *Complete the sales transaction.* The cash or personal check that was received from the customer is attached to the original copy of the purchase application with a paper clip. (See Figure 11.) The money and the completed purchase application are then placed in the appropriate drawer to await final check-out and settlement at the end of the business day.

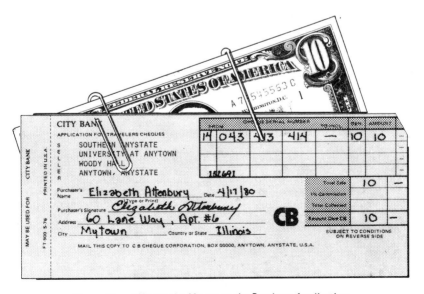

Figure 11. *Affixing the Money to the Purchase Application*

Related Information Test

Learning Objective #11:   Selling Domestic Traveler's Checks

Introduction

This test contains both objective and subjective types of test items. For the objective items (true–false, multiple-choice, completion, matching), respond on the answer sheet entitled *Answer Sheet — Objective Test Items.* For the subjective test questions (essay), write your answers in the spaces provided on the sheets marked *Answer Sheet — Essay Type Test Items.* Do *NOT* write on the question portion of the test.

True–False

If you think the statement is true, fill in the "0" under the "T" on the answer sheet. If you think the statement is false, fill in the "0" under the "F" for that statement. One point/correct response.

> *Example:*   14.   I love taking tests
>
> 14.   T   F
>   ●   0

1. A *countersignature,* as it pertains to traveler's checks, is the signature made by the customer at the time of purchase.
2. The recognized value of a traveler's check is guaranteed by the bank or other financial agency in the community where the customer purchased the checks.
3. One of the three major U.S. companies which issues traveler's checks is *Bank America.*

Multiple Choice

Each of the test items listed below is followed by four possible responses. Fill in the "0" under the letter that you think *best* completes the statement. One point/ correct response.

> Example: 82.   The moon is made from what color of cheese?
>
> A.   Blue
> B.   Green   A   B   C   D
> C.   Red   82.   0   ●   0   0
> D.   Yellow

4. The term *loose,* as used in the sales of traveler's checks, refers to:
   A. Checks that have been removed from the wallet in which they were sold.
   B. Checks that have been cashed by the customer but not yet returned to the issuing company.

C. Checks which may be sold individually or in any combination of denominations.

D. Checks which have been stolen.

5. The term *stale-dated* refers to:

   A. A check that has exceeded the legal time limit in which it must be cashed.

   B. A check that has been dated incorrectly.

   C. Traveler's checks that have not been cashed within one year of their purchase.

   D. A traveler's check that has been cashed but the date of transaction not included.

6. Which of the following types of information is not required of the *customer* on the purchase application?

   A. Printed name

   B. Printed address

   C. Social security number

   D. Signature

Completion

Complete the following items by writing in the appropriate response. Again, write your responses on the answer sheet provided and *NOT* on the questionnaire portion of the test. One point/correct response.

Example: 147.   The taste of sugar is _____.

147.   __sweet__

7. The form that is completed by both the teller and the customer at the time of sale of traveler's checks is a _____ _____.

8. The two types of wallets used to protect *loose-style* traveler's checks are the *flat* or *pocket* style and the _____ type wallet.

9. The customer's copy of the _____ _____ is saved by the customer to assist in making a claim for lost or stolen checks.

Matching

The two columns below contain definitions and terms related to the selling of domestic traveler's checks. Read the definition in the left-hand column and select the term from the right-hand column that is being defined by the statement. Enter the *letter* of the *term* being defined in the appropriate space on the answer sheet. One point/correct response.

_____ 10. Checks which are packaged and sold by predetermined denomination and dollar value.

A. Traveler's Check

B. Pre-Packaged Traveler's Checks

C. Denomination

_____ 11. The number on a traveler's check which specifies the particular bank/issuing agency on which the check is drawn.

_____ 12. The handwritten name of the individual signed by him at the time the traveler's check is cashed.

_____ 13. The dollar value amount indicated on the traveler's check.

_____ 14. A pre-paid, negotiable note.

D. Transit Routing Number

E. Countersignature

F. Purchase Application Form

G. Stale-Dated

H. Personal Check

Essay

On that portion of the answer sheet marked *Essay Type Test Items,* respond to the following questions. Write your answers in the spaces provided. (Clue: The space provided on the answer sheet is more than adequate for a correct and properly-worded response.) Five points/item.

15. Define the term *stale-dated* and explain why or why not it is important when dealing with traveler's checks.

16. What is the basic reason for having the customer initially sign each of the *loose-style* traveler's checks in the presence of the teller?

17. What guarantee does a traveler's check offer that a personal check does not possess?

Appended Item A
Learning Activities Development Sheet

Occupational Program: Teller Science

Course #1:   General Tellering

Unit #2:   Paying and Receiving

Learning Objective #11:   Selling Domestic Traveler's Checks

Learning Activities

1. Read the Information Sheet "Terms".

   A. Review the list of technical occupational information topics on the task detailing sheet "Selling Domestic Traveler's Checks".

   B. Research the topic to be discussed.

C. Prepare the organizational outline of the sheet.

D. Write the information sheet.

E. Proofread and make the necessary changes/corrections.

F. Duplicate/assemble the sheets.

2. Read the Information-Assignment Sheet "Traveler's Checks".

   A. Review the list of technical occupational information topics on the task detailing sheet "Selling Domestic Traveler's Checks".

   B. Research the topic to be discussed.

   C. Prepare an organizational outline of the sheet.

   D. Write the information-assignment sheet.

   For the assignment portion of the sheet. . . .

      1. Review the topic(s) discussed in the information portion of the information-assignment sheet.

      2. Pose probable questions and/or situational problems.

      3. Prepare an organizational outline of the assignment portion of the sheet.

      4. Write the assignment section.

      5. Proofread and make necessary changes/corrections.

      6. Complete the assignment section of the information-assignment sheet.

   E. Proofread and make the necessary changes/corrections.

   F. Duplicate/assemble the sheets.

3. Complete the assignment portion of the above information-assignment sheet.

4. Read pages 44–48 in the "Training Manual for Tellers", Fidelity Bank of Carbondale.

   A. Review the text materials.

   B. Select the sections that are appropriate to the assignment.

   C. Note section title and location.

5. Read the Task Procedure Sheet "Selling Domestic Traveler's Checks".

   A. Review the list of performance steps and standards of performance on the task detailing sheet "Selling Domestic Traveler's Checks".

   B. Prepare the organizational outline of the sheet.

   C. Write the task performance sheet.

   D. Proofread and make the necessary changes/corrections.

   E. Duplicate/assemble the sheets.

6. View the video-taped illustrated presentation "Traveler's Checks — An Informational Review".

   A. Review the information presented in the above sources.

   B. Develop a set of presentation notes.

    C. Develop a series of coordinated illustrations.

    D. Practice the presentation.

    E. Tape the presentation.

    F. Review/edit the tape and make the necessary changes/corrections.

    G. Ready the video-tape for the LAP.

7. Complete the related information test on traveler's checks.

    A. Review the materials on which the test is based.

    B. Select the types of questions to be used.

    C. Prepare the organizational outline of the test.

    D. Rough-state the questions and review the same.

    E. Write the final draft of questions.

    F. Self-take the test.

    G. Make the necessary changes/corrections.

    H. Prepare the answer key.

8. Observe the narrated slide tape demonstration of "Selling Domestic Traveler's Checks".

    A. Review the list of performance steps and standards of performance on the task detailing sheet "Selling Domestic Traveler's Checks".

    B. "Walk through" the activity to be demonstrated.

    C. Prepare a demonstration outline sheet and card.

    D. Proofread same.

    E. Duplicate demonstration outline materials.

    F. Prepare the picture guide.

    G. Select the demonstration site.

    H. "Shoot" the demonstration slide series.

    I. Narrate the slide series.

    J. Review the slide series/narration and make the necessary changes/corrections.

    K. Ready the narrated slide series for the LAP.

9. Practice the activity.

    A. Review the list of performance steps and standards of performance on the task detailing sheet "Selling Domestic Traveler's Checks".

    B. Develop a performance checksheet and list of oral test questions.

    C. Review/proofread checksheet/test questions and make necessary changes/corrections.

    D. Ready checksheet for use.

10. Take the final performance test of selling domestic traveler's checks.

    A. Review the list of performance steps and standards of performance on the task detailing sheet "Selling Domestic Traveler's Checks".

B. Identify events (performance steps and task itself) to be checked.

C. Specify oral questions to be asked (optional).

D. Prepare an organizational outline of the performance test.

E. Write the performance test instrument.

F. Proofread the test instrument and make necessary changes/ corrections.

G. Field-test the instrument.

H. Make necessary final revisions.

Agreement

The signatures of the two parties involved in the development of the learning materials for the learning activities package "Selling Domestic Traveler's Checks" confirm an agreement that the development steps specified for each learning activity will be adhered to. Any changes that might be made in the established development process must be agreed to by both parties prior to the time of change.

Student	Date

Instructor	Date

Appended Item B

Presentation Guide

Learning Objective #11:   Selling Domestic Traveler's Checks

Presentation Topics

Terms	*Visual Aids*
1. Discuss various terms and meanings	T_1 — "Terms"

Traveler's Checks

1. Definition	
2. Brands	T_2 — Major brands
3. Physical make-up and appearance	T_3 — Single check
	T_4 — Parts of check
4. Denominations and packaging	Samples of various "loose" and "pre-packaged" checks
A. "Loose" and "pre-packaged"	
B. Advantages and disadvantages of each	T_5 — Denomination and value

Purchase Applications

1. Definition and purpose	T_6 — Sample purchase application forms
2. Parts of form	T_7 — Sample — loose
3. Customer's section	
4. Seller's section	
5. Precautions	

Wallets	*Visual Aids*
1. Definition and purpose	
2. Types of wallets	Samples of various types of wallets
3. Advantages/disadvantages of various types	

Appended Item C

Name_____

Test Number_____

Answer Sheet

Learning Objective #11: Selling Domestic Traveler's Checks

Objective Test Items

True–False

	T	F
1.	0	0
2.	0	0
3.	0	0

Matching

_____ 10.

_____ 11.

_____ 12.

_____ 13.

_____ 14.

Multiple Choice

	A	B	C	D
4.	0	0	0	0
5.	0	0	0	0
6.	0	0	0	0

Completion

7. _____   _____

8. _____

9. _____   _____

Essay Type Test Items

15. Define the term *stale-dated* and explain why or why not it is important when dealing with traveler's checks.

16. What is the basic reason for having the customer initially sign each of the *loose-style* traveler's checks in the presence of the teller?

17. What guarantee does a traveler's check offer that a personal check does not possess?

Appended Item D

Demonstration Outline and Practice Supervision Guide

Learning Objective #11:   Selling Domestic Traveler's Checks

Equipment and Supplies

The following items are needed to complete the task:

- calculating machine
- money supply
- supply of assorted denominations of traveler's checks
- purchase application forms
- assortment of wallets

Procedure

Performance Steps	*Standards of Performance*
1. *Greet the customer*	The greeting is made in a friendly, courteous manner and includes the teller's offer of assistance. If the teller knows the customer's name, that should also be included in the greeting.

- What are some appropriate alternative greetings?
- Discuss a "business-like" and "personal" type greeting and why one or the other might be preferred.

2. *Take the customer's order*	The order is noted in writing and in terms of total dollar amount of checks desired and denomination(s).

- Why is an oral confirmation of the order necessary?
- What is the benefit of writing a note of the order?

3. *Count out the number of traveler's checks requested by the customer*	The total dollar amount and denomination(s) of checks are counted and totaled to equal the customer's request. If the denominations of the checks requested are the same, and the total dollar amount equals that of a booklet of checks as received from the issuing company, then the booklet of bound checks is selected for sale. However, if the request is made for two or more denominations of checks and/or is not for an amount equal to a booklet of checks as packaged by the issuing agency, individual checks are then selected, counted and totaled.

In a series of like denomination checks, the serial numbers are consecutively arranged in ascending order, and the *number* of checks sold verified by subtracting the serial number of the first check from the serial number of the last check and adding one. The *number* of like denomination checks, when multiplied by that denomination, should equal the total dollar amount requested.

- How do you keep track of the different denominations of checks during the counting process?
- What precautions can you take to eliminate errors?
- If the checks are of the same denomination, what do you do to reconfirm the total? of different denominations?

4. *Have the customer complete his portion of the purchase application*

The customer's signature and printed name and address appear in the appropriate section of the purchase application.

- Why are both the customer's printed name and signature needed?
- Why is it important that the customer press firmly when filling out the application form?

5. *Complete filling out the purchase application*

The serial numbers of the series of traveler's checks appear in the appropriate section of the purchase application.

- Why is it important that the serial numbers appear in the appropriate space and are listed correctly?

6. *Collect the money from the customer*

The total amount of money collected or personal check accepted equals the total amount of the checks sold plus one percent (1%) of the total amount purchased.

- Why is it important to collect the money *before* the customer signs the traveler's checks?

7. *Secure purchaser's signature on each traveler's check*

The purchaser signs each check in the designated place.

- What is the difficulty if the customer does not sign a particular check in your presence?

8. *Verify the signing of each traveler's check*

The signature of the purchaser appears on each check in the designated place.

- Does the customer's not signing a check in your presence in any way invalidate the check?

- What is the reason for the teller verifying the initial signing of each traveler's check?
- Must the signature always be in ink? Why not pencil?

9. *Count out the traveler's checks to the customer*

Total amount of traveler's checks equals total amount of money collected. Checks arranged in ascending order by serial number.

- What is the best way to verify the totals of checks of the same denomination?

10. *Request the customer's choice of wallet*

Customer's choice of wallet is selected and the series of traveler's checks enclosed.

- What purpose do wallets serve?
- Why are there different types of wallets and what are the advantages of each?

11. *Give the traveler's checks and copies of the purchase application to the customer.*

Customer acknowledges receipt of checks and purchase application.

- What is the best way to present the traveler's checks and application form(s) to the customer? Why?

12. *Offer instruction on cashing the traveler's checks*

The customer is asked if he or she has had previous experience in using traveler's checks and, if not, would he or she like some suggestions regarding their use. If instruction is requested, he or she is told the procedure of cashing the checks and keeping record of the transaction(s) on the purchase application(s). The suggestion is also made as to the need to keep the application and checks in different places.

- From a "customer service" point of view, why is this an important step?
- Why is it important that the traveler's checks and copies of the purchase applications be kept in separate places by the customer?

13. *Thank the customer*

The customer is thanked, wished a pleasant journey, and invited back to the bank on his or her return.

- What is the psychology behind making the customer feel good as he leaves?

14. *Complete the sales transaction*

The cash or personal check received from the customer is attached to the original copy of the purchase application with a paper clip. It is then placed in the appropriate drawer to await final check out and settlement at the end of the business day.

- If, after the customer leaves, you find there is a difference between the total amount of money collected and the total indicated on the purchase application, what do you do?

References

1. "Training Manual for Tellers." Personnel Training Unit. The Fidelity Bank of Carbondale.

Appended Item E

Final Performance Test

Occupational Program: Teller Science

Course #1:   General Tellering

Unit #2:   Paying and Receiving

Learning Objective #11:   Selling Domestic Traveler's Checks

The performance test is made up of two sections: *Performance Step Evaluation* and *Task Evaluation*. Since, in the order of performing the task, the learner will systematically complete the series of performance steps first, that section appears first. The second section deals with the evaluation of the task as a whole and completes the evaluation instrument.

Performance Step Evaluation

Directions: Below are the performance steps of the task *Selling Domestic Traveler's Checks*. Accompanying each performance step is a statement of its accepted standard of performance and a performance evaluation scale. As the learner completes a given step, read the performance standard for it and indicate on the evaluation scale how well you think he did in relation to the stated criteria. Evaluate each step in the procedure.

	Performance Steps	*Standards of Performance*

1. *Greet the customer*

The greeting is made in a friendly, courteous manner and includes the teller's offer of assistance. If the teller knows the customer's name, that should also be included in the greeting.

Performed step very well	Performed step ade- quately		Performed step poorly	Did not perform step
.	.	.	.	.
5	4	3	2	1	0

2. *Take the customer's order*

The order is noted in writing and in terms of total dollar amount of checks desired and denomination(s).

Performed step very well	Performed step ade- quately		Performed step poorly	Did not perform step
.	.	.	.	.
5	4	3	2	1	0

3. *Count out the number of traveler's checks requested by the customer*

The total dollar amount and denomination(s) of checks are counted and totaled to equal the customer's request. If the denominations of the checks requested are the same, and the total dollar amount equals that of a booklet of checks as received from the issuing company, then the booklet of bound checks is selected for sale. However, if the request is made for two or more denominations of checks and/or is not for an amount equal to a booklet of checks as packaged by the issuing agency, individual checks are then selected, counted and totaled. In a series of like denomination checks, the serial numbers are consecutively arranged in ascending order, and the *number* of checks sold verified by subtracting the serial number of the first check from the serial number of the last check and adding one. The *number* of like denomination checks, when multiplied by that denomination, should equal the total dollar amount requested.

Performed step very well	Performed step adequately		Performed step poorly	Did not perform step
5	4	3	2	1	0

4. *Have the customer complete his portion of the purchase application*

The customer's signature and printed name and address appear in the appropriate section of the purchase application.

Performed step very well	Performed step adequately		Performed step poorly	Did not perform step
5	4	3	2	1	0

5. *Complete filling out the purchase application*

The serial numbers of the series of traveler's checks appear in the appropriate section of the purchase application.

Performed step very well	Performed step adequately		Performed step poorly	Did not perform step
5	4	3	2	1	0

6. *Collect the money from the customer*

The total amount of money collected or personal check accepted equals the total amount of the checks sold plus one percent (1%) of the total amount purchased.

Performed step very well	Performed step adequately		Performed step poorly	Did not perform step
.	.	.	.	.
5	4	3	2	1	0

7. *Secure purchaser's signature on each traveler's check*

The purchaser signs each check in the designated place.

Performed step very well	Performed step adequately		Performed step poorly	Did not perform step
.	.	.	.	.
5	4	3	2	1	0

8. *Verify the signing of each traveler's check*

The purchaser signs each check in the designated place.

Performed step very well	Performed step adequately		Performed step poorly	Did not perform step
.	.	.	.	.
5	4	3	2	1	0

9. *Count out the traveler's checks to the customer*

Total amount of traveler's checks equals total amount of money collected. Checks arranged in ascending order by serial number.

Performed step very well	Performed step adequately		Performed step poorly	Did not perform step
.	.	.	.	.
5	4	3	2	1	0

10. *Request the customer's choice of wallet*

Customer's choice of wallet is selected and the series of traveler's checks enclosed.

Performed step very well	Performed step adequately		Performed step poorly	Did not perform step
.	.	.	.	.
5	4	3	2	1	0

11. *Give the traveler's checks and copies of the purchase application to the customer*

Customer acknowledges receipt of checks and purchase application.

Performed step very well	Performed step ade-quately		Performed step poorly	Did not perform step
.	.	.	.	.
5	4	3	2	1	0

12. *Offer instruction on cashing the traveler's checks*

The customer is asked if he or she has had previous experience in using traveler's checks and, if not, would he or she like some suggestions regarding their use. If instruction is requested, he or she is told the procedure of cashing the checks and keeping record of the transactions on the purchase application(s). The suggestion is also made as to the need to keep the application and checks in different places. The practice is done to facilitate making a claim if the checks are lost or stolen.

Performed step very well	Performed step ade-quately		Performed step poorly	Did not perform step
.	.	.	.	.
5	4	3	2	1	0

13. *Thank the customer*

The customer is thanked, wished a pleasant journey and invited back to the bank on his or her return.

Performed step very well	Performed step ade-quately		Performed step poorly	Did not perform step
.	.	.	.	.
5	4	3	2	1	0

14. *Complete the sales transaction*

The cash or personal check received from the customer is attached to the original copy of the purchase application with a paper clip. It is then placed in the appropriate drawer to await final check-out and settlement at the end of the business day.

Performed step very well	Performed step ade-quately		Performed step poorly	Did not perform step

. .	.	.	.	.
5 4	3	2	1	0

Additional Comments

Task Evaluation

This portion of the performance evaluation checksheet will assist you in determining if the learner has attained the objective of *Selling Domestic Traveler's Checks.* In review, the evaluation criteria for the objective are as follows:

> The domestic traveler's checks are prepared according to the underwriter's sales directions and the transaction verified by the instructor. The sequence of performance steps listed on the task procedure sheet given at the time of demonstration of the objective was followed exactly. The learner was able to explain the procedure he or she performed at the instructor's request. He or she demonstrated the complete procedure within a ten minute time period. The task was repeated a minimum of four times distributed equally over a two week time period.

As implied in the criteria statement, the learner will be evaluated in terms of his or her overall attainment of the learning objective, manipulative skill, knowledge and ability to apply it in performing the objective, professional attitudes, and perceptive skills and ability to stay within the stated time constraints.

Directions: To complete this phase of the evaluation read the various criteria statements under each heading and indicate that statement which best describes the learner's total effort as you perceive it.

1. The learner completed the task of *Selling Domestic Traveler's Checks* as follows:

   ☐ Did not complete the task in accordance with the established criteria.

   ☐ Completed the task in accordance with the established criteria.

☐ Exceeded the established criteria. Demonstrated the task in the manner of an experienced teller.

2. During the completion of the task, the learner:

☐ Could not perform the performance steps of the task.

☐ Completed the performance steps of the sequence, but with hesitation and lack of confidence. Occasionally missed a performance step or performed it out of sequence.

☐ Technically performed the series of performance steps in an acceptable manner.

☐ Performed each performance step in the sequence with confidence and ability. Adapted to varying situations with little or no difficulty.

3. During the process, the learner:

☐ Could not respond correctly to questions/situational problems posed by the instructor.

☐ Responded to certain questions and/or contrived situational problems, but with hesitation and noticeable lack of confidence.

☐ Responded properly to questions/problems that were posed, but with no additional exploration or elaboration.

☐ Responded to all requests for information. Was able to anticipate various situations and problems and suggest possible solutions to them.

4. During the process, the learner:

☐ Displayed little or no professional behavior.

☐ Observed a simulation of acceptable professional behavior.

☐ Strived to emulate professional behavior.

☐ Consistently performed in a professional manner.

5. During the process, the learner:

☐ Was almost totally unaware of almost all non-verbal communiques of the customer.

☐ Appeared to be aware of non-verbal communiques and sometimes reacted to them.

☐ Was very aware of non-verbal communiques, and once given, reacted in a positive, graceful manner.

6. In terms of time, the learner:

☐ Far exceeded the 10 minute time period for performing the objective.

☐ Did not perform the objective in the prescribed time, but exceeded it only slightly.

☐ Performed the objective within the prescribed time limit.

☐ Performed the objective in a time demonstrated by an experienced teller.

7. The learning objective was demonstrated by the learner a minimum of four times distributed equally over a two-week period.

Test #1   Date:_____

Test #2   Date:_____

Test #3   Date:_____

Test #4   Date:_____

Additional Comments:

Certification

In my professional judgment, _____ has attained the learning objective of *Selling Domestic Traveler's Checks* and is capable of performing this task in a professionally acceptable manner.

_____
                            Signature

_____
                            Date

References

Adam, James P. (Ed.) *Plato's Republic.* 2nd ed. Cambridge: Cambridge University Press, 1963.

Altman, James W. "What Kinds of Occupational Information Do Students Need?" Mimeographed. Paper presented at the Occupational Information and Vocational Guidance Conference, Pittsburgh, March 1966.

Arnold, Joseph P. and Ferguson, Edward T. *Determining Occupational Emphasis for High School Program Design.* Columbus, Ohio: Center for Vocational and Technical Education, Ohio State University, 1973.

Bailey, Larry J. *A Curriculum Model for Facilitating Career Development.* Carbondale, Ill.: Southern Illinois University. Career Development for Children Project, 1971.

Bailey, Larry J. and Stadt, Ronald W. *Career Education: New Approaches to Human Development.* Bloomington: McKnight, 1973.

Baker, Robert L. and Schutz, Richard E. *Instructional Product Development.* New York: Van Nostrand Reinhold Co., 1971.

Banathy, Bela H. *Instructional Systems.* Belmont: Fearon Publishers, 1968.

Bartel, Carl R. *Instructional Analysis and Materials Development.* Chicago: American Technical Society, 1977.

Beck, Ruth M. and Beck, James F. "A Simple Guide to the Preparation of Learning Activities Packages." Mimeographed. Trenton, N.J.: Rider College, 1974.

Bjorquist, David. "What Vocational Educational Teachers Should Know About Individualizing Instruction." Columbus, Ohio: ERIC Clearing House on Vocational and Technical Education, Center for Vocational and Technical Education, Ohio State University, 1971.

Blau, Peter M., Gustad, John W., Jessor, Richard, Parnes, Herbert S., and Wilcock, Richard C. "Occupational Choice: A Conceptual Framework." *Industrial and Labor Relations Review* 56: 28-33.

Bloom, Benjamin S. (Ed.) Engelhart, Max D., Furst, Edward J., Hill, Walker H., and Krathwohl, David R. *Taxonomy of Educational Objectives: Cognitive Domain.* New York: David McKay, 1957.

Bollinger, Elroy and Weaver, Gilbert G. *Trade Analysis and Course Organization.* New York: Pitman Publishing, 1955.

Bordin, E. S., Nachmann, Barbara, and Sega, S. J. "An Articulated Framework for Vocational Development." *Journal of Counseling Psychology* 63: 107-16.

Borow, Henry (Ed.) *Man In a World at Work.* Boston: Houghton Mifflin Co., 1964.

Bottoms, Gene and Cleere, W. Ray. *A One-Week Institute to Develop Objectives and Models for a Continuous Exploratory Program Related to the World of Work from Jr. High Through Sr. High School.* Final Report. Carrollton, Ga.: West Georgia National Conference, 1969.

Bottoms, Gene and Matheny, Kenneth B. *A Guide for the Development, Implementation, and Administration of Exemplary Programs and Projects in Vocational Education.* Atlanta, Ga.: Georgia State Department of Education, 1969.

Bretz, Rudy. *A Taxonomy of Communication Media.* Englewood Cliffs, N.J.: Educational Technology Publications, 1971.

Brewer, James M. *History of Vocational Guidance.* New York: Harper and Brothers, 1942.

Brown, James W., Lewis, Richard B., and Harcleroad, Fred F. *A-V Instruction: Methods and Materials.* 2nd ed. New York: McGraw-Hill Book Co., 1959.

Brunner, Jerome S. *The Process of Education.* New York: Vintage Books, 1960.

Budke, Wesley E. *Review and Synthesis of Information on Occupational Exploration.* Columbus, Ohio: The Center for Vocational and Technical Education, The Ohio State University, 1971.

Burns, Richard W. and Brooks, Gary D. (Eds.) *Currriculum Design in a Changing Society.* Englewood Cliffs, N.J.: Educational Technology Publications, 1970.

Buros, Oscar K. (Ed.) *Tests in Print.* Highland Park: The Gryphon Press, 1961.

Buros, Oscar K. (Ed.) *The Sixth Mental Measurements Yearbook.* Highland Park: The Gryphon Press, 1965.

Caplow, T. *The Sociology of Work.* Minneapolis: The University of Minnesota Press, 1954.

Coburn, Darrel W. *Teachers Guide for a Project Devise.* Harrisburg: Commonwealth of Pennsylvania, Department of Education, 1968.

Crites, John C. *Vocational Psychology.* New York: McGraw-Hill, 1969.

Dale, Edgar. *Audio-Visual Methods in Teaching.* rev. ed. New York: Holt, Rinehart and Winston, 1961.

Denova, Charles C. *Establishing a Training Function: A Guide for Management.* Englewood Cliffs, N.J.: Educational Technology Publications, 1971.

Doll, Ronald. *Curriculum Improvement: Decision Making and Process.* Boston: Allyn and Bacon, 1970.

Drumheller, Sidney F. *Handbook of Curriculum Design for Individualized Instruction. How to Develop Curriculum Materials from Rigorously Defined Behavioral Objectives.* Englewood Cliffs, N.J.: Educational Technology Publications, 1971.

Englehart, Max D., Furst, Edward J., Hill, Walker H., and Krathwohl, David R. *Taxonomy of Educational Objectives: Handbook I: Cognitive Domain.* Edited by Benjamin S. Bloom. New York: David McKay, Inc., 1957.

Erickson, Carlton W. H. *Fundamentals of Teaching with Audio-visual Technology.* New York: Macmillan, 1965.

Erickson, Richard C. and Wentling, Tim L. *Measuring Student Growth: Techniques and Procedures for Occupational Education.* Boston: Allyn and Bacon, 1976.

Finch, Curtis R. and Crunkilton, John R. *Curriculum Development in Vocational and Technical Education: Planning, Content, and Implementation.* Boston: Allyn and Bacon, 1979.

Fine, Sidney A. *Guidelines for the Design of New Careers.* Kalamazoo: W.E. Upjohn Institute for Employment Research, 1967.

Fine, Sidney A., Holt, Ann M., and Hutchinson, Maret F. *Functional Job Analysis:*

How to Standardize Task Statements. Kalamazoo: W.E. Upjohn Institute for Employment Research, 1974.

Firth, Gerald R. and Kimpston, Richard D. *The Curriculum Continuum in Perspective.* Itasca: F. E. Peacock Publishers, Inc., 1973.

Frost, Joe L. and Rowland, G. Thomas. *Curricula for the Seventies: Early Childhood Through Early Adolescence.* Boston: Houghton Mifflin Co., 1969.

Fryklund, Verne C. *Analysis Technique for Instructors.* Milwaukee: Bruce Publishing Company, 1956.

Frymier, Jack R. "Developing Human Potential." Mimeographed. Columbus, Ohio: The Ohio State University, n.d.

Fuller, R. Buckminster. *Education Automation.* Carbondale, Ill.: Southern Illinois University Press, 1962.

Gagné, Robert M. *The Conditions of Learning.* New York: Holt, Rinehart and Winston, 1965.

Gardner, John W. *Excellence.* New York: Harper and Row, 1962.

Ginzberg, E., Ginsburg, S. W., Axelrad, S., and Herma, J. L. *Occupational Choice: An Approach to a General Theory.* New York: Columbia University Press, 1951.

Gregg Division, McGraw-Hill Book Company and The Center for Vocational and Technical Education at the Ohio State University. *Writing Performance Goals: Strategy and Prototype.* New York: Gregg Division/McGraw-Hill Book Company, n.d.

Gribbons, Warren D. and Lohnes, Paul R. *Career Development.* Weston: Regis College Press, 1966.

Gronlund, Norman E. *Constructing Achievement Tests.* Englewood Cliffs, N.J.: Prentice-Hall, 1977.

Gronlund, Norman E. *Stating Objectives for Classroom Instruction.* 2nd ed. New York: Macmillan, 1978.

Hansen, Lorrain S. *Career Guidance Practices in School and Community.* Washington: National Vocational Guidance Association, 1970.

Harmes, H. M. *Behavioral Analysis of Learning Objectives.* West Palm Beach: Harmes and Associates, 1969.

Havighurst, Robert J. *Human Development and Education.* New York: David McKay, 1953.

Hein, Fred V., Farnsworth, Dana L., and Richardson, Charles E. *Living: Health, Behavior, and Environment.* 5th ed. Glenview: Scott, Foresman, 1970.

Holland, John L. *The Psychology of Vocational Choice.* Waltham: Blaisdell Publishing, 1966.

Hollingshead, A. B. *Elmtown's Youth.* New York: John Wiley and Sons, 1956.

Hollis, Joseph W. and Hollis, Lucille U. *Organizing for Effective Guidance.* Chicago: Science Research Associates, 1965.

Hoppock, Robert. *Occupational Information.* New York: McGraw-Hill, 1967.

Hunter, C. David. "How to Improve Your Demonstration Technique." *Industrial Education* 77: 32–33.

Jarett, Irwin, Rader, David W., and Longhurst, Philip, Jr. *Key Factor Analysis Workbook.* Raleigh: Jarett, Rader, and Longhurst, 1970.

Jordaan, J. P. "Exploratory Behavior: The Formation of Self and Occupational Concepts," *Career Development: Self-Concept Theory.* Donald E. Super, ed. New York: CEEB Research Monograph, No. 4, 1963.

Kapfer, Philip G. and Ovard, Glen F. *Preparing and Using Individualized Learning*

Packages for Ungraded, Continuous Progress Education. Englewood Cliffs, N.J.: Educational Technology Publications, 1971.

Kapfer, Miriam B. *Behavioral Objectives in Curriculum Development.* Englewood Cliffs, N.J.: Educational Technology Publications, 1971.

Kibrick, Anne K. and Tiedman, D. V. "Conception of Self and Perception of Role in School of Nursing." *Journal of Counseling Psychology*, VIII 61: 62-69.

Klausmeier, Herbert J. and Harris, Chester W., eds. *Analyses of Concept Learning.* New York: Academic Press, 1966.

Krathwohl, David R., Bloom, Benjamin, and Masia, Bertram B. *Taxonomy of Educational Objectives, Handbook II: Affective Domain.* New York: David McKay, 1964.

Kroll, M. et al. *Career Development: Growth and Crises.* New York: John Wiley and Sons, 1970.

Larson, Milton E. *Teaching Related Subjects in Trade and Industrial and Technical Education.* Columbus, Ohio: Charles E. Merrill, 1972.

Leonard, Joan M., Fallon, John J., and von Arx. *General Methods of Effective Teaching: A Practical Approach.* New York: Crowell, 1972.

Mager, Robert F. *Preparing Instructional Objectives.* Palo Alto: Fearon Publishers, 1962.

Mager, Robert F., and Beach, Kenneth M. *Developing Vocational Instruction.* Palo Alto: Fearon Publishers, 1967.

Mager, Robert F. and Pipe, Peter. *Analyzing Performance Problems or "You Really Oughta Wanna."* Belmont: Fearon Publishers, 1970.

Marland, Sidney P., Jr. "Address to Office of Education Staff." Mimeographed. Washington, D.C., December 17, 1970.

Marland, Sidney P., Jr. "Career Education Now." Mimeographed. Houston, January 23, 1971.

Marland, Sidney P., Jr. "Criticism, Communication and Change." Mimeographed. Washington, D.C., July 20, 1971.

Marland, Sidney P., Jr. "Data Gathering — A Time for Planning." Mimeographed. Washington, D.C., June 17, 1971.

Marland, Sidney P., Jr. "On Meriting a Good Opinion." Mimeographed. Washington, D.C., July 9, 1971.

Marland, Sidney P., Jr. "Statement Before the Sub-Committee on Education, U.S. Senate." Mimeographed. Washington, D.C., April 28, 1971.

Marrou, H. I. *A History of Education in Antiquity.* Translated by George Lamb. New York: The New American Library of World Literature, Inc., 1956.

Melching, William H. and Borcher, Sidney D. *Procedures for Constructing and Using Task Inventories.* Columbus, Ohio: Center for Vocational and Technical Education, Ohio State University, 1973.

Micheels, William J. and Karnes, M. Ray. *Measuring Educational Achievement.* New York: McGraw-Hill, 1950.

Miles, David T. and Robinson, Roger. "Behavioral Objectives: An Even Closer Look." *Educational Technology*, June (1972): 39-44.

Miller, Aaron J. *A Comprehensive Career Education Model.* Interim Report. Columbus, Ohio: The Center for Vocational and Technical Education, 1972.

Miller, D. C. and Form, W. H. *Industrial Sociology.* New York: Harper & Row, 1951.

Morris, Van C. *Philosophy and The American School.* Boston: Houghton Mifflin Co., 1961.

National Commission on the Reform of Secondary Education. *The Reform of Secondary Education: A Report to the Public and the Profession.* New York: McGraw-Hill, 1973.

National Society for the Study of Education. *Vocational Education.* Chicago: The University of Chicago Press, 1965.

Neagley, Ross L. and Evans, M. Dean. *Handbook for Effective Curriculum Development.* Englewood Cliffs, N.J., Prentice-Hall, 1967.

New Jersey Division of Vocational Education. *Teacher's Guide for a Model Program on the Introduction to Vocations.* Trenton: New Jersey State Department of Education, 1965.

Norris, Willa. *Occupational Information in the Elementary School.* Chicago: Science Research Associates, 1963.

Oberg, Winston. "Make Performance Appraisal Relevant." *Harvard Business Review.* January-February (1972): 61-67.

O'Hara, R. P. and Tiedman, D. V. "Vocational Self-Concept in Adolescence." *Journal of Counseling Psychology,* VI 59: 292-301.

Oklahoma Department of Vocational-Technical Education. *Career Exploration: A Guide for Teachers.* Oklahoma City: Oklahoma State Department of Education, 1970.

Oregon Division of Community Colleges and Vocational Education. *Teacher's Guide To Self Understanding Through Occupational Exploration (SUTOE).* Salem: Oregon State Department of Education, 1969.

Osgood, Charles E., Suci, George J., and Tannenbaum, Percy H. *The Measurement of Meaning.* Urbana, Ill.: The University of Illinois Press, 1967.

Osipow, Samuel H. *Theories of Career Development.* New York: Appleton-Century-Crofts, 1968.

Parsons, Frank. *Choosing a Vocation.* New York: Houghton Mifflin Co., 1909.

Peddiwell, J. Abner. *The Saber-Tooth Curriculum.* New York: McGraw-Hill, 1939.

Peters, Herman J. and Hansen, James C. (Eds.) *Vocational Guidance and Career Development.* New York: Macmillan, 1966.

Roe, Anne. *The Psychology of Occupations.* New York: John Wiley and Sons, 1956.

Roth, Robert M., Hershenson, David B., and Hilliard, Thomas (Eds.) *The Psychology of Vocational Development: Readings in Theory and Research.* Boston: Allyn and Bacon, 1970.

Short, Edmund C. and Marconnit, George D. *Contemporary Thought on Public School Curriculum.* Dubuque: William C. Brown Company, 1971.

Silvius, G. Harold and Bohn, Ralph C. *Organizing Course Materials.* Bloomington: McKnight and McKnight, 1961.

Silvius, G. Harold and Bohn, Ralph C. *Planning and Organizing Instruction.* Bloomington: McKnight and McKnight, 1976.

Simpson, Elizabeth Jane. "The Classification of Educational Objectives, Psychomotor Domain." (Unpublished) University of Illinois, Urbana, Illinois.

Skinner, B. F. *The Technology of Teaching.* New York: Appleton-Century-Crofts, 1968.

Super, Donald E. *The Psychology of Careers.* New York: Harper and Row, 1957.

Super, Donald E. and Bachrach, Paul B. *Scientific Careers and Vocational Development Theory.* New York: Teachers College Press, Columbia University, 1957.

Super, Donald E. et al. *Career Development: Self Concept Theory.* Princeton, N.J.: College Entrance Examination Board, 1963.

Taylor, Norman. *The Guide to Garden Shrubs and Trees (Including Woody Vines)*. Boston: Houghton Mifflin Co., 1965.

The University of the State of New York, The State Education Department and Bureau of Examinations and Testing. *Improving the Classroom Test: A Manual of Test Construction Procedures for the Classroom Teacher.* Albany, 1957.

Tiedman, David V. and O'Hara, Robert P. *Career Development: Choice and Adjustment.* Princeton: College Entrance Examination Board, 1963.

Toffler, Alvin. *Future Shock.* New York: Random House, 1970.

Tyler, Leona E. *The Psychology of Human Differences.* 3rd ed. New York: Appleton-Century-Crofts, 1965.

United States Civil Service Commission, Bureau of Intergovernmental Personnel Programs. *Job Analysis: Developing and Documenting Data.* Washington: United States Government Printing Office, 1973.

United States Department of Labor. *Dictionary of Occupational Titles.* Vols. I and II. Washington: United States Government Printing Office, 1965.

Winefordner, David W. "Orienting Students to the World of Work Using the Data-People-Things Conceptual Framework and the Ohio Vocational Interest Survey." Mimeographed. Nevada, April 1, 1969.

Wood, Dorothy Adkins. *Test Construction: Development and Interpretation of Achievement Tests.* Columbus: Charles E. Merrill, 1960.

Zaccaria, J. *Theories of Occupational Choice and Vocational Development.* Boston: Houghton Mifflin Co., 1970.

Zytowski, Donald G. *Vocational Behavior: Readings in Theory and Research.* New York: Holt, Rinehart and Winston, 1968.

Index